Property of
First Bap
of
Sheffield Lake, Ohio

D0853273

THE NEW LOTTIE MOON STORY

Catherine B. Allen

BROADMAN PRESS • NASHVILLE, TENNESSEE

© Copyright 1980 • Broadman Press.

All rights reserved.

4263-19

ISBN: 0-8054-6319-4

Second Edition
Sixth Printing

Dewey Decimal Classification: 266.092

Subject headings: MOON, LOTTIE//MISSIONS—CHINA

Library of Congress Catalog Card Number: 79-52336

Printed in the United States of America

FOREWORD

My dear Miss Moon:

Of all Southern Baptists past and present, you are the most famous. Please do not be offended. I know that fame was not a suitable attainment for a lady of your time and place. However, you did learn to tolerate publicity as you bartered your privacy for more adequate support on the mission field. And remember this—you did commit the totality of your life to serving God in foreign missions. You possibly did not imagine that you would serve not only in life, but also in death.

Your name is now a household presence for millions of Southern Baptists. In your name, more than $450,000,000 has been given in support of foreign missions. The Lottie Moon Christmas Offering for Foreign Missions is a cherished Southern Baptist tradition for celebrating the birth of Jesus Christ.

Strangely, the more widely your name has become known, the less well people know you. They feel free to call you "Lottie" in the casual first name-dropping status accorded remote celebrities. But perhaps no more than one million know that you were a missionary in China in pioneering times. Fewer still can accurately take the measure of your life in its own times. There is danger that you are becoming more of a product and less of a person as history marches on.

For more than fifty years, your story has been safely contained in a little red book by Una Roberts Lawrence. A swift river of words about you has flowed from this one well-worn source. After much repetition, and many generations, people began to wonder just how much of the story was the real you.

Two years ago, I was assigned to write a new Lottie Moon story. Immediately, impassioned advice hit me from two sides. One side feared that your legend had clouded your life. "Don't perpetuate that myth about her starving to death in a famine," they said. They wanted fresh, straight facts.

The other side feared that your life might cloud your legend. "Don't dare tamper with that precious story about her starving to death in a famine," they said. Yet even they wanted to reclothe the old facts in fresh meaning.

In a society that hungers for heroic figures but hastens to knock them off their pedestals, you are justified if you feel nervous about this project. I certainly was nervous.

I have sought the real you relentlessly. I have uprooted your family tree. I have searched out your words, weighed them, milked them for meaning. I have coaxed your family and friends to reveal their slightest impressions of you. I have pursued you from Viewmont to the Little Cross Roads. I have discovered that the old "legends" are truer than previously known, so I am choosing to present as many straight facts as I know. If some scoff that the new story reaches the same old conclusions—that you were a unique heroine—then they need only check my sources to see how your own times evaluated you.

Let me thank you for leaving a wide trail in word and deed. Oh, you could have been much more helpful, but you left quite a story by which today's millions and tomorrow's may know you. And they should know you.

With your permission, Miss Moon, here it is.

CATHERINE B. ALLEN

CONTENTS

KEY TO ILLUSTRATIONS

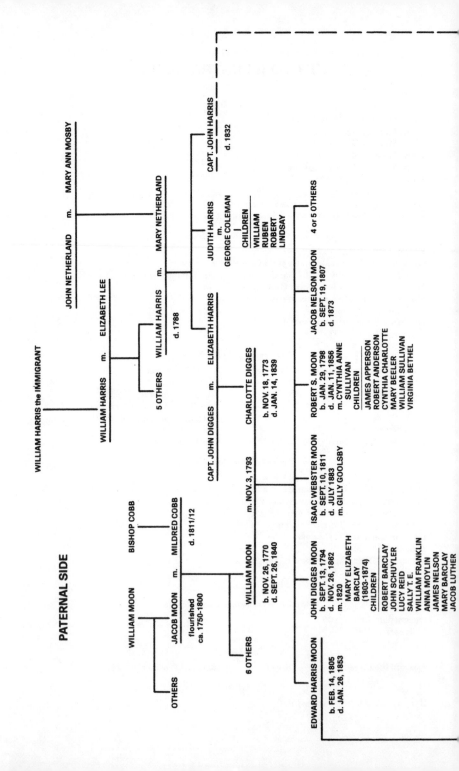

PATERNAL SIDE

WILLIAM HARRIS the IMMIGRANT

JOHN NETHERLAND m. MARY ANN MOSBY

WILLIAM HARRIS m. ELIZABETH LEE

WILLIAM HARRIS
d. 1788

5 OTHERS

WILLIAM HARRIS m. MARY NETHERLAND

CAPT. JOHN HARRIS
d. 1832

JUDITH HARRIS
m.
GEORGE COLEMAN

CHILDREN
WILLIAM
RUBEN
ROBERT
LINDSAY

ELIZABETH HARRIS

CAPT. JOHN DIGGES m. CHARLOTTE DIGGES
b. NOV. 18, 1773
d. JAN. 14, 1839

ROBERT S. MOON
b. JAN. 29, 1798
d. JAN. 11, 1856
m. CYNTHIA ANNE
SULLIVAN

CHILDREN
JAMES APPERSON
ROBERT ANDERSON
CYNTHIA CHARLOTTE
MARY BEELER
WILLIAM SULLIVAN
VIRGINIA BETHEL

JACOB NELSON MOON
b. SEPT. 19, 1807
d. 1873

4 or 5 OTHERS

WILLIAM MOON BISHOP COBB

JACOB MOON m. MILDRED COBB
flourished   d. 1811/12
ca. 1750-1800

WILLIAM MOON
b. NOV. 26, 1770
d. SEPT. 26, 1840

m. NOV. 3, 1793

ISAAC WEBSTER MOON
b. SEPT. 10, 1811
d. JULY 1883
m. GILLY GOOLSBY

6 OTHERS

JOHN DIGGES MOON
b. SEPT. 13, 1794
d. NOV. 26, 1862
m. 1820
MARY ELIZABETH
BARCLAY
(1803-1874)
CHILDREN
ROBERT BARCLAY
JOHN SCHUYLER
LUCY REID
SALLY T. E.
WILLIAM FRANKLIN
ANNA MOYLIN
JAMES NELSON
MARY BARCLAY
JACOB LUTHER

OTHERS

EDWARD HARRIS MOON
b. FEB. 14, 1805
d. JAN. 26, 1853

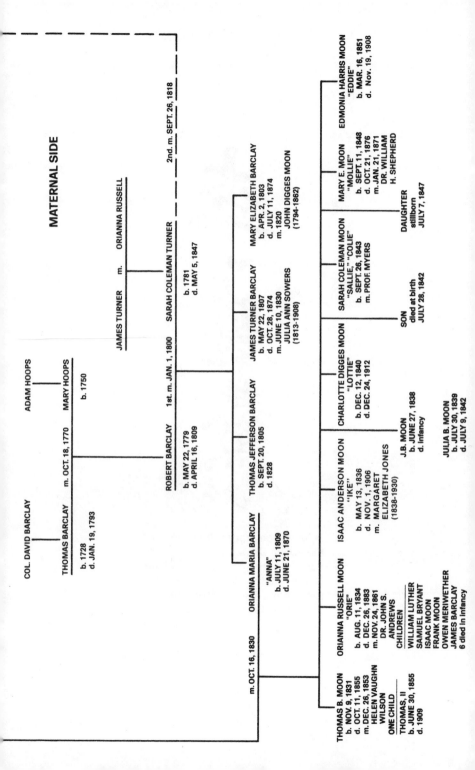

MATERNAL SIDE

COL. DAVID BARCLAY

THOMAS BARCLAY
b. 1728
d. JAN. 19, 1793

m. OCT. 18, 1770

ADAM HOOPS

MARY HOOPS
b. 1750

JAMES TURNER m. ORIANNA RUSSELL

SARAH COLEMAN TURNER
b. 1781
d. MAY 5, 1847

2nd. m. SEPT. 26, 1818

ROBERT BARCLAY
b. MAY 22, 1779
d. APRIL 16, 1809

1st. m. JAN. 1, 1800

THOMAS JEFFERSON BARCLAY
b. SEPT. 20, 1805
d. 1828

JAMES TURNER BARCLAY
b. MAY 22, 1807
d. OCT. 28, 1874
m. JUNE 10, 1830
JULIA ANN SOWERS
(1813-1908)

MARY ELIZABETH BARCLAY
b. APR. 2, 1803
d. JULY 11, 1874
m. 1820
JOHN DIGGES MOON
(1794-1862)

ORIANNA MARIA BARCLAY
"ANNA"
b. JULY 11, 1809
d. JUNE 21, 1870

m. OCT. 16, 1830

ISAAC ANDERSON MOON
"IKE"
b. MAY 13, 1836
d. NOV. 1, 1906
m. MARGARET
ELIZABETH JONES
(1838-1930)

CHARLOTTE DIGGES MOON
"LOTTIE"
b. DEC. 12, 1840
d. DEC. 24, 1912

J.B. MOON
b. JUNE 27, 1838
d. Infancy

JULIA B. MOON
b. JULY 30, 1839
d. JULY 9, 1842

SON
died at birth
JULY 28, 1842

SARAH COLEMAN MOON
"SALLIE," "COLIE"
b. SEPT. 26, 1843
m. PROF. MYERS

DAUGHTER
stillborn
JULY 7, 1847

MARY E. MOON
"MOLLIE"
b. SEPT. 11, 1848
d. OCT. 21, 1876
m. JAN. 21, 1871
DR. WILLIAM
H. SHEPHERD

EDMONIA HARRIS MOON
"EDDIE"
b. MAR. 16, 1851
d. Nov. 19, 1908

ORIANNA RUSSELL MOON
"ORIE"
b. AUG. 11, 1834
d. DEC. 26, 1883
m. NOV. 24, 1861
DR. JOHN S.
ANDREWS
CHILDREN
WILLIAM LUTHER
SAMUEL BRYANT
ISAAC MOON
FRANK MOON
OWEN MERIWETHER
JAMES BARCLAY
6 died in Infancy

THOMAS B. MOON
b. NOV. 9, 1831
d. OCT. 11, 1855
m. DEC. 26, 1853
HELEN VAUGHN
WILSON
ONE CHILD
THOMAS, II
b. JUNE 30, 1855
d. 1909

李題鰲

L. Moon

Miss Moon apparently adopted the above Chinese name. It is the name on her calling card at the United States Consulate in Chefoo, China. The phonetic rendering of that name is *Li-Ti-Ou*.

1
She Was
a Daughter of Old Virginia

Only a dozen eyewitnesses remain to describe the real Lottie Moon. Most of them remember a young child's view of an elderly giant. What was Lottie Moon like?

She was a miniature woman. In 1904 a fifteen-year-old American girl Miss Moon visited was enchanted by the little woman who could walk under her outstretched arm. She noticed that Miss Moon's feet did not touch the floor when she sat in a chair. When the two were out walking together, Miss Moon confided that she was four feet, three inches tall.[1]

Lottie's friends of young days in Virginia and Georgia invariably called her "petite." Later they noticed that she had grown "stout" or "fleshy" in China.[2] Yet the ship steward who carried her unconscious body on board for her voyage to death said she weighed no more than fifty pounds.[3]

Her deep blue eyes could dance in merriment or penetrate sharply. A firm, prominent chin line matched her strong will. Dark black-brown hair hung in long kinks down the back of the child Lottie. Later she washed it daily and slicked the curls into the severe Chinese style. Very few gray hairs ever grew on her head.

She had a cultivated voice described as deep, rich, gentle, musical. She used it skillfully to converse, sing, read dramatically, and preach the gospel.

No scribe ever recorded Miss Moon as being beautiful. Animated, attractive, charming, delightful, yes. Energetic, healthy, fearless, forceful, yes. The tiny body contained a powerful personality which overcame any physical liabilities.

11

The New Lottie Moon Story

The manners and mannerisms of Lottie Moon can best be explained in the context of her family. In turn, the family can best be understood in the setting of its ancestral estate. So, Lottie Moon's story begins at her country home, Viewmont.

Throughout most of the 1800s it was a choice address—Viewmont, Albemarle County, Virginia, on the road between Charlottesville and Scottsville. In the immediate neighborhood were the estates of two Presidents of the United States—Thomas Jefferson and James Monroe.

Viewmont was the command post for Captain John Harris, the richest man in prosperous Albemarle County.[4] From this comfortable country seat he ruled three thousand acres of prime Virginia real estate spread over ten different plantations. His domain reached to New Orleans, Memphis, and Kentucky, where he traded tobacco, cotton, and anything else that paid well.[5] It is said that he owned 800 slaves, but only 160 were counted in Albemarle County in 1830. Nevertheless, he was by far the largest slaveholder in the county.

Viewmont was already an historic site when Captain Harris took it over in 1803. The house was built prior to 1744 by Joshua Fry, surveyor, military hero, and friend of George Washington. Later it was the retreat of Gov. Edmund Randolph. In Harris's day Viewmont had survived fire and remodeling.

The Viewmont house was in character for the landed rural gentry. It was a two-storied wooden structure braced on two sides by one-story porticoes and on two ends by massive brick chimneys. Each chimney was more than twenty feet wide. Each served two rooms downstairs and two more rooms up. One chimney hid a secret staircase. Another housed a warming cupboard for the formal dining room. Handsome hand-carved paneling decorated the parlors.

The utilitarian furnishings of eight rooms were set off by plentiful gold and silver decorations. Fifteen beds, including trundles or underbeds, provided room for hospitality.

The kitchen was in the customary separate building on the diningroom side of the house. Beyond were thirty-nine slave cabins. The main house stood on a prominent hill, viewing a ring of green mountains. Viewmont's 1,500 acres rolled gently over virgin woodlands, tobacco fields, and cornfields.

(Upper) Aerial view of Viewmont estate. Modern house built from chimney bricks of the Moon home stands on the site of the original house. (Foreign Mission Board, Fon H. Scofield, Jr.)
(Lower) Viewmont (University of Virginia Library, Manuscript Division)

Grandfather of Lottie Moon:
Capt. John Harris

(from portrait, Cary N. Moon)

Grandmother of Lottie Moon:
Sarah Coleman Turner Barclay Harris

(from portrait, Cary N. Moon)

On a nearby knoll in view of the parlor was a little family cemetery. There Harris buried his first, childless wife, Frances R. Harris, on March 6, 1816.[6]

In the absence of sons to become the princes of his empire, Harris looked upon numerous nephews. One he chose was Edward Harris Moon, grandson of his sister, Elizabeth Digges. He dispatched young Edward to Memphis to learn the mercantile business.

When advanced in years, the Captain met and married a charming widow, Sarah Coleman Turner Barclay. With her came to Viewmont four children. Sarah had first been married to Robert Barclay. Barclay was from the house of wealthy Philadelphia Quakers. His father, Thomas Barclay, was Thomas Jefferson's friend and the ambassador to France and Morocco. Sarah and Robert Barclay sought their fortune in her native Virginia. On a journey back to Philadelphia to get merchandise for his store, Barclay drowned.

Sarah was left with three children and another yet unborn. Her mother-in-law, the stern Mary Hoops Barclay of Philadelphia, provided ample advice and scarce funds for the young widow. In a dream Sarah Barclay saw herself traveling to Albemarle County, following signs reading "Keep On," until she found streets of gold. Acting on this dream, she found Captain John Harris at Viewmont; and he found the children he had missed. They were married September 26, 1818.[7]

Harris's pet was Anna Maria, a little girl born after her real father's drowning in 1809. But he also doted on James Turner, Thomas, and Mary Elizabeth. Each received a maximum education, including the University of Pennsylvania medical school for James, a University of Virginia law degree for Thomas, and finishing school in Richmond for Anna Maria.[8]

In 1826 the Captain wrote his will to the advantage of his adopted children and selected nephews. Stepdaughter Mary Elizabeth Barclay had already married one of his favored grandnephews, John Digges Moon, and to them he left a choice property. James and Thomas Barclay were also to receive property. To petite, beautiful Anna Maria Barclay, he left Viewmont, which she might possess upon the death of her mother. To John Digges Moon's brother, the favored Edward Harris Moon, he left nothing—perhaps as a matchmaking maneuver. Edward soon felt it wise to return from Memphis to marry Anna Maria on October 16, 1830. Thus he became joint heir to Viewmont.

When Harris died in 1832, dozens of relatives and connections pounced greedily upon his holdings. Lawsuit followed lawsuit, with Sarah Coleman Turner Barclay Harris finally suing her own children. Although the estate was not settled until 1838 or later, there were houses and lands to spare.[9]

Edward and Anna Maria Moon had the Viewmont roof over their heads, living with her mother, as their children were born. First came Thomas Barclay Moon in 1831. Next was Orianna Russell Moon in 1834, soon called Orie. Then came Isaac Anderson Moon—Ike—in 1836.

When the next child was born, she was named Charlotte Digges Moon, in memory of her father's mother who had died shortly before. Her birthdate was December 12, 1840 at approximately 6:30 in the evening. Shortly she was known as Lottie, which she usually abbreviated from her full name as "Lotte."[10]

Four years later came Sarah Coleman Moon, named for the maternal grandmother. This daughter came to be known both as Sally and as Colie. In 1848 came Mary E. (probably Elizabeth) Moon, called Mollie and sometimes Midie. Yet another daughter arrived in 1851. She was named Robinett B. Moon, but this name was soon to be changed to Edmonia Harris Moon, or Eddie.[11]

Little Miss Charlotte was born into the eye of a hurricane of religious debate and change. Her forebears had been pious people. Captain Harris's will specified that one hundred Bibles be purchased, whatever the price, and distributed to the poor households which did not have a Bible. His widow, Sarah, held the religious reins tightly as her children began to bring spouses into the family. She was a staunch Baptist who took her children to the Ballinger's Creek and Pine Grove (later called Hardware) Baptist churches in the countryside.

Son James Turner Barclay married a Presbyterian wife, Julia Sowers of Staunton. After they honeymooned at Viewmont, her father gave them a house in Charlottesville, where James entered the drug business. Shortly afterward he became a Presbyterian, to the dismay of his mother.[12]

Mother of Lottie Moon: Anna Maria Barclay Moon
(Mrs. J. S. Andrews)

Father of Lottie Moon: Edward Harris Moon (Mrs. J. S. Andrews)

In 1832 James and Julia traded their home and three thousand dollars to buy Monticello, home of the late Thomas Jefferson. Young Barclay found the estate of his grandfather's friend and stepfather's neighbor in a run-down condition. Major repairs to house, grounds, and furnishings took vast amounts of time and money. The large family, including Anna Maria and her babies, joined the stream of strangers who constantly came to Barclay's Monticello. One servant worked full-time keeping the floors shined.[13]

Soon the notoriety and expense of Monticello became a burden. For one thing, Barclay's mother objected to the financial subsidy she must have been making to the tourist attraction. For another, the ostentatious life-style offended Barclay's deepening religious convictions.

He felt the call of God into foreign missions. Pioneering missionaries were persistently dodging their way past China's forbidding borders, and Barclay wished to join them. He was corresponding in 1834 with Karl Gutzlaff who had just worked his way into Canton and Macao. Gutzlaff assured him that his wife would be a welcome asset if God had called them to China.[14] Julia Barclay gave all her jewelry to the support of Presbyterian missions. (Not until 1836 did the Baptists send Jehu Lewis Shuck and his wife Henrietta Hall, who became the first American Protestant woman missionary to China.)

In 1835 Barclay sold Monticello at a great loss and retreated to Viewmont. The move pleased his mother, but his preparations for China drove her to hysteria. She had lost her only other son, Thomas, who had drowned mysteriously in the James River in 1828. She set Barclay up in a house and a drug shop in nearby Scottsville, and China was placed on a remote shelf of the family's lore.

Meanwhile at Viewmont, Anna Maria and Edward Moon gave birth to their children and observed the rise of religious debates. While Edward remained a devout Presbyterian, Anna Maria was aggressively Baptist. Itinerant Baptist ministers made Viewmont their home away from home. Because Baptist preaching was not available in the area every Sunday, the young and old hostesses of Viewmont invited Baptists to worship in their home.[15]

These services must have become heated discussions as the Presbyterian-turned-Baptist, Alexander Campbell, began to ply the area with cries for reformation. Entire Baptist congregations and many individuals in the area separated from their traditional beliefs. The crisis became very personal when the late Captain Harris's nephew, Reuben L. Coleman, pastor of the First Baptist Church of Charlottesville, declared himself a "Campbellite."

While Anna Maria Moon was pregnant with Lottie, a Campbellite revivalist drew huge crowds in Charlottesville and Scottsville. James Barclay warned his mother and sisters to stay away from these dangerous meetings. But he and Julia, perhaps out of friendship for Reuben Coleman, attended and found themselves willing to join forces with the new denomination which was being called the "Disciples." The people of Viewmont were indignant, but this time Mrs. Harris's fury could not stop her son. He became an elder and builder of the Disciples church in Scottsville.

The well-known Baptist divine, Robert Semple, traveled to Viewmont to warn the Baptists to resist, for "Aunt Harris" feared that her daughter was slipping under the Campbell influence. The Presbyterian pastor brought a book to Edward Moon to confirm his beliefs on infant baptism. Edward was stunned into deep religious introspection, and he came out a Baptist.[16]

So it was that Lottie Moon was born into a home whose Baptist belief and loyalty were deliberately established. Shortly after her birth, the Moons headed a movement to establish a Baptist church in Scottsville. Perhaps a desire to counteract the growing prosperity of the Disciples led Edward to give property and funds for building a substantial brick edifice for the Scottsville Baptist Church in 1842. He became a deacon and clerk, led in the establishment of a Sunday School, and often represented his congregation at Baptist association meetings.[17] In this church Edward and Anna Maria lined up Tom, Orie, Ike, Lottie, and later Colie and Mollie, in a stiff family pew, while the baby stayed home with servants. At home Mrs. Moon read religious books to the children. One was the story of Ann Judson, the first Baptist woman missionary from America.[18]

In 1847 the matriarch, Sarah Harris, died at Viewmont. She willed one hundred dollars each to the Pine Grove and Scottsville Baptist Churches, earning a lavish obituary in the Baptist press. Edward Moon, who had been exclusively in the mercantile business, now assumed the lands and slaves of Viewmont. All the family were freer to pursue their own preferences in life.

James Barclay began to preach in Disciples churches in 1848, and he agitated widely for the founding of a missionary-sending body. Although the idea seemed totally in opposition to some of the views of his friend, Alexander Campbell, it succeeded. In 1849 Barclay offered himself to the newly formed American Christian Missionary Society.

The children of Viewmont must have heard with eyes and mouths shocked wide at what their Barclay cousins told them. Dr. James returned to his vine-covered Scottsville cottage after visiting a patient. He found his wife reading the eleventh chapter of Romans as she sat on the porch. The two young sons were building a bee house. The daughter was seated on the lawn. The father began to discuss with his children the Bible's missionary teachings. Then he asked if the family would accompany him to Jerusalem to preach the gospel to the Jews. He asked each to think about the proposal overnight. Then those who wished to go were to sign their names in the family Bible on Sunday morning.

They reported to the Moons that all had signed. In 1850, Lottie Moon's tenth year, she and all the countryside sent her uncle off as a missionary. Barclay was the first, and for many years the only, missionary of the Disciples. He apparently provided most of his own support through the channels of the American Christian Missionary Society. Probably a great deal of family money helped him. He served as an evangelist, physician, druggist, and researcher. He wrote back to Scottsville of his adventures in archaeology around the Dome of the Rock and in the sewers of Jerusalem.[19]

Back in Virginia, Edward and Anna Maria handled business and family concerns of growing complexity. In general, the children were overindulged and underdisciplined. The finest tutors were brought to Viewmont to teach classics, French, and music. Edward built a valuable library, especially for the bookish and pouty Orianna.[20]

The New Lottie Moon Story

Despite the parents' best efforts, the acrimony of religious dispute left a bad impression on the children. They developed real hostility to Christian matters and stayed home from church whenever possible.

Thomas aspired to be a doctor. After being tutored, he was sent to the University of Virginia in nearby Charlottesville. Orie was given the year 1850-51 at the academically strong Troy Female Seminary in New York, but she stayed home after the birth of her sister Edmonia in 1851. Ike was preparing for the Albemarle bar.

With seven children and fifty-two slaves, a dog named Shep, tobacco growing in Virginia, a mercantile business, church leadership, property in Mississippi, and a high social standing to maintain, Edward was a busy man.[21] He cooperated with his brothers, Jacob N. Moon, who ran family mercantile and financial interests from the Memphis side, and John Digges Moon, a planter at the nearby Albemarle estate, Mount Ayr.

In November of 1852 a severe illness threatened Edward's life. From his bed in Viewmont, he told his pastor and friends, "I am ready to die. Nothing gives me uneasiness but my two grown children. No tongue can express my feelings as the thought rushes upon my mind—both unconverted. Both give signs of hostility to the religion of Jesus."[22] The children gathered at bedside showed no remorse at this emotional plea.

Edward called for his attorney and wrote his will. In it he revealed the family's high value of education and the potential for equality accorded the girls. Edward explained that he was keeping an account book on expenditures for the children's education. Already Thomas's expenses had taken $3,600, Orianna's $1,050, and Ike's $550.

Edward directed that Anna Maria take over his estate and continue to keep accounts on the children's expenses for education, clothing, and getting established in life after age thirteen. After her death, all these expenses were to be deducted from the children's equal share in the estate.[23] Edward's wealth must have been considerable, for it was not revealed in the United States Census, as were the holdings of all other men in his area. He was one of the top slaveholders in the county.

All preparations having been made for death, the disease retreated. Soon Edward was laying plans for a new driveway from the main road to the plantation house, and he left Anna Maria orders about cutting of trees. Then he departed for his regular business trip to New Orleans and Memphis. Aboard the steamboat *James Robb,* somewhere between those two cities, fire broke out. As the passengers made for shore, Edward hoisted the heavy trunk carrying his money for the trip. He had either a heart attack or a stroke and died on the riverbank on January 26, 1853.[24]

When his body came to the little cemetery at Viewmont, the Scottsville Baptist Church knew that it had lost a vital prop. The grieving family changed the name of the baby girl Robinett, who was less than two years old, to Edmonia Harris Moon, honoring the father.

Anna Maria, age forty-four, was left to assume leadership of family and support of the church. Lottie, age thirteen, entered the critical teen years in a female-run household.

Notes———— See pp. 302-303 for Key to Sources.

1. Mrs. Minnie Pettigrew Voyles, Memphis, Texas, in interview by Mrs. Frank (Leta) Ellis, 1978. Mrs. Ellis rechecked the matter of height with Mrs. Voyles October 26, 1979, at the author's request. Mrs. Voyles' sister was missionary nurse Jessie Pettigrew Glass, and Miss Moon visited their home in Fincastle, Virginia. Young Minnie, five feet, two inches herself, was pleased that she was taller than the precious Miss Moon. Other recollections of Miss Moon's height vary, though she was usually described as petite. Janie Lide, one of her closest co-workers, testified, "She was a small woman, less than five feet tall." In the summer of 1978 the author measured Miss Moon's great-niece, Mrs. Henry Davis. She was four feet, two inches tall, weighed eighty-three pounds, and closely resembled pictures of Miss Moon. Several other women descendants of Orianna Moon have been observed by the author to be unusually small.

2. Mrs. W. E. Hatcher in an interview with Una Roberts Lawrence, whose research for her book, *Lottie Moon,* is preserved at The Southern Baptist Theological Seminary, Louisville.

3. Mrs. W. E. Hatcher, "She Being Dead, Yet Speaketh," *RH,* March 6, 1913.

4. Frederick D. Nichols, "The Two Viewmonts," *The Magazine of Albemarle County History,* volume 8, 1953. A marker placed by Virginia WMU and one honoring Fry mark the location of Viewmont today on Highway 20

between Charlottesville and Scottsville near Carter's Bridge. The original house was deserted and burned in 1939, and a contemporary house was built from the brick of the two chimneys. The cemetery remains enclosed by a stone wall, but no gravestones are legible.

5. Lawrence, *Lottie Moon.*

6. See Nichols for complete analysis of the Viewmont house; Lawrence for insights into Captain Harris; 1830 United States Census for Albemarle County. See also complete abstract of Viewmont property owned by Mr. and Mrs. L. R. Walker, dated August 9, 1937, Alderman Library, University of Virginia, Charlottesville.

7. Fannie Moon Butts to Una Roberts Lawrence, and M. B. Nichols to Mrs. Lawrence, URL.

8. R. L. Coleman, "In Memoriam," a life sketch of James Turner Barclay, in the *Christian Standard,* March 20, 1875.

9. Will and probate of Captain John Harris, a handwritten ledger in possession of his descendant, Dr. Cary Nelson Moon, Charlottesville, Virginia. Also, card file at Alderman Library, University of Virginia, shows evidence of suit by Sarah Harris against Edward Harris Moon, et al. The broadside mentioned could not be located on two occasions when requested by the author. Other insights are in Edgar Woods, *History of Albemarle County, Virginia.*

10. Letters signed by Lottie Moon and addressed to her in the 1860s show that she used the spelling "Lotte." She occasionally used this spelling later in her life, but only when writing to family members. In writing to others, she signed her name "Lottie," or usually simply "L. Moon." She never signed her name as Charlotte. This name was used only in connection with school advertisements when she taught in Danville and Cartersville and in one property deed in later years. There is no clear evidence of how she thought her middle name should be spelled. For many years "Diggs" was the commonly used spelling. But this was an ancestral name always spelled by the family as "Digges."

The day of her birth is not confirmed in any primary materials. December 12 is commonly accepted among family members and the available evidence does not rule this out.

11. See Albemarle County records of the United States Census for 1850, 1860, and 1870 to establish full names and spellings. Scattered family papers and other records reflect the wide variety of nicknames. For reference to change in name for Edmonia Moon, see H. A. Tupper, *Foreign Missions of the Southern Baptist Convention.* This book's reference to Lottie as "Charlotte Mildred Moon," picked up in several Baptist papers in the period of publication is interesting. *Charlotte M.* appears on the most complete known listing of Moon children and their birthdates. This list, discovered by Mrs. Russell Thomas, also verifies the name change for Edmonia. Unfortunately, the exact date of Lottie's birth has crumbled away from the list. The list reveals that

Anna Maria gave birth a total of eleven times. J. B., born in 1838, did not survive. Julia B., born 1838, lived until Lottie was almost two, 1842, then died three weeks before Anna Maria bore a son who lived only three hours. A daughter was stillborn in 1847, between Sarah and Mary.

12. *The Christian Standard,* March 20, 1875.

13. Decima Campbell Barclay, daughter of Alexander Campbell and daughter-in-law of Barclay, wrote about the Monticello experience, defending the family against accusations of abusing the historic house. An undated typed copy, written in the lifetime of Julia Sowers Barclay, is at the Disciples of Christ Historical Society, Nashville. Mrs. Barclay gives details of the exploits of Thomas Barclay, sent by George Washington to France, and his friendship with Thomas Jefferson.

14. Letter from C. H. Gutzlaff to Barclay, Disciples of Christ Historical Society. One of the two sons born to Barclay while he lived at Monticello was named for Gutzlaff.

15. United States Census of 1850 lists the Scottsville minister, J. H. Fox, as a resident of Viewmont. Also, letter from Lottie Moon to "Dear Cary," July 9, 1910, URL.

16. *The Christian Standard,* March 20, 1875. For evidence of Edward Moon's early piety, see a letter from him to Reuben H. Coleman, May 18, 1829, from Memphis, found in LMLF. Also Edward Harris Moon obituary, *RH,* February 17, 1853.

17. Joel T. Kidd, "Scottsville Baptist Church," unpublished manuscript at Virginia Baptist Historical Society, Richmond. Also, Susie N. Blair, *Scottsville Baptist Church, A History.* References to E. H. Moon occur in Albemarle Baptist Association Minutes, The Southern Baptist Theological Seminary. Lottie wrote of her family's church life to Cary, July 9, 1910, URL. The Scottsville Baptist Church is still standing, and Viewmont's parlor furniture is on the platform.

18. Lawrence, *Lottie Moon.*

19. *The Christian Standard,* March 20, 1875. Also, Minutes, American Christian Missionary Society, 1849, 1850, and following. Also, article by Mrs. Margaret Thomson in "Christian Sunday School Journal" of July, 1852, quoted in M. C. Tiers, *Christian Portrait Gallery,* 1864.

20. William Luther Andrews, "Doctor Moon," unpublished manuscript by son of Orianna, 1936, distributed to members of the family.

21. Slave Census, Albemarle County, Virginia, 1850 Census.

22. *RH,* February 17, 1853.

23. Will of Edward H. Moon, November 27, 1852, recorded at Albemarle County Court House, Charlottesville, Virginia.

24. *RH,* February 17, 1853.

2

She Was
the Best-Educated Woman in the South

Anna Maria Moon had been groomed to behave with poise and dignity in all circumstances. In finishing school she learned to converse in French and to relish things cultural. She tried to pass on this atmosphere to her family. She did not allow her children to gossip.[1] Instead, they were encouraged to discuss ideas and things of beauty, such as their gardens, pet animals, literature, religion, and history. Rides and romps with multitudes of cousins provided social outlets.

One Sunday, Lottie and the other children connived to stay home while their mother and the slaves attended church at Scottsville, nine miles away. According to Mrs. Moon's rigid rules for Sunday, no cooking or other work was allowed after breakfast. She left home with the kitchen building locked. When she rode back up the winding drive to Viewmont, she saw smoke rising. Rushing in, she found a hot dinner on the dining table. The mischievous Lottie had climbed in the kitchen window and organized the other children as cooks, runners to the main house, and servers. Mrs. Moon was not pleased.[2]

Possibly Lottie's merriment was one of the few light touches at Viewmont. As the middle child, she was the stereotypical exception to the family pattern, differing toward the positive. Tom's personality is not well known, but he apparently had feet itchy to be gone from home. Orianna seems to have been moody and dissatisfied. Isaac seems to have lacked drive and personality. The younger girls, Colie and Mollie, were known to be restless, flirtatious, and argumentative. Eddie (as Edmonia was dubbed) was spoiled and temperamental, never knowing a father's influence. While things at home were surely not unpleasant, the seven individualists were seeking something else, and there was money for them to venture out.

Children like the Moons were expected to be well educated and well married. The boys should have taken over the farm. The girls should have reigned over large homes, plentifully staffed by slaves and populated by children—all of whom must be fed, clothed, doctored, and educated. Every known woman in the Moon family tree had followed this pattern. Girls of more limited circumstances might think of teaching school or working as governesses or seamstresses; but, of course, these should not have been possibilities for Moon girls. But the Moon girls broke out of the traditional mold.

Mrs. Moon became head of a household in transition. For a year after their father's death, the children remained more or less in residence. In the fall of 1854 the nest began to empty. Thomas was married December 26, 1853, in festivities at Viewmont. Using a bequest from his father, he then worked as a physician along the Mississippi River. His bride was Helen Vaughn Wilson, a belle of a neighboring family with connections in Dardanelle, Arkansas, where they moved. They had a son, Thomas Barclay Moon, II, in 1855. Soon after the child was born, they were on their way to California to look for gold. An epidemic of cholera broke out on their riverboat near Fort Leavenworth, Kansas. Sending Helen and the baby to safety, Dr. Tom stayed to minister to the victims. He contracted the disease, died, and was buried in Fort Leavenworth. Helen took the child to live at Viewmont for a year and for other visits there before she remarried. Little Tom was too young to remember his Virginia family, but they did not forget him.[3]

Orianna, at age twenty, embarked on a revolutionary path. She had been exposed to the feminist rumblings from Seneca Falls, New York, where the first Women's Rights Convention had been held in 1848, just prior to her studies at Troy Female Seminary.[4] Perhaps this background impressed her to enroll in the Female Medical College of Pennsylvania in 1854. The college had been advertised in the *Religious Herald*, published by Baptists and received faithfully in the Moon home. This school, founded in 1850 by Quakers, was the second institution in the nation dedicated to teaching medicine to women. Before Orie arrived only three women from the South had enrolled, and they had soon dropped out.

Medicine was not the only thing Orie learned in three years of study. Because of the controversy and social stigma related to women doctors, all persons in the school's circle had to be courageous radicals. At her boarding house, Orie learned ideas foreign to the ways of Albemarle County. Dr. Ann Preston, the only woman faculty member, was a friend of Lucretia Mott, Elizabeth Blackwell, and other leading American feminists. Other faculty were ardent abolitionists who aided runaway slaves. Because the women students were taunted and barred from practice at all Philadelphia hospitals, the Female Medical College set up its own clinic where students specialized in treating women, the courageous, or the destitute.

A number of Orie's fellow students had intentions to serve as medical missionaries. One who graduated in 1854 was rejected as a missionary applicant because she was an unmarried woman. This rejection helped lead to the establishment of the Woman's Union Missionary Society, one of the earliest missionary-sending bodies that would appoint single women. Orie, of course, was not a "professor of religion," but from these proceedings she learned of the role a woman could have in missions.

After writing a thesis on the relation between cardiac and pulmonary diseases, Orie became Dr. Moon on February 28, 1857. She and a North Carolinian were the first Southern women to earn medical degrees. Dr. Moon had not been a spectacular student, graduating sixth in the class of seven, but she had daringly attained great distinction among women of her era.[5] She must also have attained ridicule, for she said to her future sister-in-law, "My dear, you must be very brave to marry a man with me for a sister."

Meanwhile, Isaac concluded his studies at the University of Virginia and was admitted to the Albemarle County bar in 1855. He attended the Charlottesville Baptist Church as a student and was greatly influenced by John A. Broadus, pastor of the church and chaplain of the university. In 1856, after he had returned to help his mother run Viewmont, he wrote Broadus that he had decided to become a Baptist. He had evidently studied the denominational options carefully. Though he preferred uniting with the Charlottesville Baptist group, he decided for convenience to join the Scottsville church.[6] He married Margaret Elizabeth Jones of Buckingham County, Virginia, on January 29, 1857.

The fourth child, Lottie, was also sent off for an education. If she attended nearby primary schools, as some have suggested, no record was made or future note taken. In 1854 Mrs. Moon sent her to a reliable, carefully controlled school run by leading Virginia Baptists. The Virginia Female Seminary at Botetourt Springs (a resort near Roanoke) was informally connected to the Baptists of Virginia, primarily through its superintendent, Charles L. Cocke.[7]

Lottie was one of one hundred boarding students accepted for the 1854-55 term. She signed up for English and arithmetic from the preparatory department. The bulk of her studies were in the two-year collegiate program. Lottie's grades in Latin, French, arithmetic, and English were good. In two quarters she received perfect scores in French. In natural science she began with a grade of "very deficient," but she steadily improved to "tolerable" in the fourth quarter.

Playtime was painfully limited for a girl of fourteen, with only two hours a day not designated for study, meals, or chapel. For fun, the girls could go on well-chaperoned outings to the Botetourt Springs, pursue the arts, or go to Enon Baptist Church across the road. Lottie's roommate and chum, Cary Ann Coleman, was romantically involved with James Moon, a double first cousin Lottie called "Brother," so she surely found opportunity to engage in girlish gossip.[8]

Lottie returned for a second year in the fall of 1855. Her sister, listed as Coleman Moon, enrolled too. This year the school was reconstituted with improved financial backing. Now it was called Hollins Institute (later Hollins College). Lottie continued to do good work in Latin, superior work in French, and deficient work in junior mathematics. She did not attempt further science studies. In a drawing course, she ranked as "tolerable."

Despite her mixed grades, she established a reputation for being studious and intellectual. She was a charter member of the Euzelian Society, a literary organization, and she helped edit its paper. She also earned a reputation for being a prankster and wit. On April Fool's Day of 1855, she climbed the bell tower by dawn's early light and muffled the bell with bedsheets, getting the school off to a late start.[9] The prank caused much laughter, and she lost only a half-point in her deportment grade. However, the good little girl who began her Hollins career with a perfect grade in deportment was "deficient" or sometimes "tolerable" by the end.

Hollins was well regarded for its academic emphasis, unlike the ornamental atmosphere which predominated in most girls' schools of the day. A correspondent of the *Religious Herald* claimed it to be the "equal, if not superior" of any female school in America.[10]

In addition to Cocke, faculty members included such noted Baptist educators as William Pleasants and A. B. Brown. Girls were strongly encouraged to attend worship services. Chapel services were required twice daily, and attendance was reported to parents. Lottie maintained perfect worship attendance for six quarters. During the last two quarters, she was absent twenty-six times.

July 3, 1856, was graduation day for Lottie. Lottie sat with the student body dressed in snowy dresses and blue sashes. The Enon Baptist Church was packed for the occasion. Young ladies demonstrated their expertise in singing and in playing the piano, violin, and flute. Several honor students prepared essays which were read to the assembly. In the proprieties of the times, they were read not by the girls, but by distinguished men. Women did not make addresses with men present.

The only young woman to earn the "large diploma" of Hollins that year, indicating completion of the full course, prepared her essay on "Women's Rights." Observers noticed with some relief that the author "appreciates the true character of woman and understands in what her rights really consist."[11] The proper role of women was exciting some editorial debate in those early years. All Baptists of any prominence, including the professors at Hollins, agreed that the role of the educated woman was to preside in the parlor and keep silent in the church. This was the valedictory message given to Lottie Moon, along with a diploma in French. Although she did not become a full graduate of Hol-

The New Lottie Moon Story

lins, she had a high education for a sixteen-year-old. What could she do with it?

It was back to Viewmont for Lottie, where it was time for Eddie to be starting on her educational path. For a time Lottie tutored her little sister, who was eleven years her junior. Lottie also helped with the duties of running the house, heard Orie's astounding vacation reports of feminist life in Philadelphia, exchanged visits with schoolmates, and spent solitary hours reading Latin and French.

Baptists throughout Virginia, especially those in the Charlottesville area, were buzzing about a new concept of "female education" afoot near the University of Virginia. The innovators included A. E. Dickinson, associate editor of the *Religious Herald,* and John A. Broadus, pastor of the Charlottesville Baptist Church. With other leading Baptist men of the state, they decided that women should have the same educational opportunity that men had—separate, but equal. No men's school in the South exceeded the University of Virginia. In an era which seriously doubted that women had the capacity for higher education, Baptist men organized the Albemarle Female Institute in Charlottesville. It was to be run in courses, style of instruction, examinations, and degrees exactly like the nearby university. An ornamental department was also provided to add finishing touches to the young ladies who needed them. Otherwise, all courses were tough academic ones taught by men who had earned the rare Master of Arts degree from the university.[12]

John Hart, noted Baptist educator, was chosen to be principal of the Albemarle Female Institute. Crawford Howell Toy, later a controversial theologian among Southern Baptists, was enlisted as his assistant. They divided the course work into schools of ancient languages, modern languages, mathematics, natural sciences, moral philosophy, history and literature, and English and composition. Music and preparatory courses were available. This curriculum was said to be the first to depart from strict classics to include advanced academic study of English.[13]

Early faculty members, in addition to Professors Hart and Toy, included H. H. Harris (later to be president of the Southern Baptist

Foreign Mission Board), William N. Bronaugh, J. C. Hiden, and John Baker Thompson.

To this exciting new school came Lottie Moon, along with several of her cousins and old Hollins classmates. Cary Ann Coleman was again her roommate.

Girls boarded under Professor Hart's watchful eye in property taken over from the Monticello Hotel. They paid high tuition and furnished their own "napkins and towels." Lottie was in the second class admitted, beginning September 1857. She took Albemarle Female Institute by storm. Her petite form, twinkling eyes, and merry disposition made her memorable. She was considered a brain and a heretic. Other students admired her, followed her, and were slightly terrified by her. By 1858 she had earned a diploma in Latin in the school of ancient languages, but this was not the end of her studies.[14]

Young men came to call at Albemarle Female Institute, and sometimes Professor Hart permitted his students to receive the visitors. If Lottie received such visits, nobody thought to mention them. Most likely she was in the ranks of girls who unmercifully teased those who did receive male callers.

It was not unheard of for Albemarle Female Institute's unmarried professors to show attentions to young women. One such professor invited his outstanding Greek student to his apartments to snack on sweet potatoes and coffee. Another professor hovered attentively while she practiced piano. Girls were known to develop serious crushes on the eligible Professor Toy.[15] Possibly this was the nature of the relationship which arose between Toy and Lottie, who was indisputably the outstanding student of languages and a match for Toy's brilliance.

Toy taught Lottie English, and he may have been the professor who later wrote, "She writes the best English I have ever been privileged to read." He also taught ancient languages, and Lottie was one of the few women brave enough to pursue Greek. Her high-sounding essay on Greek literature has been preserved.[16] Whatever the depth of the Moon-Toy liaison, it was sufficient to leave a halo which some interpreted as romance.[17]

She delighted in informing new arrivals at the school that Professor

The New Lottie Moon Story

Hart would expect them to join the Baptist church on the following Sunday. Only after the girls fled to the patient professor in tears did they learn that Lottie was teasing. Along with other students, she attended social events at the university. The professors would chaperone these excursions which included musicals, lectures, meetings of literary societies, commencement, and promenades on the lawn to Thomas Jefferson's rotunda.[18]

One student asked Lottie what the initial "D" in her name stood for. "Devil," Lottie shot back. The nickname stuck.

Lottie had a cluster of sharp-minded friends. Of them, she wrote a clever poem on May 15, 1858. She entitled it "Our Crowd" and signed it "Deville." After writing a verse about each of six others, she said of herself,

> Last in the list is your friend Lot
> Who for naught in this world cares a jot
> Except that you'll pardon these foolish rhymes
> And of her, as a friend, you will think sometimes.[19]

The devil-may-care attitude caused concern to many in the school, where Professor Hart and Dr. Broadus maintained a high emphasis on piety.

In 1856 a strange communication had appeared in the *Religious Herald*. It was written from "Amicus" to "Miss M . . . ." The anonymous writer referred to their recent conversation. Miss "M" had flippantly professed not to care for the fate of her soul, excusing herself on the basis of not having thought about it. The writer commended Miss "M" for noble and attractive virtues and "attainment of useful and suitable accomplishments," but pleaded for her to allow God's grace to work in her heart.[20]

Whether the recipient of this public plea was Miss Lottie Moon or another Miss, Christians were trying to convey a similar message to a similarly situated Lottie. Toy's sister, Julia, one of Lottie's closest friends at Albemarle Female Institute, was later to become founding president of the Woman's Missionary Union of Mississippi. Julia and others believed their friend to be a skeptic. Lottie once told Julia as they prepared their Greek recitation on a Monday, "Ah, Julie, I was in better business than this at home yesterday lying on a haystack reading Shakespeare." Julia tried to find words to make Lottie wish she had been professing faith in Christ on that Sunday, but her courage failed her.

In December 1858 the prayers of Lottie's Christian friends were answered. Broadus was holding a series of evangelistic meetings directed to the students in Charlottesville. A group of Albemarle Female Institute students held a sunrise inquiry meeting in support of the effort. Lottie's name was on their prayer list. To the girls' great surprise, the subject of their entreaties showed up at the prayer meeting and got into earnest private conversation with Broadus.

On December 21 she made public her profession of faith in Jesus Christ during a meeting of the Charlottesville Church, and she applied for membership in that church. The only time a woman was permitted to speak before a mixed assembly of men and women was in relating her Christian experience prior to baptism. This Lottie did on December 22.[21] She mentioned that on the night before the inquiry meeting, she had been prevented from sleeping by the barking of a dog. While lying awake, she at last considered the condition of her own soul and determined to give the subject of Christianity an honest, intelligent investigation. Lottie went to the revival meeting to scoff, but returned to pray all night.

Lottie rose from the waters of the Charlottesville Baptist baptistry a noticeably different woman. "She had always wielded an influence because of her intellectual power," wrote Julia. "Now her great talent was directed into another channel. She immediately took a stand as a Christian."[22]

A schoolmate noted that Lottie seemed to be "God's chosen vessel. In his own time, he brought her to his feet, meek, submissive, ready to do any work the master assigned."[23]

Shortly after her baptism, Lottie was presiding over a student prayer meeting. She expounded verse by verse the twelfth chapter of Romans. Others commented on the quiet, sober tone that distinguished her

(Upper) Building occupied by Albemarle Female Institute, early 1850s (FMB) (Lower) First Baptist Church, Charlottesville, Virginia, building where Lottie Moon professed faith in Jesus Christ. (FMB)

behavior from that time on. There was a softer radiance in Lottie's face and a difference of spirit and purpose.

Her influence among students counted for Christ, and she was "different in all those details of the daily life which at last afforded the most delicate test of the Christian character."[24]

Broadus kept before the Baptist students of Charlottesville a constant appeal for life commitment to religious work. "The Call of the Ministry" was a frequent topic with him, and Broadus made these points: the world's need for the gospel; his hearers could supply that need; there was no reason not to do it. Many young men responded to that call. John L. Johnson, who was to marry Julia Toy, and Crawford Toy committed themselves to be foreign missionaries.[25]

In 1859 Johnson and Toy were appointed by the Foreign Mission Board of the Southern Baptist Convention to open its mission work in Japan.[26] Toy immediately left Albemarle Female Institute to attend the first classes at Southern Baptist Theological Seminary, and he completed the course in one year. The most blue-ribbon pastors in Virginia ordained them at Charlottesville during commencement season of 1860.[27]

They expected to sail in the fall of 1860, but Johnson was ill from a bout with typhoid and measles. He and his bride, Julia, missed the ship which disappeared at sea with other appointees for Japan.[28] Toy's reason for not being on that boat has never been explained. Perhaps he was looking for a bride to accompany him. The Foreign Mission Board frowned upon men braving the mission field alone. Toy seems to have been seriously interested in a young lady in Greenville, but he lost his bid to another theologian.[29] Then the Civil War flared and prohibited Johnson and Toy from fulfilling their plans.[30]

The young men who heard Broadus's eloquent calls into missions were not the only hearers. Most Baptists did not think that God called women to anything. Broadus wouldn't have thought to direct the mission call to women in the audience, except as they might ride along with husbands. But God did. Lottie Moon responded, inwardly, in the affirmative. Later she wrote of feeling led to the mission field considering Japan as her field. Some have said that there was consideration of marriage between Toy and Lottie at this time. This is barely possible, but not provable.[31]

Lottie had seen many bright girls of her circle plunge into what seemed to be a suitable marriage, only to submerge totally their gifts of intellect and personality. At least one acquaintance in similar circumstances at Albemarle Female Institute was forced by her father to marry the best of her many suitors although she did not love him. The girl thereby lost her chance to teach Greek in a college and to travel abroad.[32] There was no father to force Lottie, and she had no financial reason for rushing into marriage.

The *Religious Herald*, always full of advice to young ladies, carried a warning from "Old Maid" against convenience marriages just when Lottie may have been considering the subject. "That a lovely girl should marry any honest man who happens to ask her 'will you' simply because she thinks it may be her 'last chance,' and through fear of being called an 'old maid,' is painful to think of. Too many of our sex have already been twitted into marriage by this same silly bugbear and have found afterwards to their sorrow that though their companion was honest, yet he was far from being the one to fill their hearts' wishes."[33]

If there was a marriage proposal, Lottie was not ready for it. And, at about the same time, a gentle hint went out from foreign mission circles that consideration might be given to appointing single women as missionaries. It might not be necessary for a woman called by God into missions to go on the strength of a husband.

Lottie's own immediate course was to exhaust the possibilities at Albemarle Female Institute. Academically, she was tops. Her Latin examinations were so stunning that her professor had them reviewed by the university's faculty.

Professor Hart was so impressed by her moral philosophy exam that he wrote John A. Broadus to say it was the best he had ever seen.[34] A professor later wrote that she never failed an exam and was usually first in the class. He never again heard a woman read Greek so fluently and appreciatively. He pronounced her the most scholarly of all the graduates of Albemarle Female Institute.[35]

At school she became proficient in Greek, Latin, Italian, French, and

Spanish.[36] On Toy's recommendation, she began independent study of Hebrew,[37] and her Greek studies were largely extracurricular.

Although the standard course for the full degree at Albemarle Female Institute was three years, Lottie returned for a fourth. Before it was completed, Virginia had joined the Confederate States of America. The students at Albemarle Female Institute and at the university were preoccupied with the romance and uncertainty of Civil War. Yet Professor Hart commanded a semblance of order, and commencement exercises went off as scheduled. Five young women had put in so many extra studies according to the University of Virginia standards that the trustees thought it well to award them Master of Arts degrees. Lottie was one of the recipients. These were thought to be the first awarded women by a Southern institution or earned by women of the South. At her side was Jennie Snead, later to be Mrs. W. E. Hatcher, president of Virginia Woman's Missionary Union, who preserved the memory of the occasion. Lottie herself never displayed such laurels.[38]

As Lottie closed a chapter in her life, Broadus was able to call her "the most educated (or cultured) woman in the South." An admiring classmate wrote, "She has a mind and a wealth of knowledge that is the fortune of few women to possess."[39]

With a hint of her destiny, Lottie had earlier written in a translation from the *Aeneid* in Julia Toy's autograph book:

> While rivers shall run into the sea, while clouds shall move around the convex summits of the mountains, while the vault of the sky shall sustain the stars, always thy honor and thy name and thy praises shall continue with me whatever lands may call me.[40]

Back home at Viewmont, Lottie found sister Orianna back from the great adventure of her life. Uncle James Turner Barclay and family had returned from Jerusalem in 1858 for furlough. While in the United States, he saw to the publication of his massive book, *The City of the Great King,* regarding his archaeological work in Jerusalem. Orianna, sitting at home unable to have a formal medical practice because of public opinion, took the opportunity for travel abroad. Journeying with the Barclays back to Jerusalem, she visited France, Egypt, and many points in the Middle East.[41]

Once when walking on ship deck alone, she was accosted by a fresh young officer. He asked menacingly, "Aren't you afraid to be traveling alone?" Orianna drew a pistol from her skirts and blasted a seagull with one shot. She had no more trouble until she engaged a small boat to get her across some Middle Eastern barrier of water. The boatmen stopped in midstream to demand higher pay. Again Orianna rescued herself with the pistol. She had no reluctance to pull the gun again when an Arab chieftain insisted that she join his harem. After that, her Uncle James kept her under surveillance. She assisted him in medical work.[42]

Under the influence of the missionary spirit and the Holy Land scenes, Orianna reconsidered her hostile stance toward Christianity. At about the same time Lottie was being baptized in Charlottesville into a Baptist church, Orianna was being baptized in Jerusalem as a Disciple. A friend of Barclay's wrote the news to a Disciples publication: "Dr. Barclay's niece had grown up an open enemy to the Bible. She was a champion of Woman's Rights, with all the revolting and blasphemous claims which are sometimes given to the public through the newspapers. You will rejoice to hear that this poor, young creature has been brought to her right mind and now devours the Word she so lately despised and waits to be baptized in Jerusalem."[43]

Shortly after, Orianna left her cousins serving in United States' consulates[44] and her uncle's clinic to seek her future at Viewmont. What could she do—extremely well educated, brilliant, enlightened, well-to-do, Christian—a woman? Her sister Lottie returned to Viewmont in a similar quandary.

Notes———— See pp. 302-303 for Key to Sources.

1. Lawrence, *Lottie Moon.*
2. Lawrence, *Lottie Moon.* Also, handwritten interview notes by Mrs. Lawrence in URL.

3. Louise Haddock, "Lottie Moon's Family in Oklahoma," *The Oklahoma Baptist Chronicle*, Autumn 1977. Miss Haddock provided much additional information about Dr. Thomas B. Moon after interviewing his granddaughter, Mrs. Anna Milner, and his great-granddaughter, Mrs. Rita Watkins, of Tulsa, Oklahoma.

4. Records of Troy Female Seminary, now the Willard School, Troy, New York.

5. Records of Female Medical College of Pennsylvania, at Archives and Special Collections on Women in Medicine of the Florence A. Moore Library, Medical College of Pennsylvania, Philadelphia. Sources include faculty minutes, Annual Announcements, and Orianna R. Moon's thesis. For more information about this school, the only surviving medical school founded for women, see Mary Roth Walsh, *Doctors Wanted No Women Need Apply,* and Clara Marshall, *The Woman's Medical College of Pennsylvania.*

6. Letter from Isaac A. Moon to John A. Broadus, November 5, 1855, Broadus Papers, The Southern Baptist Theological Seminary. Isaac was listed in the Albemarle bar of 1855 in Woods, *History of Albemarle County.*

7. Records of Hollins College at the school's Fishburn Library, Hollins College, Virginia. Shirley Henn, Reference Librarian, researched Lottie Moon's grades and financial accounts and provided copies of catalogs for the Female Seminary and Hollins Institute during Lottie's attendance.

8. Lawrence, *Lottie Moon.*

9. Ibid.

10. *RH,* July 10, 1856. Also, see stories in *RH* throughout this period to see the high standing of Hollins among Baptists.

11. Ibid.

12. *RH,* June 19, 26; July 24, 31; August 7, 21, 1856; June 11, 1857, and numerous other references, 1856-61.

13. Biographical sketch of John Hart, *RH,* August 22, 1895.

14. Catalog of the Albemarle Female Institute, 1858-59, LMR. AFI became Rawlings Institute. The property eventually went to the Episcopal Diocese of Virginia for St. Anne's School, now St. Anne's-Belfield School on a different site.

15. Diary of Sarah Graves Strickler Fife, personal property of her descendant, Anne Freudenberg, assistant curator, Manuscripts Department, University of Virginia Library, Charlottesville. Mrs. Fife's diary covers her student days at Albemarle Female Institute, where she pursued a course amazingly like that of Lottie Moon, whom she probably knew well.

16. Copy shared with the author by the late Mrs. Henry Davis, grandniece of Lottie Moon. For the quote on Lottie's English, see *FMJ,* September 1880.

17. Lawrence, *Lottie Moon.*

The New Lottie Moon Story

18. Ibid., and Fife Diary.

19. From autograph album of Mollie Hill Meador (Mrs. E. J. Gresham), provided by Mrs. John Meekin Hunt, Troutville, Virginia.

20. *RH*, September 25, 1956.

21. Records of the First Baptist Church, Charlottesville, Virginia. Available from University of Virginia.

22. Article by Mrs. J. L. Johnson, HH May 1888.

23. *RH*, August 26, 1875.

24. Tupper, *Foreign Missions of the Southern Baptist Convention.*

25. John Lipscomb Johnson, *Autobiographical Notes.* Copy available in Samford University Library's Special Collections.

26. Minutes, Foreign Mission Board, 1859.

27. Biographical sketch of C. H. Toy in George Braxton Taylor, *Virginia Baptist Ministers.*

28. Johnson, *Autobiographical Notes.* Mr. and Mrs. J. Q. A. Rohrer, appointees of the Foreign Mission Board for Japan, were lost on this ship.

29. Letters from Toy to John A. Broadus, between June 1860 and October 1861, mention his pursuit of a Miss Mary (Boatwright?) in South Carolina. She was won by his friend J. A. Chambliss after her mother objected to Toy. See Broadus Papers, The Southern Baptist Theological Seminary.

30. Minutes, Foreign Mission Board, 1860 and following.

31. Una Roberts Lawrence has Lottie romantically linked to an anonymous professor in this era. This person is generally understood to be Toy. If Mrs. Lawrence had specific sources for this belief, they were not available to this author. Toy's correspondence with Broadus, who was also Lottie's friend, indicates nothing about any potential woman friend except "Miss Mary" of Greenville.

32. Fife Diary.

33. *RH*, June 30, 1859.

34. Broadus Papers.

35. Unnamed professor quoted in Tupper, *Foreign Missions of the Southern Baptist Convention.*

36. Mrs. W. E. Hatcher, URL.

37. Lawrence. Additionally Toy gave Lottie a book of Scripture in Hebrew. His inscription, written in Hebrew, said, "Lottie Moon—In Thy light do we see light." This is a quotation from Psalm 36:10. This volume is on display at The Southern Baptist Theological Seminary's Lottie Moon Room.

38. Mrs. W. E. Hatcher to Una Roberts Lawrence, URL.

39. *RH*, August 26, 1875.

40. Julia Toy's autograph book was shared by Mrs. Purser Hewitt (Julia Toy Johnson).

41. William Luther Andrews manuscript.

42. Descendants of Orianna Moon passed on these anecdotes to the author.

43. Letter from Mary R. Williams to Mrs. Alexander Campbell, August 4, 1858, published in the *Millennial Harbinger,* October 1858. Orianna's conversion is also noted by Barclay in the *Millennial Harbinger* of 1859 and in the 1859 Annual Report and Minutes, American Christian Missionary Society.

44. Consular connections are mentioned in several Disciples of Christ records, including obituary for J. T. Barclay in the *Christian Standard,* November 7, 1874.

(Upper) Hardware Baptist Church (formerly Pine Grove), where Lottie Moon was a member and taught Sunday School, near Carter's Bridge, Virginia. (Lower) Scottsville Baptist Church, essentially the same building Lottie Moon's parents help build in 1842.

3
She Was
Cast into a New Era

Wanted—*a place in a private family, by a Virginia lady, who will take charge of a class of small children. . . . Address P.O. Box 14, Scottsville, Albemarle County, Virginia.*[1]

The columns of the *Religious Herald* carried this advertisement while Lottie Moon was telling school friends good-bye in Charlottesville. The friends understood that Lottie intended "going South" to teach.[2] The recommendations of Broadus, Hart, or Toy would have been a first-class ticket to any teaching job, and Lottie had the full endorsement of these gentlemen.

Why would Lottie have felt compelled to launch a career? While the loss of Edward Moon's mercantile income reduced the family prosperity somewhat, Mrs. Moon, overseers, and Ike were farming Viewmont profitably. The value of Anna Maria Moon's personal and real estate was among the highest in the vicinity.[3]

Perhaps the prospect of quiet, rural life at Viewmont seemed dull. There, Lottie would be expected to teach Edmonia. Why not teach for pay? Vistas for all women were lifting. Girl cousins at nearby plantations were also interested in teaching. Perhaps these fortunate young women viewed teaching away from home as a lark.

Whatever Lottie's dreams, they were immediately dashed as the Civil War moved within earshot of Albemarle. Early in the summer, Mrs. Moon and Dr. Orie drove to Charlottesville to convert all available funds into Confederate bonds and currency. At the bank they learned that Confederate troops were flocking to Manassas, northeast toward Washington, while Yankee troops were congregating at a creek called

Bull Run. Orie left her mother and hurried to enlist as a military doctor. The startled enrollment officer accepted her application and, with an unknown degree of chauvinism, instructed her to wait at Viewmont until she was needed.[4]

Eager to see action, Orie heard only a vague message from the ladies of Charlottesville that they would count on her aid to nurse the wounded. She found much more appealing a direct communication from General J. H. Cocke asking for her services. She immediately shot back to him some medical proposals and asked for an appointment in a surgical hospital. She offered herself and her servant without charge, and she promised to work on the field of battle.[5]

Her wish for action was quickly granted, for the major battle at Bull Run, or Manassas, knocked Confederate wounded by the hundreds all the way back to Charlottesville. The university buildings were taken over for hospitals, and Orie was given supervision of a ward.[6] Her descendants understood that she held an actual military commission as surgeon. More likely, she held the title as a courtesy, for the male authorities never bothered to make the arrangement official.[7]

Tradition has it that Lottie, Colie, and Mollie all went to Charlottesville to nurse soldiers. However, for at least part of the time, "Lotte," as she then signed her name, was at Viewmont handling Orie's correspondence with General Cocke.[8]

Tradition also reports that Lottie had a suitor to call at Viewmont during the summer. Such courting usually involved having the young man lodge in the household for several days while friends came and went. Such a visit need not have been romantic. However, the story goes that the young man rode off to be a military chaplain without Lottie's promise of undying love.[9]

Soon the horror of war put Orie to bed for a month of collapse, and Lottie undoubtedly nursed her. In the fall, a suitor came to minister to Orie. She had met John Summerfield Andrews when she was called to consult on the surgery of his brother, wounded at Manassas. When the boy died, Orie loaned Andrews the funds to take him home to Alabama for burial. He returned to Viewmont to settle the debt and to request her hand in marriage.

Orianna was an older woman of twenty-seven, and John was three years younger. Anna Maria Moon would not consent to the wedding until she investigated his credentials. She found him acceptable, and in November 1861 the two doctors were wed at Viewmont.[10]

Otherwise, life at Viewmont was quiet and rather depressing for Lottie. She taught sister Eddie, nurturing in her a facility for foreign languages which was later to surpass her own. She kept in touch with the progress of war, especially with her cousins and her brother who were in fighting units. She promised to go to her beloved cousin Jim and nurse him if he were wounded. She may have done so, for he was wounded twice as he rode with Mosby's Raiders. She assisted her mother with the administration of the plantation, corresponded with friends, and exchanged a few visits. She planted a huge garden of annuals, cultivated roses, and knitted stockings for the soldiers.[11] To a friend she wrote, "I couldn't live without my books, flowers, and music."[12]

Another Lottie Moon, a first cousin named for the same grandmother Charlotte, spent the war much more daringly. The daughter of Edward Harris Moon's brother, Robert S. Moon, who had moved to Oxford, Ohio, served as a Confederate spy. So did her sister, Virginia. Lottie of Ohio was a beautiful, feisty prankster with a streak of steely nerve. She had gone to the wedding altar with Ambrose E. Burnside, only to say "No siree, I won't," when the minister put the crucial question to her.

But another suitor she was dallying with, James Clark, got "Lot" to complete her vows to him by producing a small pistol as they walked the aisle. Virginia Moon promised sixteen different Confederate soldiers she would marry them after the war—to keep their morale up.

During the war, Virginia Moon and Lottie Moon Clark carried dispatches across the battle lines. At one critical point Lottie Clark was captured and taken prisoner before Ambrose Burnside, now a Union general. He chivalrously released her.[13] The exploits of these two women probably raised cheers among their cousins back in Albemarle County.

During 1862 Lottie transferred her church membership from Char-

The New Lottie Moon Story

lottesville to the Pine Grove Church at the Hardware Meeting House. Mrs. Moon had moved her membership to Hardware from the Scottsville Church two years earlier because it was closer to Viewmont. Lottie taught Sunday School at this church, interested in both white and Negro children.[14]

To a friend, she wrote her hopes that the men would get on with the battle. "The women and children can take care of themselves. Far better all perish than bow the neck to the tyrant's yoke!"

Her faith was tried and deepened by the sorrows falling all about her. "I do not believe that any trouble comes upon us unless it is needed, and it seems to me that we ought to be just as thankful for sorrows as for joys," she wrote. She recalled Broadus's prayer, "Send us affliction and trouble, blight our dearest hopes if need be, that we may learn more fully to depend on Thee."[15]

Orie and John Andrews went to Richmond, where John's military assignment took him, but soon Orie returned to the shelter of Viewmont. In October 1862 the first of her twelve sons was born.[16]

For approximately two years Lottie seems to have lived a nondirective existence at Viewmont, immersed in her family and in the national crisis. Then she became impatient to seek her own destiny. In October of 1863 she was seeking employment as a private tutor for a sixteen-year-old girl in Valdosta, Georgia. John A. Broadus, now a professor at The Southern Baptist Theological Seminary in Greenville, South Carolina, was asked to provide a letter of reference.[17]

This is one of the more definite clues to several vague ventures into tutoring. These must have occurred during the Civil War years between 1863 and 1866. Lottie's first biographer understood that she taught briefly in a private family in Alabama. A family in South Carolina recalls that she was their tutor. In the Greek Revival mansion of Mrs. John E. Dennis in Bishopville, Lottie had the back bedroom upstairs on the left. A window overlooked enormous cotton fields. She was governess for several young children of the family. For a schoolroom, she used a windowless little brick outbuilding which had a huge fireplace. This Presbyterian family could have learned of Miss Moon from Broadus in nearby Greenville.[18]

In Farmington, Georgia, was another family who never forgot Miss

Moon's services. She tutored young Percy Middlebrooks, the only child of a wealthy Baptist father. Lottie lived in a room added to the back of the house. In her contract, she was guaranteed two hours each afternoon for private rest, meditation, and Bible study. When the geese wandered up from the barn to her annoyance one afternoon, she gave Percy five cents to drive them away. Thereafter, Percy arranged for the geese to disturb Miss Lottie's Bible study every afternoon, so that he could earn more money. The Middlebrooks family considered Miss Lottie as a very pious young lady.[19]

However widely Lottie's wartime tutoring experience might have ranged, she seems to have been at Viewmont as the Confederacy crumbled. Orie and John were back at Viewmont for the birth of a third son when news came of Robert E. Lee's surrender not far away at Appomattox. Yankees filled the countryside. Raiders and rumors of raiders panicked the residents of Viewmont. Word came that nearby Carter's Mill was in flames and that Viewmont would be next. The household spun into action. They loaded all food and clothing onto a wagon. The elderly house servant, known as Uncle Jacob, drove it twenty miles into the woods for hiding. Mrs. Moon gathered all the family silver and jewels. She thrust the treasures into Lottie's trembling arms with orders to bury them in the orchard.

Then the frightened family awaited their doom. But the raiders never came. The dust kicked up by a traveling herd of sheep had caused the false alarm. With a sigh of relief, John Andrews went to find Uncle Jacob and the wagon, which he did safely. Lottie went to dig up the treasure, which she could not find. In later years, plows occasionally turned up a valuable piece, but most of the heirlooms were lost forever, as was the glory of Viewmont.[20]

Mrs. Moon assigned four hundred acres of Viewmont and a house to Isaac and Mag (his wife Margaret). These Ike sold to a double first cousin. Then he leased woodlands and two fields from his mother, with the agreement that he would build a small house on them. It must have grieved the family to see the great estate begin to pass out of their hands, even if to cousins.

Some of the Viewmont servants, as the slaves had always been called, stayed on under Mrs. Moon's protection; but the old economy was gone. The mistress of Viewmont leased out all her remaining property except for her house, orchards, and cemetery, in return for her choice of one-third of the crop raised on the land. She could not collect debts owed her, so she was soon in debt to cousins who had sources of income other than land.[21]

Painfully Mrs. Moon gathered funds to send Edmonia and Mollie to the Baptist-related Richmond Female Institute (later part of the University of Richmond). There they were confined during holidays because their mother had no cash for transport. Orie and her family decided to seek their fortune in John's less devastated family territory of northeast Alabama.

As the fragmented family painfully readjusted to a disrupted postwar economy, what was previously an idealized option for Lottie now became a necessity. She needed a job. Lottie's friends advertised her search for a school in which to teach. If she thought of the mission field, she knew it was impossible. Not only would the Foreign Mission Board not appoint single women, but it could not appoint anybody. It had survived the war only by the determination of Maryland and Kentucky Baptists and by missionaries who took secular jobs.

If Lottie grieved for the bygone social system, she never mentioned it. It is more likely that she viewed the new day as a challenge and opportunity. The prospects for a well-educated, independent-minded woman were much more favorable in postbellum than antebellum times.

Even in the conservative Baptist community, leaders understood what the shortage of men and the collapse of the economy would mean. In pulpit and press, they began to urge women to prepare for education, careers, wage earning, and independence—"as much as is proper for women." It was even suggested that women might "find their calling."[22]

Notes——— See pp. 302-303 for Key to Sources.

1. *RH*, summer of 1861 (this advertisement appeared repeatedly).
2. Mrs. W. E. Hatcher to Una Roberts Lawrence, URL.

3. United States Census, 1860.

4. William Luther Andrews manuscript.

5. Letter from Orianna Moon to General J. H. Cocke, July 19, 1861, Cocke Papers, University of Virginia Library.

6. Letter from Lottie Moon to General John H. Cocke July 27, 1861, Cocke Papers.

7. Search of officers' records of Confederate Army revealed commission and career of John S. Andrews, but not of Orianna Moon Andrews.

8. Cocke Papers.

9. Lawrence, *Lottie Moon;* Fife Diary.

10. William Luther Andrews manuscript.

11. Recollection of John A. Broadus, quoted by Lizzie H. Woodbury in *WR,* March 20, 1879. Letter from William P. Louthan to "Miss Lottie," July 31, 1861 (in files of Mrs. Russell Thomas) shows her reputation as an honor student and "bright Christian."

12. Letters of Lottie Moon to Kate Fife April 3, 1862, and May 29, 1862, Fife Papers, University of Virginia Library.

13. Ophia D. Smith, *Oxford Spy Wed at Pistol Point,* and Anna Mary Moon, *Sketches of the Moon and Barclay Families.*

14. Minutes, Hardware Baptist Church (Pine Grove Baptist Church), Virginia Baptist Historical Society.

15. Lottie Moon to Kate Fife.

16. William Luther Andrews manuscript.

17. Letter from Y. M. Barnsale (?—illegible) to John A. Broadus, October 24, 1863, Broadus Papers.

18. Correspondence and interview 1978 with Embra Dennis Hearon, Bishopville, South Carolina, descendant of Mrs. Dennis. Miss Hearon's grandmother told her the story of Lottie Moon as governess, but she has no idea of the dates or the connections which brought Lottie to Bishopville. The Dennis house and a small outbuilding which may have served as a schoolhouse still stand.

19. Interview 1979 with Mrs. Nellie Carson, Anderson, South Carolina, relative of the Middlebrooks family.

20. William Luther Andrews manuscript; Lawrence, *Lottie Moon.*

21. Deeds reflecting these arrangements are recorded in Albemarle County courthouse, but the transactions are confusing and incomplete.

22. *RH,* November 23, 1865, and many issues following.

Lottie Moon about 1870 (FMB)

4
She Was
a Devoted and Successful Teacher

With good judgment, Lottie sought employment in a border state where money was more plentiful than in the deep South. She applied to the Danville Female Academy, operated under the arm of First Baptist Church in Danville, Kentucky. Pastor and principal, Duncan H. Selph, wrote for John A. Broadus's endorsement of Miss Lottie Moon on March 21, 1866. He was looking for an efficient teacher and commanding disciplinarian. Probably, Miss Lottie got to Danville for the term beginning September 1866.[1]

Her move to Danville and Selph's willingness to give free education to daughters of Baptist ministers rendered destitute by the war called the school to Virginia's attention. It was recommended as one of the best institutes in Kentucky.[2]

Danville offered a preparatory department, an academic department, training in music and foreign languages, and lessons in the ornamental arts. Miss Lottie's assignment was in the preparatory department.

Because so many students were granted scholarships by the tender-hearted church, finances were uncertain. Lottie was unhappy at first with the prospects at Danville, but she was prevailed upon to stay. For the 1868-69 term her sister Mary (Mollie) joined her as a teacher.[3]

Management of the school was turned over to A. S. Worrell, noted Greek scholar, who quickly moved on to a school of greater prestige. Then the church pastor, Henry McDonald, operated the school until Herbert Davis was induced to take it over. Miss Lottie made a favorable impression on all her bosses, particularly Worrell.[4]

The New Lottie Moon Story

Prior to the 1869-70 term, the Danville Female Academy was merged with another school in town. The new school was managed by the Presbyterians, who called it Caldwell Institute. The head of this collegiate school, Lewis G. Barbour, invited Miss Charlotte Moon to take the chairs of history, grammar, rhetoric, and literature. She accepted for the term of 1870-71.[5]

In addition to her schoolwork, Miss Lottie became active in the First Baptist Church of Danville. She moved her church letter there from Pine Grove (Hardware) in April 1868.[6] Miss Lottie has been said to have served as the pastor's assistant. It is not evident whether this was a formal arrangement, whether teaching in the church academy ranked her a church staff member, or whether she simply made herself indispensable as a Sunday School teacher. She taught a class of adoring girls in their young teens. Her students were later to recall that she was very popular and that she taught them the twenty-third Psalm.[7]

In Danville she began to fall under the spell of faraway China. A Southern Baptist medical missionary to China, G. W. Burton, had come to Danville at the beginning of the Civil War. The funds he generously sent back to his co-workers in China helped sustain them during the war and its aftermath. Lottie undoubtedly had many opportunities to learn from him, and she came to know A. B. Cabaniss, former China missionary who was secretary of Kentucky Baptists and agent for foreign missions.[8]

Meanwhile, the situation at Viewmont was steadily worsening. Sad letters came to Danville from Anna Maria Moon. A debt was hanging over the land, and Mrs. Moon had been unable to pay interest for two years. She suggested that Lottie use her surplus salary to pay the interest in return for receiving title to part of the land. She had to ask Lottie for cash to meet expenses.[9]

Colie was in Bristol, probably teaching. Eddie and Mollie (Mary) had been able to complete diplomas at Richmond Female Institute. Mollie's essay was read at the 1867 commencement. Eddie earned diplomas both in mathematics and in English literature and moral philosophy. Her essay, "Beauty and Fashion," was read at the 1868 commencement.[10] The young ladies were able to keep up appearances by swapping and altering dresses.

After schooling, Mollie taught briefly in Danville with Lottie and then in various places in Virginia, considering herself highly independent.[11] Eddie was "at home" with her mother, her brother Ike, and her sister-in-law, Mag.

Everyone was engaged in a fight to keep the wolf away from the door. Mrs. Moon's personal wealth stood at one-fortieth of its prewar corpus.[12] The few remaining servants sent word that they missed "Miss Charlotte," though her absence was probably vital.

Added to the strain of finances, Mrs. Moon's heart was broken when Mollie and Colie left their Baptist upbringing to become Roman Catholics. She poured out her grief in letters to Lottie. Lottie wrote back urging toleration. Mrs. Moon studied her levelheaded Lottie's advice and replied, "I admire the spirit, but I do not believe in the Catholic religion. I think it is a misnomer to say religion." She detested the rosaries Colie and Mollie brought to the house.[13]

Family tradition says that the girls were attracted to Catholicism by a handsome and famous music teacher, Nicholas Couch. He tutored the girls on several Moon plantations. Cousin Anna Moylin Moon was similarly influenced to become a Catholic.[14]

Among the troubles Mrs. Moon passed on to Lottie was sadness over a breach with Orianna. As a grandmother, Anna Maria objected to her daughter's child-rearing techniques, but the willful Orie wanted no meddling.[15] Only Lottie gave Mrs. Moon complete satisfaction and hope. She was brilliant and accomplished within acceptable boundaries.

Mrs. Moon had done her best to give each child a privileged start in life. Unable to do more, she turned her face to the wall of Viewmont to die. Lottie rushed home before school was out in 1870. Her mother died on June 21, as Lottie stood by weeping. Pastor J. C. Long of Hardware thought Mrs. Moon's departure was a model of perfection. She was calm, clearheaded, joyous, beautiful, and full of faith. Despite the family's tears, the church's mourning, and the dread solemnity of the final hour, Long thought it a most uplifting occasion.

"She was a woman of quiet and unobstrusive manners; modest, but very firm in her opinions, full of silent energy, with an invincible love of right," Long wrote. "During the life of her husband, she fully sympathized with him in all his efforts to promote the cause of Christ, and after his death his mantle seemed to rest on her."[16]

Lottie, through her tears, agreed with Long. She wrote the news for John Andrews to break to Orianna. "The worst—no, the best has come. She died peacefully and happily. For about three days, there was no pain. The last moments were, of course, sad, but I think I can never fear death after seeing her triumph over it."[17]

At death, Anna Maria had spoken words of peace to her children, hoping to heal the raveling edges of the family unit. Lottie tried to transmit her wishes to others.

Although Mrs. Moon died with property mortgaged and leased, there was hope for clearing the title to Viewmont. It should have provided a tidy source of income and inheritance. All the children and the son of deceased Tom were to share equally in the estate. A premium was first to be paid to Eddie and Mollie, who were not self-supporting.[18]

Settlement of the estate was to drag on as late as 1884. Isaac was the executor, and he became head of Viewmont. Apparently unable to make it pay off, he turned to schoolteaching and various businesses. For a time in the 1870s, John and Orianna Andrews took over the old place. Eddie, and sometimes Colie, called it home for at least ten more years. It is impossible to say how much inheritance ever fell to Lottie. She had some discretionary income through most of her life, but she also needed pay for her work.

While at Viewmont in that summer of 1870, Lottie learned from Eddie the details of her religious life. Amid the denominational diversity of her family, Eddie had become a Baptist by choice. She seemed a bit impulsive in the summer of 1867 when she accosted J. C. Long at the Hardware Church and begged him to baptize her that very day. Although she was young and very romantic, he was impressed by the earnest glow on her face. She was baptized in a beautiful outdoor baptistry by the creek near the church. She was received as a member at Hardware, but she was not recorded in the roll book until November 1870. At college, the Baptist atmosphere reinforced her and gave her

(Left) Dr. John S. Andrews and Dr. Orianna R. Moon Andrews, about 1861 (Mrs. Mary Virginia Andrews to WMU) (Right) Anna Cunningham Safford

missionary information and teachings.[19]

While out riding in Albemarle County one summer afternoon in 1870, Eddie and Lottie discussed what their fates would be, now that their mother was dead. Eddie revealed her dream of being a missionary to China. Lottie acknowledged that she had felt the same interest, but she had squelched it because she had promised to care for her nephew, Tom, in case his widowed mother should die.

At the end of the pivotal summer of 1870, Lottie, age thirty, returned for one more year at Caldwell Institute in Danville. The pay was good and the accommodations fine. She developed a rare friendship with a colleague, Anna Cunningham Safford. Miss Safford taught the academic subjects Lottie found most troublesome—mathematics, natural philosophy, and astronomy. "A. C." Safford was as strong a Presbyterian as Miss Moon was a Baptist. She was the daughter of a Presbyterian minister who had done missionary work in the South. Anna was three years older than Lottie, smart, well educated, full of leadership ability, pursuing a career in teaching, and beset by shortened family finances. Among a faculty whom Anna called "radicals," she and Lottie held a precarious place because of their Confederate background. Their superior abilities led L. G. Barbour to retain them despite some opposition which seems to have existed.[20]

After each failed to proselyte the other, Lottie announced that she would not permit Anna to be a Baptist. Denominational difference understood, the two friends shared many confidences. Neither foresaw marriage (Lottie's friend, Dr. Toy, had by this time returned from studies in Germany and was on the faculty of The Southern Baptist Theological Seminary). Each had committed her life to doing the work of God. The only question was where and what that work might be. Each had considered foreign missions, but neither the Presbyterians nor the Baptists were yet warm to the idea of single women missionaries.

That left the homeland, and the South was a needy field. Christians were greatly concerned about destitute and despairing churches, about former slaves who could barely hold their own in life, and about women who no longer had men or property to support them.

Lottie pondered seriously how she as a woman could best render

Christian service in this situation. She must have been greatly stimulated and confused by the hot turmoil raging in Baptist publications on this question. The influential *Religious Herald* deliberately kept the "women's question" before its readers across the nation. The editors considered the complex issue crucial to the day. The many angles of debate paralleled Lottie Moon's quandary about how to live her life in a changing society.[21]

How could a woman earn a living? The *Herald* editorialized that the "sudden and violent change in the Southern society" had brought "sufferings to females for want of suitable employment." The editor urged, "By all means, let us have female professors of languages, philosophy, astronomy, and mathematics. Let titles be duly accorded to them. Let them be more liberally rewarded." He also wanted new spheres opened to women. "We are the advocate of woman's rights—not of such rights as would concert her into a man—but of those by which her powers may be developed . . . the opportunity to be employed in some avocation, adapted to her sex, healthful, useful to society, and remunerative to herself."[22]

Then arose another question. If a woman could become so competent in the secular realm, would her role change in the church? Here the *Herald* became a cautious advocate. Hot and plentiful letters to the editor insisted that woman be kept on a pedestal at home and at church. The editors acknowledged that the gospel was equally adapted to men and women and its privileges equally conferred on them, but their spheres of labor should be different. They thought that women should preach by the eloquence of pious life. "Women are not only permitted, but are required to teach the word of the Lord privately," they said. The one area completely closed to women was public administration of the gospel.[23]

The gate was open for endless debate. Every Bible passage and interpretation yet to be advanced in the next hundred years appeared in the denominational press while Lottie was teaching school. Did the Scriptures forbid females from voting and speaking in church meetings? Baptists were divided in practice and belief. A leading evangelist of the day, A. B. Earle, encouraged women to kneel in public aisles, pray aloud,

The New Lottie Moon Story

and bear public testimony of their faith. When the erudite, widely published author, Sallie Rochester Ford, reported this custom approvingly, she was soundly attacked—"nothing personal"—by John A. Broadus of Virginia. S. H. Ford, Sallie's famous husband, a Baptist editor, and her son struck back with strong defenses.[24]

On the other hand, John A. Broadus issued a long biblical exposition which drew the conclusion that women must keep silent in the church. But this by no means stopped the debate on all sides by men and women, clergy and laity.

One correspondent acknowledged that there could be no wrong in women speaking up if men were not available to do the job. Then came debate on the propriety of female prayer and missionary society meetings.[25]

Mrs. J. W. M. Williams, wife of the innovative and powerful pastor in Baltimore, took advantage of the unsettled state of mind to push the cause of women's missionary societies. Baltimore women were far advanced in this movement. Mrs. Williams pointed out that women missionaries were proclaiming the gospel effectively in foreign lands. A woman missionary of another denomination had visited Baltimore and modestly addressed a public meeting of women while seated. Mrs. Williams and other listeners became convinced, by her message on women's work in foreign lands and by her example, that women could proclaim the gospel. Mrs. Williams said to women, "You may not be required to go to a heathen land, but if it is your duty, and you thus use your talents, it will become your sweetest privilege to teach the truth . . . Ye who have been taught of Jesus, can ye not tell others of him? Ministers cannot do all that is needed . . . ."[26]

"The women question" controversy did not solve Lottie Moon's personal dilemma about how to respond to God's working in her life. From Danville, Kentucky, where she pondered "the women question," came a lengthy proposal bearing the initials "L. M." The editor of the *Religious Herald* published the rather radical idea in two installments, commending the articles appreciatively "to the careful attention of our readers, especially of our city bishops."[27]

"L. M." gave a detailed study of what other denominations were doing in establishing religious orders for women. She explored several historic orders of deaconesses in Europe. Then she cautiously suggested that each church, especially those in large cities, set apart and sustain two deaconesses. "These could make it their business to minister to the poor and suffering, establish Sunday Schools, sewing schools, night schools, mother's meetings. In a large city, such an instrumentality would be invaluable in reaching the poor, the degraded, and the ignorant."

"L. M." agreed, "Our Lord does not call on women to preach, or to pray in public, but no less does he say to them than to men, 'Go, work today in my vineyard.' " In case someone would object to the deaconess plan because women were not interested, she said, "Let this good work, for which we are pleading, be but inaugurated by our churches, and we predict that willing hearts and ready hands will be found, glad to offer themselves for a life of consecration. All such women would ask would be the assurance of a modest maintenance."

Pointing out that other denominations were more effective in using the labors of Christian women, she said, "Shall we who think we hold a purer gospel neglect any of the means of its advancement?"

A few months later, a *Herald* editorial restated the proposal that city churches appoint and support professional deaconesses. Others championed similar ideas, and a few churches reported trying women in local missionary roles. But no church offered such an opportunity to Lottie Moon. So she and Anna Safford launched their own project.

Academic education for women was still an unsupplied need in the deep South. Lottie's distant cousin, Pleasant Moon, was a merchant in Cartersville, Georgia. He and other leading men of the town established a board of trustees to open a school for girls.

When Lottie heard of the opportunity, she recognized that she and Anna had all the qualifications needed to run a first-class institute. As soon as the 1870-71 term closed in Danville, they were on the train to Cartersville.[28]

Lottie lived with her cousin at first, then moved to a house more convenient to the school. Class was hastily set up in an old cannery with one large room and two small ones. During June, the trustees advertised that Miss A. C. Safford and Miss C. Moon would be associate principals of the Cartersville Female High School. It was promised that they would enforce obedience, order, and ladylike deportment. Primary and intermediate departments would offer the rudiments and common branches of education. An advanced department would be equivalent to the best female colleges, with instruction in ancient and modern languages. Though nonsectarian, the school would teach the Bible weekly. It was to be a day school, but boarders could be housed privately.[29]

The young ladies were said by their previous employer to be "competent, conscientious, faithful teachers, good disciplinarians, and reliable women." For additional references, Lottie pointed to John A. Broadus and C. H. Toy, both of The Southern Baptist Theological Seminary; A. S. Worrell, now president of a woman's college in Lexington, Kentucky, and editor of the Baptist *Western Recorder;* and J. C. Long, pastor in Charlottesville.[30]

School opened on July 3, 1871, with Lottie presiding over the primary department, preparing girls "to take their places in society as true, intelligent, earnest women."[31] Seven pupils enrolled at first, but the student body rapidly grew to more than one hundred. Misses Moon and Safford invested their own funds in books, piano, organ, and scientific apparatus, as well as in improving and beautifying the building.[32]

Anna joined the Presbyterian congregation,[33] and Lottie moved her church membership to the Cartersville Baptist Church. She taught the young women in Sunday School and spent many hours visiting and aiding destitute families in the community. The pastor, R. B. Headden, an ardent supporter of missions, considered her his right hand. The town was elated, and the lady principals agreed to stay on another year.

Lottie must have entered the 1872-73 school year with reduced enthusiasm. Her baby sister, Edmonia, had, without warning, gone to China to serve as a Southern Baptist missionary. While correspondent

Edmonia Moon (Mrs. Charles Goode)

for Richmond Female Institute's missionary society, Eddie had become a pen pal of Martha Foster Crawford, wife of Tarleton Perry Crawford. The Crawfords had been missionaries in China since 1851, and for nearly ten years they had served in Tengchow, a treaty port in North China. Eddie and Lottie developed a special interest in Mrs. Crawford's mission school work.

Upon arriving in Cartersville, Lottie had written James B. Taylor, corresponding secretary of the Foreign Mission Board in Richmond, about the forty-five dollars in gold the sisters were annually providing for Mrs. Crawford's school. Lottie was to pay one-third, while Eddie, who always seemed to have more money (perhaps due to the way their mother's estate was handled) paid the remainder. Also, Lottie contributed to the fund to erect a Baptist chapel in Rome, Italy. By standards of the day, Lottie and Eddie's contributions to missions were outstanding. Lottie always admonished the Foreign Mission Board not to reveal her name as donor.[34]

In 1849 the Board had appointed a single woman, Harriet Baker, to serve as a missionary in South China.[35] It was an experiment pronounced unsuccessful. From that time until 1872, the Board had a definite policy of not considering single women applicants. Three forces worked to change this policy.

First, the concept of "woman's mission to woman" was gathering steam in Baltimore. Following the suggestions of her son, Rosewell H. Graves, Southern Baptist missionary in Canton, and following the example of other denominations, Mrs. Ann Graves had organized the Baptist women of Baltimore. The organization included such notables as Alice and Annie Armstrong, their mother, and Mrs. J. W. M. Williams. Pastors of the city backed them strongly. The Woman's Mission to Woman organization spurred interest among women in other states. Where the women organized, increased funds flowed to the Foreign Mission Board. With those funds went influence.

Behind the movement was the idea that the cloistered women of China (and other lands) could be reached only by women missionaries. Wives of male missionaries could have only limited time and mobility to do time-consuming house-to-house witnessing. Single women were needed for the job. Up to this time, the Foreign Mission Board had given little consideration even to married women. They were not examined in connection with their husbands' appointments, had no official standing as missionaries, and were not expected to do much on the field. However, their presence was considered in the setting of salaries.

In more innovative denominations, single women sometimes had the status of "assistants" to men or "sisters" to the men's wives. The idea of a woman going afar without the protection of a man was not thinkable. It was assumed that if a single woman were appointed, she would have to be connected to the household of a missionary family.

Early in 1872 Martha Foster Crawford urged Mrs. J. W. M. Williams and the women of Baltimore to push for the appointment of two single women to do woman's work with her. She mentioned that she was in correspondence with a young lady desiring appointment (undoubtedly Edmonia). The Crawfords offered a home for ladies who might work with them.[36]

A second factor that changed the Foreign Mission Board's policy was the death of James B. Taylor. His successor, Henry Allen Tupper, was a courageous friend of women's work. He took office in January 1872. At the same time, it was made known that Rosewell Graves in Canton and James B. Hartwell of Tengchow would welcome female co-workers. When the Foreign Mission Board met with Tupper's leadership, two of the brethren remarked that times had changed; and with the times, their opinions about female missionaries had changed. "This change is in harmony with the Scripture," said one who observed the Board in action. "There was doubtless a wider sphere for the activities of pious women in the service of Christ in the apostolic times than there has been for centuries past among evangelical Christians."[37]

At least one Virginia Baptist woman, Kate F. Evans of Amelia County, had been recently appointed a missionary by Northern Baptist women rather than by her own denomination because of the Foreign Mission Board's policy; and she was drawing support from Southern women.[38]

Then an ideal circumstance arose for testing the appointment of single women. Since mid-1871, the Board had been dealing with Mr. and Mrs. N. B. Williams, a young couple seeking appointment to China. Mrs. Williams was the daughter of parents who had represented Southern Baptists in China. Her sister, Miss Lula Whilden of South Carolina, wished to accompany the Williamses to Canton. The Board could hardly refuse this familial arrangement, so the first crack appeared in tradition.[39]

Though not announced, word of this arrangement leaked to Viewmont and the ears of Edmonia Moon.[40] In the fall of 1870 Eddie had tried her hand briefly as a private teacher in Clinton, Green County, Alabama, but was now frittering her life away at home.[41] In March of 1872 she was stunned when her close cousin, Anna Moylin Moon, left home to enter the Convent of St. Joseph's in Wheeling, West Virginia.[42] Eddie, at age twenty-one, immediately sent an urgent inquiry to H. A. Tupper. If there were another single lady going to China, she wished to go also. Eddie sent along a letter from Mrs. Crawford stating that she would be welcome.

Tupper made a noncommital acknowledgment on April 1, but by April 9 he had called a special meeting of the Foreign Mission Board to consider her inquiry.[43] She made no formal application and stood no examination, but Eddie's professor at Richmond Female Institute, C. H. Winston, gave her a sterling recommendation. "Her standing as a pupil was excellent and she gave evidence of strong, well-trained intellect. Her character was marked by reserve, independence, firmness mixed with deference, candor, and honesty," Winston said. "She had a dash of originality and romance."[44]

It was understood that the young lady had offered to pay her own expenses for travel and for living until support could be arranged. At Tupper's suggestion, that support was already in sight. On April 4, 1872, women of five churches in Richmond organized mite societies to furnish Miss Edmonia's support.[45] Her salary was set at four hundred dollars a year—less than the full six-hundred-dollar missionary's salary because she expected to live with the Crawfords in Tengchow.

As of April 9, 1872, Edmonia Harris Moon was a Southern Baptist foreign missionary. In frenzied preparations, the family helped Eddie pack and rush to Baltimore. There she met Mr. and Mrs. Rosewell H. Graves; Mr. and Mrs. James B. Hartwell, three children, and two Chinese traveling with them; Mr. and Mrs. N. B. Williams, and Miss Lula Whilden. On April 17 in the Eutaw Place Baptist Church of Baltimore, Baptists gathered to send the missionary force off with ceremony and prayer. The next day the party boarded the train to the West Coast via New York, and on May 1 sailed from San Francisco.[46] By June 1872 Edmonia was in China. Her letters to Lottie and other family members began to lure Lottie to follow. Learning of Miss Eddie's talented sister, T. P. Crawford let the Foreign Mission Board know that she should be appointed.

In January 1873 Lottie was in confidential communication with H. A. Tupper, and they became lasting friends. Lottie wanted to be sure she could be appointed a missionary before she dared tamper with her prospects in Cartersville.[47] Perhaps she was not sure whether foreign missions, with the restraints imposed on single women, would be as fulfilling a work as running her own school.

On the other hand, she had Mrs. Crawford's testimony that missionary work among women was exclusively a woman's domain. A Christian woman in China could have her own work without imposing on man's domain. Chinese women rarely attended public services conducted by a man until after conversion at the hands of a woman.[48]

Eddie wrote her: "I cannot convince myself that it is the will of Heaven that you shall not come. True, you are doing a noble work at home, but are there not some who could fill your place? I don't know of any one who could fill the place offered you here. In the first place, it is not every one who is willing to come to China. In the next place, their having the proper qualifications is doubtful."[49]

Then Eddie described her exotic surroundings, the open door to evangelize, the need of China for education, and the pleasant social contacts with other missionaries.

To further Lottie's sense of call to China, her missions-minded pastor, R. B. Headden, returned from the February 1873 meeting of the Middle Cherokee Baptist Association thoroughly fired up. At his suggestion the pastors there had agreed to preach on the need for laborers to work in the foreign fields white unto harvest. When Headden preached on this theme at Cartersville, Lottie Moon left her front-row pew to pray in her room all afternoon. Later, she told Headden that his sermon cemented her determination to go to China. She told others that she heard her call to China "as clear as a bell."[50]

A. C. Safford answered a call to China also. She wrote to her relatives about her plans to go as a Presbyterian appointee to Soochow, China. "This thing is not the romantic resolve of a young, foolish heart. It is the result of prayerful deliberations by a matured woman who has known much of life," wrote Anna. She also explained what she and Lottie told the Cartersville School trustees—their school was not paying off.[51]

Misses Safford and Moon were under contract to remain with their school unless it proved unprofitable. Although the school was widely acclaimed a success, the principals displayed account books to show that their personal investment was not producing handsomely, thanks to a too-low tuition. As Anna said, they had great popularity, honor—everything but a support. The trustees were reluctantly, but legally, convinced to let the teachers go without a fuss. Having settled matters with the trustees on June 2, they announced their plans to the students.

That was not pleasant to do. Lottie was loved by her little students. She was hardly bigger than they were. Her dark hair fell in pretty long curls. Her jolly disposition took the edge off her strict discipline. Despite her thirty-three years, she looked young. Her methodology was to make learning fun and to give rewards rather than punishment. Students prized the cards of merit she gave them for good recitations.

As customary, all the students gathered in the big schoolroom for the day's concluding lectures. Misses Moon and Safford stood at the rostrum and announced their plans to be missionaries to the heathen in faraway China. Yes, this meant they would no longer be the children's teachers. As the students comprehended this thought, they dissolved in tears. One later wrote, "For us younger ones, death seemed to have entered our school."[52]

On commencement day, June 12, the largest crowd ever assembled in Cartersville watched as the missionary candidates marched one hundred charges into the Presbyterian church. The Methodist pastor spoke on "Seek ye first the kingdom of God." On the same day the newspaper published details of the "successful but not remunerative school" and confirmed the principals' planned departure. The next day a public lecture was held to raise funds to buy out the Moon-Safford investment in the school. Gifts and messages of love flooded the women, and these were acknowledged in the community press.[53]

Not a few people (said to be non-Baptists) in the town bitterly resented the way in which Lottie and Anna deserted their high calling in Cartersville. Much was said about the waste of such excellent women on the uncaring heathen, while good Southern girls needed education so desperately.

On the other hand, the move served as nothing else had to elicit missionary interest and support in Georgia. On Lottie's last Sunday in Georgia, the Cartersville Church marked the occasion. Dr. Headden preached on missions. At the close of the service, the congregation sent a generous fifty dollars to the Foreign Mission Board.[54] Lottie was hardly out of town before the women of First Baptist Church met to organize for her support. They were possibly the first woman's missionary society among Georgia Baptists. Other societies were soon formed and wanted to help.

On July 7, 1873, Charlotte Digges Moon was officially appointed a missionary by the Foreign Mission Board in Richmond.[55] By July 17, 1873, announcement was made in the denominational papers that Miss Lottie would be joining Miss Eddie in Tengchow. Georgia Baptists were asked to assume the bulk of Lottie's support as Virginia had assumed Eddie's.[56]

Lottie's old home church in Albemarle County took no note of her going to China (nor had it noticed Edmonia's appointment). But it did make lavish record of her handsome donation to the Virginia Baptist Memorial Fund for education. Lottie had routed her donation through the Hardware church. The clerk was instructed to express to Sister Moon "the kindly regard in which her memory is held by us."[57] It was the first time a woman had been mentioned in the church record other than upon enrollment or dismissal. The Albemarle Baptist Association did note with pride that Miss Moon was the third missionary to go out from their circle.[58]

Lottie headed for China by way of Lauderdale County, Alabama, where Orianna was living at the Alabama-Tennessee state line with her growing brood. For a month she rested and rambled around the countryside with her nephews. Probably she picked up tips on doctoring which she would need in China.[59] The sisters shared letters from Ike at Viewmont; from Mollie, who had married Dr. William Shepherd of Norfolk in 1871; and of course from Eddie. (Colie's path is unclear. It is said she briefly entered the Catholic convent at Wheeling.)[60] Lottie and Orie discussed God's working in their lives and rejoiced in Lottie's plans.

From Alabama, "L. M." wrote an appeal for people to join her in China. "Young brethren, can you, knowing the loud call for laborers in the foreign field, *will* you settle down with your home pastorates? So many could be found to fill your places at home; so few volunteer for the foreign work. For women, too, foreign missions open a new and enlarged sphere of labor and furnish opportunities for good which angels might almost envy." She quoted proof of this last sentence from a lady missionary in a private letter, then continued: "Could a Christian woman possibly desire higher honor than to be permitted to go from house to house and tell of a savior to those who have never heard his name? We could not conceive a life which would more thoroughly satisfy the mind and heart of a true follower of the Lord Jesus."[61]

Her train journey from Florence, Alabama, to New York, to San Francisco commenced on August 15. She stopped briefly in Albermarle County to see family and in Baltimore, where she surely saw the women's leaders of the city.[62] She found the overland travel to be the hardest part about going forth to be a missionary. In San Francisco she received word of the Cartersville Woman's Missionary Society's plans to support her, and she stopped to get a photograph taken for friends there.

Her colleague from Danville days, A. S. Worrell, was living near San Francisco. He entertained her until time for sailing on September 1. He sent this message back to Virginia: "Miss Moon was once a member of my family, and a most devoted and successful teacher. . . . It has been a cherished purpose with Miss Moon, for years past, to be a missionary to the heathen; and now that her desires in this regard are about to be gratified, she is quite happy, and says that in going to China to join her sister, she feels as if she were going home. A lady of fine intellect, of rare culture, and of splendid social gifts, she lays herself on the altar of sacrifice to glorify him who purchased her with his precious blood. Virginia never reared a truer, nobler woman. May heaven abundantly bless her in her noble mission."[63]

Notes——— See pp. 302-303 for Key to Sources.

1. J. William Jones to John A. Broadus, February 19, 1866, shows how Lottie's friends helped her gain employment. Duncan H. Selph to John A. Broadus, March 21, 1866, with attached circular for Danville Female Academy. Both in Broadus Papers, The Southern Baptist Theological Seminary.

2. *RH*, July 19, 1866.

3. Letter from Mary Moon to Captain J. H. Stafford from Danville, May 22, 1869. Letter is the property of Lila Watson, Darlington, South Carolina, retired missionary to China. Captain Stafford was Miss Watson's relative.

4. Records of First Baptist Church, Danville, Kentucky. Worrell wrote his impressions in the *Evangel*, quoted in *RH*, September 18, 1873. Development of the Danville Female Academy can be sketchily traced through advertisements in *WR* and in biographical studies of Worrell and other presidents. See *WR* for March 23, 1867, and September 5, 1868, for example. Henry McDonald was later professor at Georgetown College, where he was a colleague of Bettie D. Fowlkes, one of Lottie's best friends.

5. Catalogs for Caldwell Institute, 1870-71 and 1871-72, available in archives of Centre College, Danville, Kentucky.

6. Church records, First Baptist Church, Danville, Kentucky. The author is indebted to Bill Weatherford, student at The Southern Baptist Theological Seminary; Mike Crain, the Baptist pastor at Hyattsville, Kentucky; Lee N. Allen, professor of history at Samford University; Paul Debusman of the library staff at The Southern Baptist Theological Seminary; and Mrs. William Vaught of Danville Church, for exhaustive research on persons and experiences of Danville.

7. Mrs. C. P. Terhune to Una Roberts Lawrence, February 15, 1924; Mrs. M. C. Butler to Mrs. J. M. Collier, January 19, 1929. Both in URL.

8. Letters from G. W. Burton to J. B. Hartwell place Burton in Danville

during Lottie Moon's tenure there. Letters available in Hartwell Family Papers, Library of the Yale University Divinity School. Correspondence from Lottie Moon to A. B. Cabaniss published in *WR* through the 1870s indicates a personal friendship between them.

9. Letters from Anna Maria Moon at Viewmont to Lottie Moon at Danville, January 7, 1869, and December 28, 1869, LMLF.

10. *RH,* July 4, 1867, and July 9, 1868.

11. Letter from Mary Moon to Captain J. H. Stafford from Bedford County, Virginia, January 15, 1870.

12. United States Census, 1870.

13. Letters from Anna Maria Moon to Lottie Moon and from Mary Moon to Captain J. H. Stafford. William P. Louthan to Lottie, 1861 (owned by Mrs. Russell Thomas), indicates that Mary's religious experience was typically Baptist at this point.

14. Letters from Fannie Moon Butts to Una Roberts Lawrence, URL.

15. In addition to Anna Maria Moon's letters in FMB files, family troubles are pointed up in a letter from Mrs. Moon to Lottie December 27, probably 1866, now framed and preserved by Charlotte Churchill, Crewe, Virginia.

16. Anna Maria Moon obituary, *RH,* August 25, 1870.

17. Letter from Lottie Moon to John Summerfield Andrews, undated but probably June 21, 1870, LMR.

18. Will of Anna Maria Moon, May 20, 1870, with complete inventory of property at Viewmont, recorded in Book 28, pages 265 and 296, Albemarle County courthouse.

19. *RH,* January 4, 1877. Also, unpublished article by William Luther Andrews, March 5, 1913, furnished by Mrs. Henry Davis.

20. Letters from Anna Cunningham Safford to members of her family, in files of the Historical Foundation of the Southern and Reformed Churches, Montreat, North Carolina.

21. *RH,* January 11, 1866.

22. Ibid., February 9, 1871.

23. Ibid., May 14, 1868.

24. Ibid., February 16, 1871, and March 9, 1871. Many articles spun off this controversy over a period of months.

25. Ibid., October 5, 1871.

26. Ibid., February 24, 1870.

27. Ibid., March 23, 1871, and April 13, 1871.

28. Margie Black, secretary for the Middle Cherokee Baptist Association, Cartersville, Georgia, is the chief researcher and source of data concerning Lottie Moon in Cartersville. The author acknowledges her extensive labors in discovering this information.

29. *The Cartersville Semi-Weekly Express,* June 30, 1871.

The New Lottie Moon Story

30. Ibid., July 7, 1871.

31. Ibid., June 30, 1871.

32. *The Standard and Express,* June 12, 1873.

33. Records of First Presbyterian Church, formerly Friendship Church, Cartersville; investigated by Margie Black.

34. Lottie Moon to J. B. Taylor, July 10 and July 18, 1871, and Lottie Moon to H. A. Tupper, May 25, 1872, LMLF. See Martha Foster Crawford's appeal to "Young Ladies of Female Colleges," *RH,* May 13, 1869.

35. Minutes, FMB.

36. *RH,* April 25, 1872, May 2, 1872, and June 26, 1873.

37. Ibid., April 25, 1872.

38. Ibid., January 30, 1873 and February 27, 1873.

39. *Baptist Courier,* May 9, 1872, and *RH,* April 25, 1872. Lee N. Allen, *The First 150 Years: First Baptist Church, Montgomery, Alabama, 1829-1979.*

40. *Baptist Courier* hints of this appointment made in July 1871, August 3, 1871.

41. Tupper, *Foreign Missions of the Southern Baptist Convention.*

42. Robert C. Nash to Ruth Ann Archer, May 3, 1979, quoting from records of the Sisters of St. Joseph of Wheeling. Anna Moon became Mother Superior of the convent.

43. FMB Minutes.

44. Tupper, *Foreign Missions of the Southern Baptist Convention.*

45. Juliette Mather, *Light Three Candles.*

46. *Baptist Courier,* May 2, 1872; *WR,* January 27, 1876. Eutaw Place Baptist Church was the home church of Rosewell Graves, his mother Ann, the Armstrong family, and others instrumental in the development of women's work in missions.

47. Lottie Moon to H. A. Tupper, January 13, 1873, LMLF. Tupper's responses are reflected in copy books, FMB.

48. Martha Foster Crawford letter, *RH,* February 25, 1869.

49. Edmonia Moon to Lottie Moon, May 19, 1873, and other correspondence, LMLF.

50. Recollection by Lizzie S. Cobb, October 16, 1898, found in Minutes of Woman's Missionary Society, First Baptist Church, Cartersville, Georgia. See *Minutes,* Middle Cherokee Baptist Association, 1873. The Association met at the Oothcalooga Baptist Church in Adairsville, according to Margie Black in letter to author, May 16, 1979. See *CI,* November 26, 1903, for Headden's recollection that three or four young men decided to enter the ministry at the same time as Lottie's decision. Also, Katharine James to Una Roberts Lawrence, February 3, 1923, URL.

51. A. C. Safford to her sister, June 10, 1873, Historical Foundation of the Presbyterian and Reformed Churches.

52. Recollection by Mrs. W. P. Larramore (Florida L.), a student at the time of the resignation. This letter has been placed with the Minutes, Woman's Missionary Society, First Baptist Church, Cartersville. Margie Black has seen Miss Moon's cards of merit in private collections in Cartersville.

53. *The Standard and Express,* June 12, 1873.

54. *CI,* August 21, 1873. Minutes have been preserved from the first meeting of the Woman's Missionary Society in August 1873, throughout Lottie Moon's career. The Cartersville women faithfully corresponded with their missionary, and that correspondence was recorded with the minutes. These letters are the property of First Baptist Church.

55. FMB Minutes.

56. *RH,* July 17, 1873; *CI,* August 7, 1873.

57. Minutes, Hardware Church (Pine Grove), Virginia Baptist Historical Society.

58. *RH,* September 25, 1873. Prior to Lottie this association had produced G. B. Taylor, Italy, and Edmonia Moon.

59. William Luther Andrews manuscript.

60. Exhaustive inquiries fail to verify Lawrence's statement in *Lottie Moon* that Sarah Coleman Moon followed her cousin Anna Moylin Moon into the convent. Except for a brief time in Washington, D.C., alluded to in Lottie Moon's correspondence, and verified in the 1877 City Directory of Washington, D.C., this sister is lost.

61. *RH,* August 28, 1873.

62. *The Sun,* Baltimore, August 19, 1873. Lottie was joined en route to Baltimore by Miss A. C. Safford and by two Presbyterian men missionaries who conducted them to China.

63. *RH,* September 18, 1873.

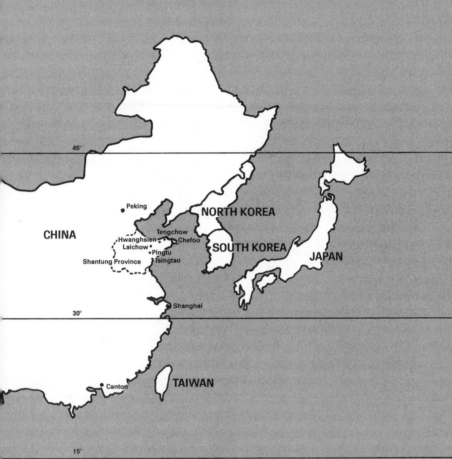

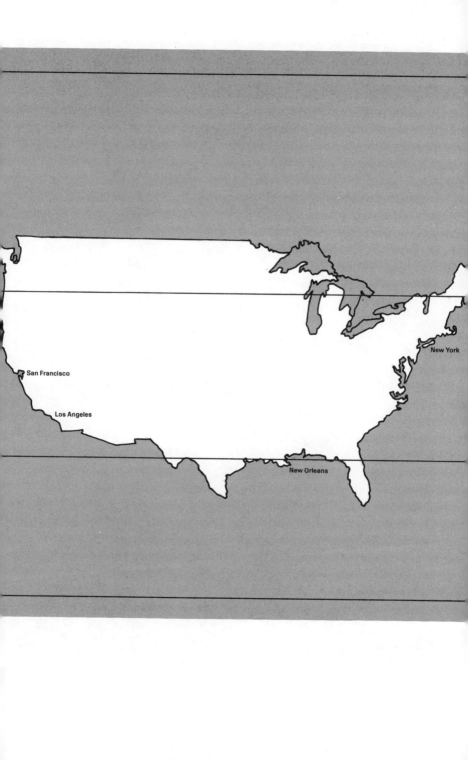

Lottie Moon, 1873, retouched
(Virginia Baptist Historical Society)

5

She Was
Full of Faith and Promise

he sun was shining on the sparkling waters of the San Francisco Bay when the *Costa Rica* steamed out at noon September 1, 1873. A cluster of long-faced missionaries of several denominations, all bound for the Orient, waved good-bye from the rear of the ship. These missionaries never expected to see the shore of America again or to embrace the loved ones left there.[1]

Lottie Moon, although on board, did not stand with this group. She had measured the realities of her departure weeks before. She was commissioned to stay in China until total breakdown or death. So she had cut her ties in Virginia and shed her tears along the central railroad route to the Pacific. Now the pain of leaving dimmed behind the future's bright glow.

The ship's gong sounded for lunch. Lottie reluctantly left the beautiful scenery sailing past and entered the dining room. A few minutes into the formal meal, the room started to swim before her eyes, and she made a rapid escape from the table. From that moment, she fought a twenty-five-day bout with seasickness. Annoyed at her weakness, she insisted on sitting through dinners of endless courses which she came to hate.

She was not too sick to enjoy the interesting assortment of colorful passengers. Bright conversation, lectures, card games, chess, anagrams, and quiet reflection filled the hours. Only one gale ruffled this phase of the trip, and during it Lottie was too sick to count the danger.

She thankfully sighted land at Yokohama, Japan, on September 25. The next day Lottie Moon set foot on foreign soil for the first time. The rapid jumble of Oriental language filled her ears, and she was excited beyond measure. A gentleman in the party cut through the throng of chattering drivers and settled her into a ricksha. She felt like a baby in a carriage as a miserable-looking Japanese man ran through the enchanting streets with her in tow.

Arriving at the Grand Hotel, she found herself for the first time surrounded by people who could not understand her language. Not daunted, she searched out an English-speaking man who helped her over the language barrier. For several merry hours, she toured the streets and fingered silks and lacquers in the shops, then rode a ricksha back to the *Costa Rica*.

Next the steamer halted at the port of Kobe. There, Church of England missionaries showed her the sights of ancient pagodas and conducted her to worship services. Then she sailed on to Nagasaki, seeing the temples and shrines with Church of England hosts. These experiences were ever a delight to Miss Moon. She considered Japan the most beautiful of countries.

The trek from Nagasaki to Shanghai should have taken forty-eight hours. But on the first night out, the ship was struck by a hurricane. As Lottie hung on in her cabin, she heard glass shatter in the dining room; then she listened as the deck around her cabin broke away bit by bit. The next day the storm blew relentlessly until the ship's rudder was lost. Then the ship blew aimlessly back over its old course.

While the crew fought to save the ship, gentlemen missionaries valiantly tried to protect the ladies. The ship's surgeon and other passengers quelled their hopelessness with strong drink. All agreed that the end was near. Miss Moon, already expecting to die in the cause of missions, was prepared for the end to come then. Calmly she told others, "I should scarcely be surprised to see a divine form walking upon the mad waste of howling water, saying 'It is I, be not afraid.' " But death by shipwreck was not God's will. The storm quieted, and the *Costa Rica* limped back into Nagasaki, where Lottie was too exhausted to go ashore. Later on, Dutch Reformed Church missionaries invited her to dinner and croquet, and on Sunday she prayed for the Queen at the Church of England.

The next attempt at Shanghai was peacefully completed. On October 7 Matthew T. Yates, the distinguished Southern Baptist missionary in Shanghai, and Mr. and Mrs. Tarleton Perry Crawford of Tengchow came aboard to welcome Miss Moon to China. The greeting party conducted her to the comfortable Yates home, where Mrs. Yates made her at ease. Christians of Shanghai immediately called on her. Lottie felt festive.[2] China at last! Shanghai was the main foreign port of the area and was the strongest center of missions except for Canton. United States business interests were headquartered here, and the foreign community was powerful.

The amiable Lottie was charmed by the Yateses and pleased by T. P. and Martha Foster Crawford. All were legendary figures to her. They were considered old and broken-down by this time, being in their fifties and having survived more than twenty years in China. Lottie drank in every word, knowing that they had paid dearly for the experience they had to share.

What of Miss Edmonia? Lottie was hungry for news of this beloved sister who had braved the way to China. Edmonia awaited her in Tengchow. There she was said to be supervising masons and carpenters rebuilding the Crawfords' house. The home had to stretch to accommodate the growing family of young ladies.

Crawford had taken Lottie's arrival as an excuse to handle personal business in Shanghai, and Mrs. Crawford would naturally be needed to accompany a woman's arrival. So Edmonia stayed behind.

News of Eddie was exciting. All the callers from the extended missionary circle in Shanghai spoke cheerily of the pretty young woman and jokingly chided Crawford for allowing the dainty creature to be buried in musty old Tengchow. "She will die or go crazy there, Mr. Crawford. Why not send her to work in Shanghai?" If such comments caused raised eyebrows and sharp glances between Mrs. Yates and Mrs. Crawford, Lottie did not detect the meaning. She only heard that Eddie was mastering the difficult Chinese language with incredible speed, that she was teaching in a newly organized Sunday School, and that she had declined a proposal of marriage from an attractive gentleman in Shanghai.[3]

The New Lottie Moon Story

Though eager to get to Eddie and to her field of service, Miss Lottie had to wait while T. P. Crawford's business dealing (probably concerning private real estate holdings or a nasty lawsuit then brewing) delayed their departure. She stifled her impatience and decided to learn while waiting. Mrs. Crawford, familiar with Shanghai from her first term of service, took her to visit a Chinese family. Lottie encountered there her first scalding Chinese tea and began to master elaborate Chinese courtesy.

Receiving a visit from a Chinese Christian woman at the Yates' home, she fought to like her first taste of Chinese food. The woman gave her boxes containing delicacies made for the Chinese feast of the moon. Intending to eat them out of politeness, Lottie recoiled at the oiliness and hastily shut them away.

The Chinese pastor in Yates' field came to meet the new American missionary. Lottie noticed with some surprise that he was a man of refinement, benevolence, and good sense.

At last Mrs. Crawford took Lottie to the ship bound for Shantung Province, leaving T. P. to follow later. Again the sea struggled to keep Lottie from her appointment with Tengchow, but both she and the ship weathered the typhoon.[4]

Shantung Province was almost encircled by a seacoast nicked by several good harbors. The terrain varied from stark purple mountains to golden rolling plains. Few trees broke the landscape. The temperature could range from deep, snowy freezes to sunstroke heat. Many rivers and streams watered fields of wheat, millet, sorghum, and sweet potatoes—the main food crops.

The area was estimated to be the most densely populated spot on earth. Confucius had been born and buried in Shantung, and many pilgrims visited the place. Chinanfu was the capital of the province, but Chefoo was becoming a leading port.

In 1858 treaties opened several Chinese ports, including Tengchow and Chefoo, to foreign trade and to foreign missions. Foreign powers had forced China to admit their subjects for residence in these ports and for travel as far inland as they dared go. Foreigners were subject not to Chinese authority but to their own nations' representatives. Yet in treaty ports, China was obligated to protect foreigners. Americans in Shantung Province were answerable to their consul in Chefoo, which had been only a tiny fishing village before the treaty. The American treaty (and others) guaranteed toleration of Christianity for Chinese as well as for Americans.

Lottie's ship put in at Chefoo, and she caught her first look at this place of importance to her future. Most mission boards who had work in North China maintained contacts in the city. Doctors were usually available, the climate was healthy and clean, and foreign social contacts were plentiful. Many missionaries from other parts of China vacationed in the city.

One Southern Baptist missionary family lived in Chefoo. Lottie met James Boardman Hartwell, his second wife, and his children. Although still very influential in Tengchow, the Hartwells had moved to Chefoo soon after arriving with Edmonia Moon the previous year. Mrs. Hartwell had taken sick on the trip over and had not had a well day since. Hartwell continued to reach fifty-five miles away to Tengchow to direct a school and church. His North Street Baptist congregation was led in his absence by an ordained native pastor, Woo Tswun Chao. Though tiny, it was the largest (with approximately sixty members), oldest congregation related to Southern Baptists in the province, having been established in 1862.

While in Chefoo, Lottie visited Presbyterian mission points. Suddenly she was surrounded by eager Chinese children touching her, examining her, and peppering her with meaningless sounds. Her Presbyterian hostess interpreted, "What is your age?" Then she explained, "You don't have to answer, but do but do not be offended. It is a customary question to ask a stranger." Lottie also learned that the children were curious to know whether she was male or female, whether she had a mother-in-law, and what her name was. Lottie's quick ear and tongue tried to form answers to these routine questions. The seeming Chinese nosiness did not dull her attraction to the beautiful children. Rather, she was stimulated to learn.[5]

The customary route from Chefoo to Tengchow was overland. Tengchow was originally to be the treaty port for Shantung, but foreign boats could not safely navigate its ancient silted harbor. Overland travel usually was accomplished by foot, by sedan chair, by donkey, by wheelbarrow, or by shentze. For such a long trip—usually two days—shentze would be best.

The shentze was a cruel initiation for the untried missionary. The contraption looked like a covered wagon slung on poles instead of wheels. It was a sort of basket turned on its side with mouth pointed forward. It was covered by a thick cloth which more or less weather-proofed the inside. The shentze poles were fastened on mules in front and behind. One or more drivers walked beside to guide the beasts through narrow, rutted trails. Inside the housing, the passenger lay back on mountains of bedding to cushion the jolts. The ride was violent and often sickening.

On October 25 a haggard, thirty-three-year-old Lottie Moon arrived in Tengchow, her home for the next thirty-nine years. Tengchow was much too proud and ancient a city to celebrate the arrival of another despised "foreign devil." In fact, all foreigners had been utterly unwelcome ever since Hartwell had offended the leading citizens when he first tried to obtain property in 1861. No foreign commerce had taken hold in Tengchow, even though it was a prefectural city with a harbor. To this city flocked thousands of young men to take the Chinese equivalent of civil service exams. Based on classic, unchanged forms of memorized Chinese literature, the literary exams were the only path for upward mobility. Fixed on antiquity rather than current progress, the population was stagnated at 80,000.

The massive, gray stone walls of Tengchow dated from before the birth of Christ. Much folklore and literature hovered over the history of the town known traditionally as Penglai. At the stony harbor was a walled Water City. A water gate could admit sampans for protection. Immediately adjoining was the thickly walled main city, which was sided by a pleasant pebbly beach.

Inside the main city lived the tiny foreign population. Lottie brought the Southern Baptist census to six. The Northern Presbyterian mission numbered scarcely more. There were no other foreigners except an occasional drifter or visiting missionary.

Tarleton Perry Crawford (FMB)

Martha Foster Crawford (FMB)

(Upper) Tengchow, showing walls of Water City and main city (Ruth C. Thornhill) (Lower) Tengchow, or Monument Street Baptist Church, built by T. P. Crawford in 1872. Miss Moon's Little Cross Roads residence was nearby, and she worshiped at this church 1873-1912. The monument gate is the Chee monument or the Pi Fong on the Little Cross Roads. (FMB)

As recently as 1870 missionaries had been forced to retreat to Chefoo in the face of their planned annihilation. Only weeks before Lottie arrived, the women missionaries had halted their visiting when Chinese soldiers whipped the townspeople into a murderous frenzy. Lottie was to become keenly aware of this recent history.[6] Such hostility, the limited social contacts, the stagnant intellectual climate, and the isolation of the place all contributed to an atmosphere that often literally destroyed Westerners.[7] A Presbyterian leader said at this time, "No man lay or clerical will hold out in this place without a clear call of God to labor for the souls of men."[8]

As Lottie made a leap of faith into this environment, the mules lurched and clopped over streets paved with worn-out millstones. She sized up thoroughfares barely wider than an alley. Dull, forbidding walls lined the streets, betraying nothing of the houses and gardens hidden behind.

Tengchow was quieter and cleaner than Shanghai. Although Lottie had to lift her skirts and step carefully to avoid sewage in the streets, she saw that Tengchow was a relatively hygenic city. Not a tree or flower or tall building broke the harmony of low thatched and tiled roofs. Looming overhead was an architectural giant, the Chee Monument, a splendid Oriental gate.

Nearby rose two "offenses" to the landscape. One was an American-style church with a steeple. Crawford had proudly completed it the previous September, paying for it with his own money and leaving the Foreign Mission Board indebted to him for three thousand dollars. Close by rose the second incongruous building—a two-storied American-style house. This was what Crawford had added to his compound in order to accommodate the new recruit.[9]

Edmonia welcomed her sister with effusive and relieved cheer. Quickly she filled in Mrs. Crawford on the construction progress. The place was livable, and Edmonia scratched her name into her bedroom window glass.[10] Lottie comprehended the housing situation, and within one week she dispatched her first letter to H. A. Tupper and the Foreign Mission Board. She reported that she had arrived, found Tengchow cleaner and less odorous than expected, like the climate, was

The New Lottie Moon Story

well, and wanted a house of her own.[11]

"Stir up the hearts of our sisters in Richmond so they shall build for my sister and myself," she pleaded. The same request quickly went out in letters to support points throughout Virginia and Georgia.

Eddie and Lottie wanted to operate a boarding school for girls. Mr. Crawford insisted that he had ample property on his place for any work the young ladies wanted to do, but they quickly disagreed. "Each separate building is a new point of entry into the city," Lottie sharply reasoned. She saw no reason to centralize all work under Crawford.

Crawford and the Foreign Mission Board believed that young single women must live in the household of a married couple. The Moon sisters soon learned how that arrangement looked to polygamous Chinese. Lottie was well accustomed to fending for herself in the world. She wanted out. But there was little choice unless funds could be raised for a separate establishment.

For a foreigner to buy a house in Tengchow took sleight of hand or a miracle. Crawford had acquired his house by sleight of hand and had had to defend it with violence. Crawford pointed out that Miss Edmonia had been sent to him with no advance warning and with no housing funds. He had accommodated her as best he could. That had been in a confining, damp, spartan eleven-by-thirteen-foot cell in a building separate from his main house. There Edmonia contracted a devastating series of illnesses that were to ruin her health permanently.

When Crawford learned that Miss Lottie would be coming out with no housing allowance, he took it upon himself to tear down Edmonia's little room and make the two-storied addition to his house. This action had brought forth a mob intent on murder and destruction. Missionaries held them back with guns. The tall structure violated the privacy of all surrounding neighbors. Chinese men could envision the white man up high spying on their wives in their walled courts.[12]

By armed force Crawford prevailed, so Lottie and Edmonia each had an upstairs bedroom. Each also had a downstairs study, as did the Crawfords. In a study, a missionary received Chinese visitors, taught them, and conferred with his personal teacher who doubled as a secretary.

In addition the house had a parlor, a dining room, a chapel, various hallways, a kitchen building, servants and school students' quarters, and guest rooms built in Chinese style for Chinese visitors. The compound had a total of thirty-six rooms.[13]

Lottie was soon to meet another member of the mission, the remarkable Mrs. Sallie J. Holmes. She lived with her young son, Landrum, in a small adapted Chinese house a short distance from the Crawford estate. Sallie Holmes was the real pioneer of North China. Prior to treaty openings in 1860, she and her groom were the first Westerners to stake out Chefoo and Tengchow. When the J. B. Hartwells joined them in late 1860, it was agreed that the Holmeses would settle in Chefoo while the Hartwells took Tengchow.[14]

Sallie had just buried a baby daughter and was pregnant when her handsome husband rode out with a man of another mission to placate a robber band. Holmes was brutally murdered. Sallie remembered a vow she had made when they were weighing their odds for survival: "I would not go back. I would stay here and work." This she did, contrary to all custom and advice. She gave birth to Landrum in June and moved to Tengchow in July 1862.

Except for a visit to America for Landrum's health, she had remained at her post. As a widow with some independent means, she had her own house and compound. She in many ways had the most spunk and the most impact of all the missionaries. Lottie's usual word for her was "vigorous."

Mrs. Holmes ran a girls' boarding school and had turned over to Eddie Moon a little boys' day school. Mostly she boldly traveled the countryside doing women's evangelistic work and house-to-house teaching, covering as many as four hundred villages in a year. Just slightly older than Lottie, she took charge of training her in the ways of woman's work.

T. P. and Martha Foster Crawford were the third couple to pioneer in North China. They arrived in 1863 after a decade in Shanghai proved too much for their health. Martha, an Alabama schoolteacher, had received from God a clarion call to China in a day when a single woman could not be appointed. She was one of the first to make in-

(Upper) Sallie J. Holmes (Sketch by Louise Barbour from engraving in *Kind Words*) (Middle) Open sedan chair *(Ruth Thornhill)* (Lower) Mule cart (Ruth Thornhill)

quiry about appointment, and her pastor was dealing with the Foreign Mission Board about her case when T. P. Crawford, a Kentucky bachelor, asked for appointment to China.

The Board's matchmaking secretary told Crawford that there was a young lady missions volunteer in Alabama. Without knowing her name, Crawford galloped almost directly to her side. Never a man to stand on ceremony, he wasted no time in pointing out the practicality of a marriage. Considering the options, Martha, and eventually her parents and minister, agreed that Crawford's proposal was providential. The bridal pair romantically promised to catch up on the courtship later and were wed and off to China in nine months.[15]

By the time Lottie Moon entered their family circle, Crawford was pastor of Monument Street Baptist Church in Tengchow. He had organized it in 1866 with Chinese from Hartwell's church, a Presbyterian, Mrs. Holmes, Mrs. Crawford, and their Chinese helpers.[16] Now its membership was about fifty. Crawford's specialty was street preaching and dealing with inquirers who visited the chapel in their compound. A man of many varied interests, he had unusually progressive views on the role of women in missions.

Mrs. Crawford assisted her husband in worship services by sitting with and working with the women who dared to attend. Primarily she was an effective evangelist to women. Sometimes she traveled with Mrs. Holmes on evangelistic tours, but each woman had her own territory. On the side she handed out medicine to nearly two thousand patients a year. Except for her and an occasional Presbyterian doctor, no other medical aid was available closer than Chefoo. Regardless of the standing other married women might have had with the Foreign Mission Board, Mrs. Crawford was one whose effectiveness and zeal ranked her with the most respected missionaries.

Edmonia briefed her smaller but older sister on this cast of characters who were to play major roles in the rest of her days. In seventeen months Eddie had suffered a rude awakening to them and to mission life in China. The Moons were the first new blood to flow into the North China mission since before the Civil War. The missionaries welcomed them with pitiful gratitude. But having had exactly no experience in orienting newcomers, they simply threw them into the swim, expecting them to bounce and float with veteran toughness. It was survival of the fittest. The missionaries early predicted that Eddie would wash out. But having taken the main shock, she could help Lottie survive.[17]

When Edmonia had arrived the missionaries were dismayed at her youth and immaturity. However, they were too desperate for help to object much. They expected her to work, and she did. But they quickly begged for another young woman to come be her partner. They hinted that a little more experience would help and that dedication and enthusiasm were necessities. The Crawfords, upon learning of Lottie, joined Eddie in urging her to come to their rescue and wrote H. A. Tupper to help recruit her.[18]

The old hands recognized in Lottie a perfect missionary. "Miss L. Moon is a highly cultivated, very pious, self-sacrificing woman," noted Mrs. Crawford. Mr. Crawford informed the Foreign Mission Board that Miss Lottie entered her new life in the best of spirits and "with firm and sober delight." "She will prove a true missionary, or I'm a poor judge of character," he wrote.[19] Lottie wrote, "At our very doors is the work we crave."[20]

Obviously the new recruit had to learn Chinese immediately. Within a week Lottie attacked the task. The standard method was to engage a personal teacher, a man educated in Chinese classics who could speak little if any English. The teacher came to the student's home for daily recitations, pointing out Chinese characters with his scholarly fingernails grown many inches long. Learning was up to the student, who suffered privately for many candlelit hours.

The languge of Tengchow was Mandarin. The written language, which few Chinese could read at all, was the same throughout the empire. Speech varied greatly. Even within the Tengchow field were many dialects. The spoken language was based on a tonal system totally different from Western tongues. With two years of practice, most Americans could communicate well enough to function. Most made no attempt to master the written language and therefore always had a teacher. The teacher was essential for preparing lessons, sermons, publications, and business correspondence in Chinese.

To the advantage of the Moons, both Mrs. Holmes and Mrs. Crawford were whizzes at the spoken language. Mr. Crawford fancied himself a scholar. He had fashioned a new shorthand system of writing and was miffed that other missionaries in the realm had not furthered its adoption.[21] In Tengchow's Presbyterian mission family was Calvin W. Mateer, who wrote many aids with which the next generation of missionaries learned the language with greater ease.[22]

Edmonia, still a child when she joined the mission, surprised everybody with her speed in learning.[23] In less than a year, she was teaching Sunday School and taking over Mrs. Holmes's boys school. Miss Lottie was slower to get the language, but "still not slow," according to Mrs. Crawford. Lottie had better facility with the written character than with the strange tonal speech. Once she caught on she quickly mastered all the dialects of the region.

Learning and accepting the culture of the Chinese was often a harder lesson than the language. Edmonia went to the foot of the class in this regard. She was utterly unprepared to recognize the difference between Western culture and Christianity. She considered the unchristianized to be uncivilized. Lottie, too, arrived in China thinking the Chinese to be an inferior race, but she recognized that they were not devoid of culture.[24] She was willing to learn from it and able to grow in appreciation for it. When Williams' *Middle Kingdom* came to hand, she virtually memorized this massive work which was for years the standard reference on China.

Lottie had heard of the bound feet of Chinese women, but seeing the custom shocked her deeply. "Their deformed feet and tottering walk are but a type of their narrow minds and degraded morals," she wrote Tupper.[25] She expected to reach the minds of women through schools; then they would give up the inhumane fashion. "The greatest blessing we could bestow upon this people is the Christian education of the future wives and mothers," Lottie thought.[26]

She saw that respectable women of Tengchow would not come to church, even though the Crawfords had erected a privacy wall between men and women and separate doors for them to enter the building.[27]

The New Lottie Moon Story

Women of the better classes were not seen on the street but had trades-people come to their compounds. Woman-to-woman evangelism was the only hope for these women and for the merry Chinese children who were irresistible to Lottie. She loved their shining black eyes and comical pigtails.

Mrs. Holmes and Mrs. Crawford, along with Eddie, arranged for Lottie to visit in some of the homes of Tengchow, but the opportunity was limited. So in her third week they took her on her first trip to the country.

"We're going on a picnic, Miss Moon," Mrs. Crawford announced at breakfast. All the ladies would go. The veterans would preach;[28] the young ones would observe; everybody would enjoy the lunch out-of-doors.

Mrs. Holmes gallantly led the traveling procession, mounted on her braying donkey. Mrs. Crawford, Miss Edmonia, and Miss Lottie each rode in an open sedan chair carried by coolies. A Chinese deacon from the Monument Street Church walked beside.

They jostled through crowds at the market. Lottie drank in the sights of vendors displaying immense baskets of vegetables, peddlers carrying baskets on poles suspended on their shoulders, and mule trains carrying fuel and grain.

Suddenly the party found themselves surrounded by a throng that included many women. People were joking and making merry during a theatrical production that was shaping up. The foreign procession attracted only laughing interest.

Mrs. Holmes called a halt in a quieter suburb. The coolies set the chairs upon the ground. Lottie could not speak with the people, but she was useful in attracting a crowd of curious men and boys. The Chinese deacon then held them captive for a sermon. One of the chairbearers was a Christian, and he added his testimony.

Meanwhile, the other women missionaries split among the few women peering from their gates or edging down the street. Their objective was to gain an invitation into a home or to attract a group of willing listeners. Their plot was broken by a rude young man who loudly ridiculed the Chinese deacon, so the procession mounted for an attack elsewhere.

Several villages later Lottie had the experience of being the first foreigner ever seen by the people. This was an advantage of the Teng-chow region. Within reach were millions who could be lured by a curious-looking foreigner. And these millions had never heard the gospel. The simple villagers received the foreigners cordially. In the relaxed rural life of the more distant villages, women freely circulated on the streets.

It was lunchtime, but the missionaries could scarcely eat for the opportunity to present the Bread of Life. "The scene was doubtless as novel to the Chinese as to ourselves," Lottie wrote to her friends. "They crowded so close as to touch us. The knives and forks seemed to awaken special attention. It is a habit of the Chinese to comment freely on all they see, and their unsophisticated remarks are often amusing, though personal."

Before the crowd could wander away, the missionaries began teaching the women and children. The usual procedure in an uncultivated field like this one was to teach a hymn. "Happy Land" was the one sung today. A child learned it perfectly and was rewarded with a hymn sheet printed on red paper. Then others clamored to learn for the reward.

Lottie quickly calculated the hundreds of similar villages that awaited her touch. Mrs. Holmes said, "We can't stay here all day. Let's go!" So from village to village the picnic party went.

To counter this pleasant small success, Lottie experienced icy hatred when a man ordered women in his area away from her and Mrs. Holmes. But she also learned persistence and strategy, for Mrs. Crawford had wisely taken position in another area of the village. All the ladies who could speak Chinese had their hands full with interested hearers Mrs. Crawford attracted. At last Mrs. Holmes walked triumphantly to the donkey and exclaimed, "This village is conquered!"

Lottie was exhausted and indescribably thrilled by the picnic. As she journeyed home at sundown toward the blue sea dotted with purple islands, she knew she had found her life's work.[29]

By March, with the aid of a Chinese woman church member, Mrs. Mung, Lottie Moon was brave enough to work on her own in the city. She considered herself an evangelist for women, and she was gaining skill. Mr. Crawford suggested a good line for the inevitable question about her destitution in not having a mother-in-law. "Mothers-in-law are too hard to get along with. I'm afraid they will beat me," Lottie learned to joke. This always brought a sympathetic laugh, for Chinese women were painfully controlled and abused by the mother-in-law system. However, they pitied and consoled Lottie for being unmarried at her advanced age.[30]

Mrs. Mung helped Lottie gain admittance to a few homes in Teng-chow. Taking care to use good Chinese etiquette, they would call on the ranking woman of the house—the oldest mother-in-law. Usually younger women and children would be permitted to gather with them. Sometimes friends and neighbors would be invited in.

If the hostesses were busy, they kept on with their sewing or mat-weaving while listening to Lottie "explain books." If they were at leisure, they smoked, always offering Lottie a pipe. Although she politely declined the pipe, she nevertheless unwillingly inhaled huge quantities of smoke in the unventilated rooms.

Once situated, Mrs. Mung did most of the talking. She explained the basic distinctives of Christianity, especially the resurrection, Lottie struggling to follow and learn the speech. Then Lottie read from the catechism Mrs. Crawford had written some years before.

Daily this routine was repeated until Lottie was receiving invitations and visitors. She also developed nerve and proficiency in going from house to house. On the street, any passing woman or child would receive a friendly greeting in hope that the contact would result in an invitation to a home. As often as not, she was rewarded with the curs-ing epithet: "Foreign devil!"

While eager to make herself a welcome guest, Lottie did not tolerate discourtesy toward herself. When some boys on the street surrounded her with disorderly and rude conduct, she drew herself up to her full four feet, three inches, lectured them on their behavior, and pointedly told the leader he had no manners. The boys thusly shushed, she soon had them chanting the catechism and the hymn "Happy Land."[31]

In addition to learning the languages and the evangelistic ropes, she helped in Crawford's Monument Street Church. She attended services to greet and teach any women who might come. At this time Crawford was beginning classes to train potential preachers. These men occasionally came from their country homes to Tengchow for classes. If their reports indicated needs for women's work, the ladies of the mission followed through.

In Sunday School, Lottie taught the "infants." Crawford quickly had Lottie seeing the wisdom of his theories on making Chinese support their own churches and programs without foreign subsidy. Like Crawford she was writing, "The greatest obstacle today to the spread of the gospel in China is the belief that money is to be made by joining the church."[32]

During Chinese New Year holidays early in 1874 Mrs. Lan, a Baptist with children in both Mrs. Holmes's and Mrs. Crawford's schools, went to her native village for a visit. Soon she was calling the Tengchow missionary women to help her deal with crowds of inquirers who responded to her witness.

First, Mrs. Holmes on a donkey and Eddie in a chair went to Mrs. Lan's aid. Then Mrs. Crawford, a Presbyterian woman, and Lottie joined the effort. When they reached the village, eight miles away, they saw an unusual crowd spilling out of the Lan house. On the streets little groups of men and women earnestly studied hymns and the catechism together. The harvest was great, but three of the missionaries had other duties; so they left the Misses Moon to complete the job.

Lottie fought down a wave of loneliness and homesickness as she watched her friends leave the village, though she knew that Eddie's fluency and sociability and Mrs. Lan's status in the village guaranteed them safety. With characteristic discipline she reminded herself that even with limited language she could do much, and she turned energetically to the work.

By Sunday she and Eddie had set up the first worship service ever held in the village. Mr. Mung, the faithful deacon from Tengchow, preached. A Chinese girl led the singing. It was a day of triumph.

The next day Eddie and Lottie headed for home in open sedan chairs. The weather turned cold, and winds from the sea whipped them into severe discomfort. By the time they arrived home, Eddie was weak and ill with what developed into typhoid pneumonia. Further cold-weather trips were ruled out for her, and any village work was doubt-ful.

Lottie could only rejoice to be back in a bed. "You cannot imagine how I felt after doing without even the most ordinary comforts," she wrote. The harsh, physical strain of country work was more than she could cope with at this early stage. Other ladies might prefer country work, but Lottie said, "My heart turns longingly to the city homes grimly closed against us, forbidding our entrance, and hating us with a hatred that would vent itself in blood if only they dared."[33] She felt sure that progress was being made when fewer people called her "foreign devil" and more called her "foreign lady-teacher."[34]

Before her first year was up, death touched her little circle of friends. The Presbyterian ranks had been painfully thinned by the departures of several whose health had broken. One man was suffering an emotional collapse. Then Mrs. C. R. Mills, one of the earliest pioneers in Teng-chow, died, leaving four little children, one a deaf-mute. The Baptists mourned with their friends. Also, the Presbyterian ranks were thunder-struck when a once-friendly village very nearly murdered one of the missionaries, and a consular trial was required to force the Chinese authorities to punish the offenders.[35]

At about the same time Chinese soldiers took to racing their horses threateningly near Mrs. Holmes's house. Having recently had her little son, Landrum, assaulted by two Chinese officals, she may have been overzealous. In her usual take-charge way she pelted the soldiers with stones and injured the eye of one of the horses. The soldiers complained to the United States consul, and Mrs. Holmes was forced to apologize.[36] Lottie had cause to ponder the struggle for physical survival in the face of many hazards.

After a few rough episodes with soldiers on the streets, Lottie and Edmonia adopted a policy of firm friendliness. For a time, the soldiers would crowd around and beg boisterously for books. Unsure of their intent, the women decided to supply their requests and talk in the most gentle and kindly fashion. After a while they won the respect and friendliness of the men. "It is unpleasant to a lady to be surrounded by these rough soldiers, but certainly it is far more agreeable to be treated kindly by them than to have them call me foreign devil and threaten to kill me as they used to do at first," she wrote Tupper.[37]

It was obvious to everybody that T. P. Crawford was in precarious condition physically, mentally, and emotionally. A high-strung, combative individual by nature, he tilted at every windmill as well as at life's major crises. Lottie wrote to the homeland that Mr. Crawford must have reinforcements and a vacation. Even Presbyterian missionaries felt it their duty to warn the Foreign Mission Board of his impending breakdown.[38]

Edmonia's health steadily declined. She became irritable, cranky, and constantly bedridden with colds. On the horizon loomed the possibility that she might have to leave the field, but she wrote that to part with her beloved China would be impossible. She continued to conduct her school for little boys. Schoolmarming for her meant hiring, equipping, and supervising a Chinese teacher. Often the teacher was not a Christian, possibly used opium, and had to be watched carefully. Weekly or more often, Eddie would hear recitations, give examinations, and check up on the teacher. The curriculum consisted of Chinese classics with the addition of Bible memorization, hymn singing, and the catechism. Some of the missionaries experimented with teaching science and mathematics. Edmonia surmised that a major defect in Chinese education was its total ignorance of the outside world. Thus, she wanted to add geography to the curriculum and contemplated publishing a geography text. With her own funds, she ordered an organ from Georgia. She taught singing to her students and had some private musical enjoyment as well.[39]

Lottie continued to share her sister's dream that one day the two of them would be operating a collegiate-level school for girls of the upper class. But she began to comprehend the difficulties lying in the way. Mrs. Holmes was achieving success in her girls' boarding school, but only because Mrs. Crawford's boys' school would not admit applicants unless girls of the family came to Mrs. Holmes. The typical Chinese family saw no use whatsoever for a girl to be educated. Although being able to read was a novelty for a girl, it was not a necessity. If a family were fortunate, it betrothed or married its girls at a very tender age.

The New Lottie Moon Story

Even though a promised girl might not be bidden to join her groom's household for many years, she must be ready to go. Being away in school would complicate this relationship. Also, how could a dutiful mother see that her schoolgirl's feet were kept properly bound? And with a girl at school, who would handle the lowest chores of scullery around the house? Only a family under Christian influence, or a family needing to get rid of an unwanted mouth, would send a girl to school.[40]

Lottie could see that much evangelistic work and personal persuasion needed to accompany the school, so she began pleading for a pair of single women to join her. Learning from her sister's experience and also that of Presbyterian women, she insisted that a lone woman would suffer in morale and health. "Send two, now" became her motto. "Tengchow is a particularly appropriate field for women missionaries."[41]

Although much time was still absorbed in study, and although she had constant opportunity to work, Lottie felt pangs of despair after a year. She poured out a river of words to family, friends, missionary societies, and the Board back home. To her special society at Cartersville, she wrote, "Your missionary has begun to wonder why you have sent her no words of cheer, but yesterday there came a letter. . . . In your native land, surrounded by those who speak your mother tongue and whom you have known from infancy, you can scarcely form an idea how we in this foreign country look forward to the mail and how a chill, a feeling of despondency, will arise when there is nothing for us. The older missionaries say they are forgotten at home, that hardly anyone cares for them; and they tell us newcomers that it will be so with us in the lapse of time."[42]

Writing to her Cartersville friends and others, she painted the picture of her work—visiting, always with another woman. Bearing the gaze of rude men on the street ("It does not matter about being polite to a devil, you know"). Answering endless questions. Seeing naked boys playing in the creek. She reported with pride that she had five homes in the city where she taught serious students the catechism.

Not all was work in Tengchow, however. Lottie enjoyed swimming in the sea, riding sidesaddle on a donkey, walking on the city wall, exploring the Water City, collecting seashells, and embroidering.[43]

Often, the Baptist and Presbyterian missionaries would gather for a social evening. The Mateer home or the large Crawford home would be chosen because of the space needed for ten adults and six children. Draperies would be drawn, and the guests could imagine themselves at a typical American party. Lottie or Eddie would play the organ and sing or perhaps read poetry. Sometimes the group would play charades or swap the latest publications from the West. Inevitably, the talk would turn to shop, but the evenings were good therapy for everybody.[44]

Usually the same group, or at least the women, would meet weekly for an English prayer meeting.[45] Occasionally visitors, perhaps the children of traveling missionaries, would lodge with the Crawford establishment for a few days. For instance, Edmonia greatly enjoyed a visit from the teenage daughter of Presbyterians in Chefoo, whom she coached in her schoolwork.[46]

While Lottie was learning to have an impact on China, she created a sizable impact on the United States. As the first mature, well-known single woman to be dispatched by Southern Baptists, her writings signed "L. Moon" stimulated much interest among the women of the Convention.[47] H. A. Tupper skillfully turned this interest into the formation of woman's missionary societies, which he constantly championed. Her going to China and his election to the Foreign Mission Board spurred the formation of central committees in each state to promote women's societies. Lottie's letters became the curriculum studied by these. Each letter was copied and shared many times and was often printed in one of the Baptist state newspapers. Writings by Mrs. Crawford, who was even more prolific, were also eagerly devoured; but women did not tend to organize on her behalf.[48]

The request by the Misses Moon for a house of their own fell on attentive ears. With Tupper's encouragement, a Moon House Fund was established. Lottie thought that $2,000 would be sufficient, but Tupper set the goal at $3,000. Virginia, headed by the Richmond societies pledged to Edmonia, was asked to contribute half the amount, while Georgia, stimulated by Lottie's Cartersville women and led by Second

Baptist Church of Atlanta, promised the other half. The women earnestly coalesced around this goal, took their appeal to the Baptist papers, and soon raised more than $2,500.[49]

Lottie and Edmonia notified the Board that they "could live" on a reduced salary of $450 while boarding with the Crawfords, so that the remainder of their $600 allowance could help swell the fund.[50]

The Southern Baptist Convention of 1874 heard much discussion of the Moons. J. C. Long, soon to gain fame as professor at Crozer Theological Seminary, rose to testify to Miss Edmonia Moon's piety and self-sacrifice. R. B. Headden of Cartersville acquainted the brethren with Miss Lottie's singular qualifications and devotion to her calling. Of course, in the halls it was well known that Dr. Broadus considered Miss Lottie the "most cultivated woman I ever saw."[51] Such reputations helped the pastors of the land see the merit of the "woman's mission to woman" idea being pushed by Tupper and several leading pastors.

Personal concern for missionaries on the field was a vital ingredient in the fund-raising system of the day. In late 1875 a serious financial crisis arose. The missionaries in North China ran out of credit, and the Board in Richmond had no money to send. Tupper threatened to recall the missionaries. He held out to the stingy churches a poignant picture of the brilliant young ladies laying their lives on the line and of the broken-down old veterans hanging on for hope of aid. Actually, he did not overstate the case, and his appeal was dramatic enough to resolve the immediate crisis. Women's societies filled their mite boxes more urgently as they were acquainted on a very personal level with the Moons' plans.[52]

Late in 1874 Lottie had a bout with sickness. Eddie continued in very uncertain health, first with eyes, then with throat, then with conditions of the lungs. After seeing a doctor in Chefoo, Eddie rested there. Then she was ordered to Shanghai for further advice and rest. The senior missionaries thought it well for Lottie to accompany her sister before she too fell victim to the stresses of mission life.[53]

In Shanghai she reveled in the progressive work of Dr. Yates and admired his new chapel. A short hop from Shanghai was Soochow, the field of Miss A. C. Safford, Lottie's dear friend. Here Lottie and Eddie learned some of the risks and thrills of living inland away from treaty port protection. "The more I see of mission life, the more impressed I am with the amount of hard work—real drudgery—of these noble veterans," Lottie wrote.

The rest did little for Eddie but greatly revived Lottie. She returned to Tengchow encouraged with increased enrollments—Eddie's school had fourteen pupils—and the belief that she would live to see the success of work in North China.[54]

She was soon able to enjoy countryside evangelistic tours with more appetite. After Edmonia gave up traveling, Lottie became Mrs. Holmes's steady partner. In the fall they set out on donkeys over a terrain that reminded Lottie of the central United States. As usual they carried bedrolls and a supply of ready-to-eat food. It was harvesttime and they had a hard time getting hearers, but Lottie enjoyed the sights of grain being cut and threshed. Reaching their final destination, Lottie Moon and Sallie Holmes moved into a temple and priest's house offered them free of charge. Ignoring the yard full of hideous idols, they made their apartment in a low, tile-roofed building more elegant than their usual country places. The floor was earthen. The windows were covered with paper. "The circumstances would suggest an utter absence of comfort, yet we find ourselves more than contented," Lottie wrote.

In one room was a fire which sent heat through flues to a masonry bed in the other room. This bed, called a kang, was standard equipment in every Chinese house. Actually it was a platform covered with matting. Because it offered the only dry, heated surface in the house, the occupants sat, ate, and slept on it. Lottie usually used her bedroll as a backrest by day as she sat cross-legged on the kang. Then at night she would unroll the bedding to sleep on it. She learned that it was a fairly comfortable system, except when the kang cooked her in warmer weather.

To this apartment by night came inquirers and a Chinese Christian man who conducted preaching services. In the low room two candles burned. In one corner a table accommodated the pastor and his books. The pastor calmly puffed away at his pipe along with other men, until the crowd gathered in the dim light. Lottie and Sallie waited patiently for the pastor to lay aside his pipe. "We will sing 'Must Jesus Bear the Cross Alone,' " he said. Following singing, preaching, and praying, the group remained to chat. Lottie's imaginative mind was captured by the drama and simplicity of the service in dim, flickering light.

In another village she heard the familiar shrill cry, "The devil-women have come." At length women flocked around in such curiosity that Lottie laughed out loud. "Are you a woman?" a woman asked, pointing to Mrs. Holmes. Satisfied at this point, the women heard the gospel in a friendly way. After eleven days and forty-four villages, the travelers returned home, Lottie wiser and more appreciative of the life of country evangelists.[55]

Miss Safford returned the Moons' visit in the summer of 1875. She slept in Lottie's bedroom while Lottie moved downstairs. Although somewhat crowded, everybody was refreshed by her presence. She came bearing many ideas for women's work, which also included children's work. On her suggestion, Lottie asked the Baptist women's societies to send her Sunday School and trading cards with color pictures. She distributed these as rewards to children who learned hymns or Bible verses.[56]

In another venture Lottie undertook to publish a Sunday School paper for children. The Foreign Mission Board appropriated money for the publication, and Lottie wrangled plates for illustrations from the American Tract Society.[57]

Upon arrival in China, Lottie had stepped into a colossal dispute between the two men of the mission. It was to hover cruelly over her entire thirty-nine-year career. Edmonia had doubtless been indoctrinated into the background as she traveled to China in company of J. B. Hartwell, one of the two combatants. Although she tried to steer clear of involvement, Eddie soon found that all Americans and many Chinese in the area were well versed in the dispute. Unwittingly, the immature girl added bits to the gossip. T. P. Crawford, her host and the other half of the feud, came to suspect that she was loyal to the opposition.

Basically, the problem was that Hartwell's and Crawford's "souls crossed each other at right angles."[58] During the Civil War, the China missionaries had to make a living in secular work. Hartwell left his church in Tengchow to work as an interpreter in Shanghai. Crawford, who had made a tidy fortune in Shanghai real estate, went to Tengchow to occupy Hartwell's field. After the war, Crawford did not extricate himself from loans and business ventures he had entered into with Chinese Christians in Hartwell's church.

The two couples living in the one house brought the wives into permanent conflict. The men violently disagreed about everything from the order of worship to whether Mission Board money should be used to pay Chinese pastors and teachers. Because of their differences, the Foreign Mission Board waived its usual requirement that all missionaries in an area work together through one treasurer. The Board dealt with Hartwell and Crawford as if they were in different lands.

Crawford started his own church, but Tengchow was no longer big enough for the two jealous men. When Mrs. Hartwell died, and her survivor went wife-hunting in the United States, the situation should have calmed down. Instead it worsened as Hartwell continued to control his North Street Church through correspondence and by funding of Chinese Pastor Woo.

As Hartwell and Mrs. No. 2 returned to Tengchow, the fatal battle again began to rage. One of Crawford's investments was in a company run by the leading financial pillar in Hartwell's church. Crawford came to hold liens on all of the Chinese man's property. Amid tangles of charges and countercharges, Hartwell tried to mediate.

Soon after Lottie Moon joined the scene, the Chinese churchman sued Crawford in consular court. The court found that Crawford was in a position to take everything from his opponent, which Crawford said he would do if not paid in one year. The native then prepared to kill Crawford, and Crawford believed that Hartwell was involved.

Crawford asked Hartwell and his church to discipline its lawbreaking member. Instead, the church censured Crawford. After this blow, even the best men from other missions could not drag Hartwell and Crawford to the negotiating table. Failing to effect a biblical peace, Crawford felt justitied in notifying Hartwell that Hartwell would henceforth be "as a heathen and a publican" to him.

The New Lottie Moon Story

The smelly mess was incredibly complex. Lottie and Eddie Moon never wrote of it directly at this time and probably did not understand it, but they were certainly aware and wounded. Through it all, Lottie remained loyal to Crawford, who she thought conducted himself like a gentleman under fire. (She must not have known the extent of his private business.) She was supportive of the heartbroken and confused Mrs. Crawford. She thought it disgraceful that Hartwell spread the bad news about his colleague all over China and the United States.

The unfortunate controversy would not die even after the second Mrs. Hartwell's health took that family back to America. Hartwell brought charges against Crawford before the Foreign Mission Board. Crawford remained quiet. Miss Moon agreed with Mrs. Holmes that the two men should be separated in their work and that she would choose to go with the Crawfords.

The Foreign Mission Board, futilely trying to grasp the situation from Richmond, dictated that two churches of Tengchow should be combined under Crawford's supervision. Matthew T. Yates was instructed to go up from Shanghai to bring about the merger. After failing to accomplish this objective, Yates reported to Richmond that personality conflicts between Crawford and Pastor Woo (Hartwell's stand-in) made the merger impossible. Also, the North Street Church would not yield until Hartwell's plans about returning to China were known.

In view of a merger of churches, Lottie and Edmonia Moon moved over to occupy the long-vacant Hartwell house on North Street. Pastor Woo lived in the compound, conducted a school there, and led worship services in the chapel. The comfortable house had been locked during Hartwell's long absence. It was considered Foreign Mission Board property, and the Misses Moon were very eager to be gone from the Crawfords. It had grown tedious to all parties for the single ladies to be living year after year as guests.

Lottie suggested that she would vacate the North Street place if Hartwell should return. If not, it would be to the best interests of the Baptists if this location were maintained rather than buying a new place with the Moon House Fund, which was now invested in China.

When Hartwell discovered her move, he exploded to Richmond and to her. Lottie stood firmly and calmly. She wrote graciously to Hartwell and lengthily to the Board. She said, "The Board will understand why I scrupuously refrained from giving any hint of the difficulties in Shantung. Now that I know the affair has been brought before the Board . . . I can speak out on matters in which the Board are deeply concerned."

Lottie showed her intention to remain a member of Crawford's church but to be supportive of the Hartwell-Woo North Street Church. She then concisely, forcefully, but impartially outlined the situation regarding property and congregations as if a lawyer before the high court. The document was the sort that was to make Miss Moon famous among the Board members.

Miss Lottie wrote a soothing private note to H. A. Tupper. "I am sure you are much grieved at the unfortunate alienation between brethren. May I remind you, if it be any comfort, that it is said of Paul and Barnabas that, 'the contention was so sharp between them that they parted asunder from one the other.'" She assured him that other mission boards had their own disputes. Then she gently suggested that a quiet withdrawal of one of the parties usually solved the situation.[59]

In effect, that was accomplished as Mrs. Hartwell proved unable to return to China. The Board saw things Lottie's way and noted that "they arrived at the foregoing conclusions after having patiently and painfully reviewed the whole subject." Although the Board went to great lengths to clear the character of both parties, Hartwell continued to bicker until he resigned in 1879 to work with the Chinese in California. Crawford did not cease dabbling in business affairs that invariably left the Chinese feeling victimized. Most importantly, the Misses Moon stayed in the North Street house and began a considerable ministry to the women of that church.[60] Years later someone assessing Miss Moon's life in China said, "The most remarkable thing was that she was in the middle of a lifelong feud between two colleagues, and throughout she remained the friend of both families."[61]

Lottie was now a fully oriented, responsible member of the mission. Both the Crawfords were in critical condition after the internecine row, and they retreated to Japan during the months of August and Septem-

The New Lottie Moon Story

ber 1876. In their absence, Lottie administered Mrs. Crawford's booming school and her medicine service. Many of the students were ill, but Lottie coped admirably. It was a matter of some significance that she, Eddie, and Sallie Holmes—three lone single women—were able to run affairs smoothly, even when the Foreign Mission Board's final decisions regarding the property feud arrived and needed interpreting to Pastor Woo. In her many communications to H. A. Tupper, Lottie revealed a bubbling happiness with the progress of her work.[62]

More and more frequently came the word, "Miss Lottie Moon is out preaching in the country." The woman of 1876 was fully at home in China, fully comfortable with the language, fully toughened to the rigors of foreign living, and fully committed to her work of evangelism.

Mrs. Holmes and she were invited by a Chinese pastor, Mr. Dzoong, to visit his village twenty-five miles from Tengchow. Lottie felt great affection and appreciation for this brother who was supported by native Christians. A few years earlier she would not have been able to say of him, "I have never met anyone who seemed more fully to realize in his character the words, 'He had been with Jesus and learned of him.' "

Using a donkey and a pony for transportation, another donkey loaded with bedding, baskets of food, and other baggage, the two friends set out. En route they gathered a crowd of thirty women and girls for teaching. Next they permitted a class of schoolboys to come to them. Lottie gave books to the boys and drilled them in the catechism. Throughout their trip, as usual, Lottie had to assure women of her sex before they would come near for teaching.

At Mr. Dzoong's village they were provided the ancestral hall of a fine home for their classroom. Accustomed to only a doorstep or open street, they were thrilled at this luxury, complete with hot tea, graciously served. On Sunday, as was their custom, they ceased traveling and conducted worship services where they were. Mr. Dzoong preached to the men; Mrs. Holmes took the women; and Lottie got her usual preference of teaching the children.

Several villages later, the crowds were so immense and so hospitable that Lottie broke one of her cardinal rules. "I hope you won't think me desperately unfeminine, but I spoke to them all—men, women, children. I should not have dared to remain silent with so many souls before me sunk in heathen darkness," she wrote later to the Foreign Mission Board. When the large crowd overflowed the hall, she adjourned to the yard and pleaded with the Chinese to turn from idolatry to the true and living God.

Later the women joined Mrs. Holmes and Miss Moon on the kangs in their rooms while Mr. Dzoong held services in the hall. The two missionaries retired with groans. "I can never forget that night," Lottie wrote. "The smoke-blackened walls, the window that would not open, the stifling atmosphere, the living creatures (insects) that crawled over us!—such a night I never passed. We could not but laugh at the situation."[63]

After more nights in this fashion, Lottie's throat was feeling very ill-used, and she was predicting another missionary on the retired list before long.

The trip home was livened up by two little girls who were being sent to Mrs. Holmes's school. The girls were stowed in big baskets slung on either side of the donkey. "The little creatures were so merry," Lottie recalled. She felt that their cavalcade should have made a charming picture.

The contentment and purposefulness Lottie Moon enjoyed at this time were not to last. Gently she was forced to recognize the true state into which her sister had sunk. Edmonia was not only chronically ill, but she was also suffering drastically from what later generations were to call "culture shock." Since her arrival in China she had fought to throw it off, but now she succumbed to it.

Her departure from the United States had been cruelly rushed. Never having been out of her native environment, she had been suddenly thrust among strangers for a confining, three-month trip. Immediately she was subjected to the disillusioning and disgusting feud between Crawford and Hartwell. She also had opportunity to observe the ambivalent way in which the Hartwells dealt with their Chinese assistants in the travel party.

By the time she landed in Shanghai she thought that she was going crazy and begged to be put on the return ship to America, promising that her brother Isaac would repay all charges. Mrs. Yates, her hostesss, immediately pronounced her unfit for China and so warned Mrs. Crawford by mail. However, a doctor who observed her for some days insisted that she was not crazy, but merely "hysterical." J. B. Hartwell decided that she was T. P. Crawford's problem, since his wife had invited her out, and that Crawford should decide what to do with her. Although Hartwell warned H. A. Tupper at this time, he did not describe the situation to the Crawfords.[64]

With grim foreboding, Martha Foster Crawford welcomed Eddie to Tengchow and was pleasantly surprised and invigorated by her charming presence. Her skill with the language, her excitement, and her piety put their minds at ease.[65]

Then came one debilitating illness after another—impossible to diagnose today, but sounding like asthma or tuberculosis. When Eddie wrote her symptoms to her doctor-sister and two doctor-brothers-in-law, they immediately asked her to come home to Viewmont.[66]

The worry about Edmonia gave the mission double cause for rejoicing when Lottie joined the force and Eddie perked up. But the girl who had lived all her life with servants responding to every whim did not fit well into Mrs. Crawford's inflexible household. Her failure to conform to meal schedules, her desire for absolute quiet in the house, her temper, her crossness with the Chinese—all irritated the Crawfords. The living conditions gave Eddie (and Lottie) no personal freedom. Mrs. Crawford sniffed self-righteously that Eddie did not appreciate all that had been done for her. She never blamed Lottie but felt sorry for her.

Nerves were stretched to the breaking point by the time of Miss Safford's visit in 1875. Anna soon learned that turning in her bed made the bedstead creak, which made Eddie furious, which then aroused the whole household. No wonder Lottie insisted on getting into private housing. She tried to keep peace, not apologizing to Mrs. Crawford but trying to make amends.

After illness cut into the work that Eddie could safely accomplish, Mrs. Crawford pronounced her good for nothing as a missionary.

When the Moons moved to North Street, Lottie did the work of two, feeling grateful that Eddie could make a home for them both. The boys' school grew, and a start was made on a girls' school. But the least crisis could bring on trouble; and a major crisis, such as when a crowd of soldiers stoned Eddie as she walked outside the city wall, was a disaster.[67]

It was decided well before wintertime of 1876 that Edmonia could not survive the winter in Tengchow's damp cold. Plans were made to send her to Japan. In October, before the Crawfords returned from their rest and recreation trip to Japan, Eddie had gone to Shanghai to join Mrs. Yates for a trip to Japan.

In the company of Mrs. Yates, something mysteriously happened to confirm her idea that Eddie's problem was more serious than China missionaries could cope with. Mrs. Yates sent word to her husband, who telegraphed Lottie to join the women in Nagasaki, Japan, immediately. Terrified, Lottie threw her belongings into a trunk and within four hours was gone from Tengchow.

Whatever she found in Japan convinced her that Eddie must go home permanently. All the missionaries concurred and wrote the Foreign Mission Board that charming Miss Eddie had given her best effort but was physically unable to tolerate the climate.[68]

The Misses Moon arrived home on December 22, 1876, just in time for a tender family Christmas at Viewmont. Eddie was promptly put to bed by the Drs. Andrews, who were then occupying the old home. Brother Isaac and Mag came over from Church Hill, another family estate where Ike was teaching school. Dr. William Shepherd brought from Norfolk his motherless little Mamie. His wife, Mary (Mollie) Moon, had died and been buried in October while her sisters were en route home. Sister Colie was working as a counter for the Treasury Department in Washington, D.C. She came as soon as possible, full of delightful talk about her adventures. Except for Eddie's serious illness, the family scene would have been perfect. Dr. Shepherd prescribed a remedy of massive doses of cod liver oil and whiskey, and her chances for survival improved.[69]

Everyone agreed that Edmonia's China days were over, but Lottie wanted to be on the next boat back. However, there was no money in the Foreign Mission Board treasury to send her. Also, there was important public relations work for Lottie to do. At the same time Edmonia had to leave China, it was noticed that three other missionaries—a sizable cut of the China force—had left the field because of illness. This created a breach of confidence with many Baptists who wondered why these missionaries were not dedicated enough to die on the field. The family members who accompanied them home, such as Lottie, were utterly without excuse. Tupper, missionaries on the field, and other friends had to work hard to placate those who had no sympathy.[70] Lottie made contact with the women's societies who had been so supportive of her and Edmonia. Of serious concern were the Virginia women whose special missionary was now fallen.

H. A. Tupper, by now a great admirer of Miss Lottie, exchanged lengthy letters with her about every imaginable type of mission business. The Hartwell-Crawford problem still simmered; Lottie vented her opinion that Hartwell had said enough. The matter of the Moon House Fund had to be decided in a way that would please the donors; many options were explored. From Tengchow and all Shantung Province came lurid tales of famine, suicide, cannibalism, infanticide, and disease; Lottie did what little she could to stimulate the flow of relief money.

Many friends and family around the country invited her to visit. Usually she had to decline even so gracious a bid as was sent from John A. Broadus in Louisville where Southern Seminary had moved. There is some hint that Broadus and Tupper at this time encouraged Crawford H. Toy to drop by Albermarle County during a promotional tour for the seminary. Whether he did is impossible to know. However, the Toy-Moon friendship seemed interestingly rekindled from this time until 1882.[71]

The most immediate problem for Lottie was getting back to China. Many pleas went from Richmond via Baptist newspapers, but contributions were not forthcoming. At length, the Moon House Fund sponsors agreed that it was pointless to keep such a sterling missionary in this country while that money lay in the bank. Women of Richmond authorized the use of their house contributions for transportation and promised to pick up Lottie's support.[72] In mid-October Lottie again said good-bye to Virginia. She was Mrs. Tupper's guest for three days in Richmond while visiting the women's societies and conversing at length with her friend, the secretary of the Foreign Mission Board. Tupper sent off this "modest, intelligent, devoted woman" with a tribute in the *Foreign Mission Journal* and other papers: "It was good to be in the company with one who feels specially called to labor among the far-off heathen, and who, after experiences of its hardships and difficulties, returns to her work, not merely with cheerfulness, but with a spirit of quiet Christian exultation."[73]

Miss Moon took the train to New York, where she visited leaders in the nerve center of woman's work for woman, the Woman's Union Missionary Society. She was entertained by the Union's famous Mrs. T. C. Doremus.[74] In the company of a congenial group of single women appointees for China, she eagerly made the voyage—for home.[75]

Notes———— See pp. 302-303 for Key to Sources.

1. Lottie Moon to friends, October 9, 1873, and Lottie Moon to her sister Orie, September 30, 1873, LMR. For insight into a typical missionary's attitude about departure, see T. P. Crawford's letter in *RH*, June 25, 1868: "I shall never see you again in the flesh. I expect to live, to suffer, and to die. I cannot leave till God calls me . . . on high."

2. Letter from Lottie Moon, October 11, 1873, Cartersville Minutes; *Baptist Courier*, December 11, 1873.

3. *KW*, July 22, 1873; Lottie Moon to friends, October 9, 1873.

4. *Home and Foreign Journal*, February 1874.

5. *FMJ*, June 1880.

6. *CI*, March 5, 1874; Martha Foster Crawford to H. A. Tupper, June 16, 1873, TPCLF.

7. Irwin T. Hyatt, Jr., *Our Ordered Lives Confess.*

8. C. W. Mateer, May 27, 1874, in foreign missions correspondence of Presbyterian Historial Society, microfilm roll 198.

9. Descriptions of the Crawford structures may be found in MFCD. Details of the financing are scattered throughout Minutes of the FMB and TPCLF.

10. Handwritten notes of William Carey Newton forty years later mention Edmonia's name carved into the window.

11. Lottie Moon to H. A. Tupper, November 1, 1873, LMLF.

12. Anna Seward Pruitt, *Up from Zero.*

13. MFCD.

14. *WR,* March 6, 1884.

15. Tupper, *Foreign Missions of the Southern Baptist Convention;* Tarleton Perry Crawford, *Fifty Years in China.* William B. McGarity, *CI,* September 14, 1893, said, "She was about the first single lady to apply."

16. Hyatt, *Our Ordered Lives Confess.*

17. MFCD.

18. T. P. Crawford to H. A. Tupper, and Crawford's report of December 31, 1872, TPCLF.

19. Martha Foster Crawford described Lottie in her diaries. T. P. Crawford to H. A. Tupper, November 17, 1873, TPCLF.

20. Lottie Moon to H. A. Tupper, November 1, 1873, LMLF, FMB.

21. Lottie Moon, December 3, 1873, Cartersville Minutes; MFCD.

22. Hyatt, *Our Ordered Lives Confess,* treats Mateer along with Lottie Moon and T. P. Crawford.

23. Pruitt, *Up from Zero:* "She was speaking like a native in six months."

24. Lottie Moon, October 11, 1873, Cartersville Minutes; Lottie Moon to H. A. Tupper, October 24, 1873, March 13, 1875, and November 1, 1873, LMLF.

25. Lottie Moon to H. A. Tupper, November 1, 1873.

26. *Home and Foreign Journal,* February 1874.

27. *RH,* January 9, 1873; *CI,* March 24, 1874.

28. Both Presbyterian and Baptist women missionaries of this era commonly used the word "preach" to describe their witnessing on public streets and in private homes. "Mrs. Holmes and Miss Lottie Moon are out preaching in the country," said *RH,* January 7, 1875.

29. *Home and Foreign Journal,* March 1874.

30. *CI,* June 11, 1874.

31. Ibid.

32. Lottie Moon to H. A. Tupper, November 2, 1875, LMLF.

33. Lottie Moon, March 7, 1874, Cartersville Minutes.

34. *CI,* June 11, 1874.

35. *RH,* June 11, 1874; *Woman's Work for Woman,* July 1874; *FMJ,* September 1874.

36. Correspondence from Sallie Holmes, July 15, 1874, and following, to American Consulate, Chefoo, China. Volume 3A, 1874-79 of Miscellaneous Correspondence, Record Group 84, National Archives.

37. Lottie Moon to H. A. Tupper, February 25, 1876, LMLF.

38. *Home and Foreign Journal,* March 1874.

39. R. B. Headden to H. A. Tupper, May 5, 1875, LMLF. Edmonia Moon to Orianna Moon Andrews, August 11, 1876, LMR. Edmonia Moon to John Sum-

merfield Andrews, September 26, 1874, from papers given by Mary Virginia Andrews.

40. *KW,* July 15, 1877.

41. *FMJ,* July 1874.

42. Lottie Moon, August 8, 1874, Cartersville Minutes.

43. Lottie Moon, September 8, 1874, Cartersville Minutes.

44. *RH,* August 17, 1876.

45. *WWW,* May 1876.

46. Edmonia Moon to John Summerfield Andrews, September 26, 1874.

47. *RH,* July 22, 1875, contains only one of many examples of Lottie's writings published in the *Herald* of Virginia, *Christian Index* of Georgia, *Western Recorder* of Kentucky, and *Foreign Mission Journal.*

48. Mrs. Crawford was the most frequent missionary correspondent of *Kind Words,* though Lottie Moon occasionally wrote. This publication taught missions to children.

49. *RH,* September 17, 1874, and *FMJ,* November 1874, are examples of Moon House Fund promotion.

50. *CI,* October 1, 1874.

51. *CI,* October 1, 1874; *RH,* May 21, July 21, October 15, 1874; and other reports of 1874 Southern Baptist Convention.

52. *WR,* July 24, December 2, 1875.

53. *FMJ,* May 1875.

54. *FMJ,* June 1875.

55. *CI,* January 21, 1875.

56. MFCD.

57. Lottie Moon to H. A. Tupper, December 28, 1874; *FMJ,* December 1874.

58. MFCD. For a complete study of the Hartwell-Crawford difficulties, see Hyatt, *Our Ordered Lives Confess.* Hartwell Family Papers and JBHLF contain documentary material.

59. Lottie Moon to J. B. Hartwell, October 11, 1875; Lottie Moon to H. A. Tupper, March 24, 1876 (two letters), LMLF.

60. *Baptist Courier,* August 10, 1876.

61. W. W. Adams Notes, WMU.

62. Lottie Moon to H. A. Tupper, May 27, 1876; MFCD. C. W. Mateer of the Presbyterian mission preached in Crawford's church during his absence.

63. *Baptist Courier,* June 29, 1876.

64. J. B. Hartwell to H. A. Tupper, July 2, 1872, "Strictly Confidential," JBHLF.

65. MFCD records Mrs. Yates' warning to Mrs. Crawford and Mrs. Crawford's subsequent feelings about Edmonia.

66. Edmonia Moon to Orianna Moon Andrews, August 11, 1876.

67. *Baptist Courier*, August 13, 1876.

68. MFCD; Mrs. Crawford to H. A. Tupper, November 13, 1876, TPCLF.

69. Lottie Moon to H. A. Tupper, January 29, 1877, LMLF

70. *FMJ*, April 1877; *Baptist Courier*, September 27, 1877.

71. Lottie Moon to J. A. Broadus, April 17, 1877; C. H. Toy to J. A. Broadus, August 1, 1877, Broadus Papers, Southern Seminary.

72. Resolutions of Woman's Missionary Society, October 9, 1877, LMLF.

73. *Baptist Courier*, November 8, 1877, and *FMJ*, November 1877.

74. Lottie Moon to H. A. Tupper, October 20, 1877, LMLF. Mrs. Doremus was called "one of the most remarkable laywomen in the whole history of American Protestantism" by R. Pierce Beaver in *All Loves Excelling—American Protestant Women in World Mission*.

75. Awaiting her steamer in San Francisco, Lottie made arrangements for receiving and caring for the Hartwell children, who were coming from China to join their parents in the United States, where they had hastened on account of Mrs. Hartwell's declining health.

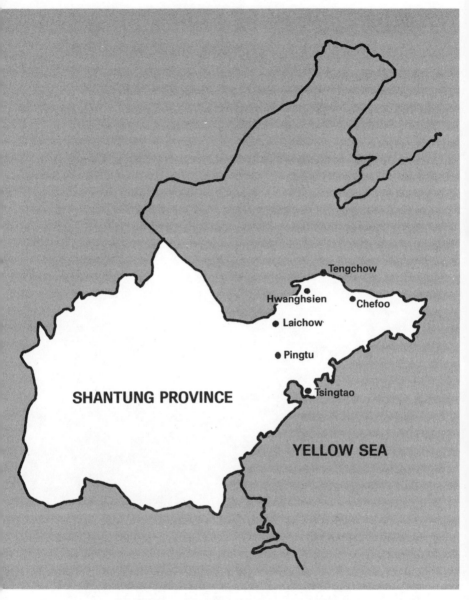

Maps showing Lottie Moon's places of work and travel, Shantung Province, North China

Lottie Moon, about 1877, charcoal sketch by a cousin
(Virginia Woman's Missionary Union)

6
She Was
a Professional

It was a different Lottie Moon—Miss Moon—who sailed for China on November 8, 1877. In contrast to the eager neophyte run by faith alone four years ago, this woman was clothed in skill and confidence. She was a thoroughly professional missionary both in mind and emotion. Among the thirteen other missionaries on board the *Tokio Maru*, she was an object of respect.[1]

She would settle in her private home, pick up a definite work as a schoolteacher, walk calmly in the face of danger, and speak and mingle comfortably with the Chinese people. With the ship gliding smoothly across untroubled waters, Lottie Moon had a delightful trip.

Pausing in her beloved Japan, Miss Moon had fun with Northern Baptist missionaries, observing approvingly that their attractive church building blended with local architecture and custom. She was enchanted by the beautiful and polite people. But she wrote to Henry Allen Tupper, "Now I honestly believe that I love China the best. Actually, which is stranger still, I love the *Chinese* best."[2]

Taking a studied look at the Woman's Union Missionary Society's mission compound for single women, she added to her growing bank of impressions about how a woman of her status might make the greatest contribution. After sailing through the Inland Sea, which she considered to be a fairyland, she was ready for China.

In Shanghai, Matthew and Eliza Yates welcomed their friend and briefed her on China shoptalk. Yates was the senior Baptist missionary in China. Recently he had been one of the hosts for the first General Conference of Protestant Missionaries in China. An unprecedented

The New Lottie Moon Story

forum, the meeting in Shanghai did much to set the direction for strategy in all denominations. Lottie must have regretted missing the historic discussions, which had taken place during her absence in America with Edmonia. She secured the book of proceedings, and the Yateses sketched in the background.

Martha Foster Crawford had been one of four women among forty-five program guests. She wrote an impressive paper on women's work, which was read before the audience by her husband, in the custom of the times.

T. P. Crawford presented a paper entitled "The Advantages and Disadvantages of the Employment of Native Assistants." According to form, Crawford mainly saw disadvantages, and he argued them in a way that ruffled the good feeling of the meeting. In the published proceedings, the paper was accompanied by an editorial note explaining the general disagreement with his paper, after a debater called it "self-contradictory and destructive."[3]

Eliza Yates acquainted Miss Moon with the Woman's Missionary Association which was organized during the all-China conference. The association grew out of the increasingly significant prominence of women as a distinctive mission strategy—a definite movement of which Lottie was feeling herself very much a part. Mrs. Yates had been elected president. Miss A. C. Safford was vice-president and instigator of a new publication, *Woman's Work in China.* They wanted Lottie to be a contributing editor, and she consented.

In Shanghai Miss Moon admired the new chapel which the Yateses were dedicating, then slipped off to the interior to visit Anna Safford at Soochow. Miss Safford never failed to energize her old friend with fresh ideas for the work.[4]

When the steamer for Chefoo set Miss Moon on Shantung soil, a snowstorm was raging. Helen C. Nevius, matriarch of the Presbyterians in Chefoo, bundled Lottie into layers of wadded garments. Looking like a Chinese mandarin, Miss Moon lumbered into a shentze and set off for Tengchow in the Christmasy blizzard. A Chinese Baptist brother escorted her to a safe arrival on December 22. "It is worthwhile to go away from China to get such a welcome," she told her three co-workers.[5]

When Lottie left Tengchow, Baptists had barely penetrated the crusty, though crumbling, population. The upper-class people were too haughty to receive missionaries, while the poorer classes were too busy seeking out a survival to worry about religion.

Lottie found the situation slightly improved. The famine had brought starving and dying people in from the countryside, and inflation had hit everybody. Thus chastened, the Chinese were able to notice the relief ministries performed by missionaries. Lottie's own heart was touched by the suffering. H. A. Tupper forwarded to her care the several small contributions that had come to the Board for relief—$5.50, some stamps, and a single earring. She spent some of the relief gifts directly on food for the needy at her doorstep and gave most to a formal relief program of English Baptists. She was very pleased with the unusual showing of benevolence when the Tengchow church took up a collection to feed the hungry. Having done what she could, she accepted the famine and horrid sights of starvation as a Chinese problem which would have to be lived with.[6]

In the Crawford household she met two children whom the old couple had adopted for their declining years. Minnie, age fourteen, and Alfred (or Freddie), age seven, were English orphans who had been stranded in Japan. During the Crawfords' vacation in Japan, Mr. Crawford had arranged to adopt them, thinking that his wife needed to become a mother. Mrs. Crawford accepted them sight unseen. Now in addition to her mob of boy boarding students, her ministry to the sick, and her far-flung women's evangelistic work, Mrs. Crawford was caring for two troubled, dull children.[7]

Crawford was smarting over reviews of his book *Patriarchal Dynasties*. For him it was a momumental work which had assumed more importance than his missionary task. Using Chinese perspectives, he suggested a new chronology for the book of Genesis. Southern Baptist friends and scholars took the book with a large grain of courtesy to the honored missionary but with little seriousness. Seeing her friend's disappointment, Lottie loyally ripped off a stern rebuttal to the reviewers, calling on her Hebrew to show that Crawford might have a point.[8]

Lottie found Sallie Holmes crushed with grief. Her son Landrum was preparing to leave in the company of the Presbyterian Mateers to be educated in the United States. To him the United States was a completely foreign country where no one knew or loved him. Mrs. Holmes was torn between her love for the boy and her concern for the Chinese women. She was running a well-established boarding school for girls and the largest Baptist itinerating circuit. With amazing fortitude, Sallie decided not to leave her work. But her heart followed Landrum, and she was a woman in distress. Lottie wrote to her friends in Richmond asking them to assume responsibility for Landrum.[9]

Ever mindful of the heroic examples of her colleagues, Lottie gave her whole self to the work. Picking up the threads of her sister's dream, she wanted to establish a girls' boarding school for the higher classes of people of Tengchow. This center of work would put her in contact with a widening circle of personal evangelism. This is the work she had done in the United States; she would simply relocate it in China. In February 1878 the school opened with five pupils. Soon the number grew to thirteen. But they were not the fine young ladies she had dreamed of.

Although schoolwork was a widely accepted strategy of missions in China at this time, there were many obstacles. For boys, all their hopes for advancement were tied to learning the ancient literary classics on which the "civil service" exams were based. This fact made missionary objectives run counter to Chinese objectives in school. Mission schools took valuable time from classics to teach Christianity. Sometimes they added subjects such as mathematics, science, and geography. For some, this curriculum secured the limited supply of jobs related to foreign business. But it made most dependent on missionaries for employment as teachers or assistants.

After fifteen years of experience with the Chinese literary curriculum, Mrs. Crawford boldly ruled that the Bible would henceforth be her main textbook. This move broke the hearts and the chances of her prize pupils, but it soon succeeded.[10]

In girls' schools, the problem was not what to teach but how to get girls in school at all. Even for Christians, school tended to interfere with the main business of being female: getting feet properly misshapen, getting married, and doing the work relegated to the lowest form of humanity.

One way to get pupils in spite of these obstacles was to pay families for letting their children come. Southern Baptists stopped short of this. But they did assume all costs not only for instruction, but also for life support. As Lottie opened her school, the missionaries set a rule that parents had to pay for their children's clothing, often rags. That left only lodging, food, medicine, books, and teacher for Lottie to provide. It took all her persuasive powers all across the countryside to assemble a class on this basis. As a result some of the students were rescued from prostitution or virtual slavery. Upper-class people could not be convinced to put their daughters in school.

Miss Moon's school operated in a row of Chinese rooms in her North Street compound. Most of the building had been improved with plank floors and glass windows. Kangs big enough for five girls each dominated each sleeping room. The kangs were heated from fireplaces in the kitchen, where a cook stirred up simple meals of millet and vegetables. Supervising the Chinese servants who helped with the school, especially the cook, was a headache. At one point the food was so bad that four students went home to mama.

Lottie outlined a course based on reading, arithmetic, and geography. The texts were the one-hundred-page catechism prepared by Mrs. Crawford, the hymnbook compiled and composed by Mr. Crawford, and *Peep of Day,* a children's book of Bible stories adapted from English by Mrs. Holmes. Lottie embellished these courses by giving singing lessons, using Edmonia's organ.

Memorization was the basic method of instruction. In classic Chinese style, all the girls read and quoted aloud simultaneously, making a jarring noise. Miss Moon hired a pretty young Chinese woman to coach the memorization. When the venerable Miss Moon entered to give examinations, the girls raised the volume of their labors louder and higher to show respect.

For the examination, a girl turned her back to Miss Moon, then shouted out her memorized recitation. According to Chinese practice, the turned back was necessary to keep the student from reading the teacher's book of big Chinese characters. Soon Miss Moon could proudly report that students were able to recite the entire book of Mark or Matthew. Doubtless she could, too![11]

The New Lottie Moon Story

The great hope in all these efforts was that girls would find their way to being professing, practicing Christians. At least three of Miss Moon's early students became baptized believers. But many who might have made the leap toward Christianity were beaten back into tradition by parents or mothers-in-law. Part of Miss Moon's chronic heartbreak was to see a promising girl married off to an opium eater or an aggressive ancestor worshiper.[12]

The foot-binding issue was a constant trial. At the very age a girl should be coming to school, the mother would begin the process. With bands of cloth, she bent the four small toes under the ball of the feet and drew them mercilessly toward the heel. After months of tightening, the bones would break and, with good fortune, heal into a three-inch foot with a pointed big toe. Girls were in constant pain, and infection often caused rotting, illness, and even death. During this time a girl would not be spared her share of the chores even if she had to crawl or drag herself across the dirt floor.

Miss Moon threw all her influence into enlisting schoolgirls who had not been bound, but she did not require unbound feet for admission. Once a bound-foot girl was in school, Miss Moon launched a diplomatic battle to free her. One girl's Christian future father-in-law gave permission for her to be unbound, as approximately one-third of the students were. The girl's feet grew normally. Then the groom was furious and demanded that Miss Moon rebind the feet. Thinking she had the father on her side, she staunchly refused. But the father wavered under pressure from his wife and son. "Then you can take her away tomorrow," puffed Miss Moon in righteous indignation. "I usually abide by the parents' decision, but it would be a refinement of cruelty to bind the feet of a grown girl. I refuse to have such suffering inflicted under my roof. I will not be a witness to it!" She forced the family to back down, and she delivered an impassioned sermon on how the bound foot was inconsistent with the Christianity the father professed.[13]

In those days of uncertain missions finance among Southern Baptists, Miss Moon had to struggle to keep her school supported. Women's missionary societies were encouraged to sponsor one or more students. To these sponsors Miss Moon wrote colorful letters about the chosen child's problems and progress. This was laborious work which brought in approximately fifteen dollars a year per child to the Foreign Mission Board. Some of the girls were named for their sponsors—Lois, Mary, Emma, Eva.[14]

Miss Moon enjoyed little daily reward for her efforts. The girls had been trained from infancy to excel in hot temper and quarreling. The household was never peaceful. She understood the necessity the oppressed girls felt for fighting, but she tried to show a Christian example of peace. She was constantly arbitrating.

Meanwhile, she was at war with dirt, vermin, and germs. Eventually she accommodated to having a generous amount of uncleanliness in the girls' living quarters. Her school at its worst was much more hygienic than the homes at their best, so she endured hopefully for the day of a higher class of student. With amazing accuracy, she predicted that it would be twenty years before her ambitions would be fulfilled.

Yet she loved the girls and became involved in their strivings on a very personal level. On one occasion she was tricked into taking a sickly five-year-old child. Having received the tot, she couldn't part with her. Lottie wrote like a proud mama of her development into a fat, rosy, merry picture of health. Although the child was entirely too young to fit into the schoolroom routine, she became Lottie's special love and had free run of the place.[15]

Operating a school was a burden, but it did not consume all of Lottie Moon's time. Nor did it adequately fulfill her calling to give Chinese women the uplifting message of Jesus. Neither did many of the other responsibilities attached to being a missionary, but these regularly arose. In this period of her life, Lottie came to have a more prominent role in decisions affecting the mission group. Because of her well-known writing skills, it was she who usually penned the reports or queries to Richmond.

Immediately upon arrival in 1877 she had settled down in the North Street property formerly occupied by J. B. Hartwell. The mission held what amounted to a lifetime right of rental because of substantial improvements Hartwell had made on the buildings. With the Moon House Fund in hand, she wanted to clear the title and purchase the establishment outright. In classic Chinese fashion, purchase proved impossible, but she did succeed in getting the rent reduced. Next she tried to buy another suitable tract. Again, it was impossible to establish clear title or to find the person with the right to sell. After two years of negotiations, Lottie was convinced that she should stay at North Street and was eager to be done with the tedious discussions which were distracting her from her work.[16]

At the same time, T. P. Crawford eyed the plump Moon House Fund which he as mission treasurer had not been asked to handle. He found it necessary to call for repayment of his loan to the Foreign Mission Board for building the Monument Street chapel. Lottie graciously wrote to the leading Virginia and Georgia women who had raised the Moon House Fund. She convinced them that their donation would be well used in paying off the church building, since both she and her school students worshiped there. By 1881 the matter was settled, and the rented North Street compound was her home.[17]

Related to the property issue was a bit of old business about church merger. During the famine the famed English Baptist missionary, Timothy Richard, was forced to leave his church in Chefoo while doing relief work. In February after Miss Moon returned, T. P. Crawford summoned from throughout the province members of the English church, the North Street Church (with many of its members fifty miles away at Shangtswang), and Monument Street Church. This time Crawford presided over a peaceful vote in favor of merger, with the understanding that members might withdraw if Richard returned, which he soon did.

The new church was constituted as the Tengchow Baptist Church. However, as soon as Crawford left the area in the summer, the merger began to dissolve. Some of the old North Street members, remembering Hartwell, were complaining and wanting to meet separately. Lottie suspected that some wanted to slip Confucian custom into their worship and steadfastly refused to permit them to use the North Street chapel. She feared the influence they might have over the girls' school. Miss Moon assumed leadership in halting the schism in the church, dealing sternly with a troublemaking man and girl and writing Richmond and Shanghai for help.

Practically speaking, it was too much to think that one church in Tengchow could minister to members who lived not in the city, but up to fifty miles in all directions. So Miss Moon assisted the true Christians of North Street Church in establishing themselves as a church in the village of Shangtswang, keeping their heritage as the oldest Baptist church in Shantung Province. The merger maneuver had served to flush out some unfaithful members and to eliminate the old personality conflicts. Miss Moon firmly told the Board, "No more church mergers!" But she had used the experience to learn to influence the Chinese men without violating her own sense of feminine propriety and without making the men "lose face."[18]

Lottie kept close, though somewhat delayed, touch with happenings in the United States. When she read that the *Biblical Recorder* had announced the end of the days of missionary hardships, she undertook some missionary education. "When it comes to living in native houses with dirt or brick floors, sleeping on native beds, and eating only food prepared in the native style, *this* most people would consider a hardship," she wrote. She portrayed the loneliness and psychological isolation felt by a missionary. "Almost daily he is brought into contact with those who hate him and who would take his life if they dared."[19]

Lottie recognized that all these hardship factors were worse in the interior than in a city like Tengchow. She counted the cost of interior life and found herself not fully able to pay it. She stayed close to Tengchow, but added increasingly to her trips to the country.

Mrs. Holmes, who put nothing ahead of country work, hooted when she read in the *Religious Herald* the opinion that missionaries suffered poor health because they did not adopt the native life-style. She simply wrote with acid pen for an immediate appropriation to build a pigsty under her bedroom window. And she apologized for her folly in using carbolic acid and other disinfectants.

Mrs. Holmes's philosophy was to be her American self, to live in the outlying villages closely with the people a large part of the time, but retreating to American refinements in her Tengchow home. Probably Mrs. Holmes was the predominating influence in leading Lottie more and more to the rural circuit.[20]

One morning, a year after her return to the field, Lottie awoke

The New Lottie Moon Story

dreading a country tour she had promised to take with Sallie. She sent a message across town to Mrs. Holmes's house. "Don't you think the weather is too threatening? It's cold and awfully windy. Shall we go or not? I think it the better part of wisdom to stay."

The runner shortly came back with a laconic reply from the indomitable Mrs. Holmes: "Go." Soon the ladies were in their sedan chairs. They ordered their bearers to take them to as many villages as possible up to a ten-mile station, where they expected to camp for the night. They met with such responsive audiences that night fell before they could reach their intended shelter. The chair bearers enterprisingly found a village home which would accommodate them for the evening. This was a rare piece of good fortune. The host was hospitable, and the missionaries were quickly surrounded by boys, girls, and women. Although it was time for rest, the Holmes-Moon team immediately moved into battle formation. Mrs. Holmes ordered the boys to the yard, and soon Lottie could hear her putting them through the catechism in her usual vigorous style.

Back inside, Lottie, on the kang, taught the women and girls. To her great delight they were eager pupils who begged for books. Even the host requested a New Testament. The next morning they taught up to the moment of their departure for another long, productive day in other villages. At sunset Lottie announced to Mrs. Holmes very positively, "I will do no more missionary work today. I'm exhausted!" But as the chair bearers ran off to find a house for the night, she found herself surrounded by curious people. "It's impossible not to speak, when we have the words of eternal life," Lottie sighed, and fell to the work.

Much later the ladies were conducted to their room. It was small—nine by nine feet. The walls and rafters were black from the smoke of many years. The kang was of simple mud covered with dirty matting. The floor was dirt. A paper window could not be opened to admit air, and the doorway could not be closed. It opened into the chair bearers' room—certainly an unfortunate arrangement. Crude though the room was, the tired women sank onto the kang and received a crowd of visitors. Soon they had to divide forces—Holmes in the yard, Moon inside. Invited to a neighboring house, they found a hot, crowded, tobacco-smoke-filled room. "How can you do it?" Lottie wearily cried to Mrs. Holmes, who commenced to speak with fresh vigor. The wearisome visit ended with the family escorting the ladies back to their room—a show of high honor. They hung a shawl over the open door and slept pleasantly on the mud bed.

As soon as the shawl came down at morning, the tiny room filled with visitors who wished to observe breakfast. "Miss Moon, please note that we are being observed by thirty people. I've counted them!" said Mrs. Holmes. Indeed, two were in the doorway with dozens crowded behind. Four boys stood on a table for a better view. "Now look. Some boys are tearing holes in the window," Lottie said. "We are a wondrous sight, I suppose."

She later wrote H. A. Tupper, "Have you ever felt the torture of human eyes beaming upon you, scanning every feature, every look, every gesture? I felt it keenly."

But she chatted on with an old woman beside her on the kang. "Do you know what I have been doing?" Miss Moon asked. "I have been counting the people in this room."

The woman looked disconcerted and apologized. "We have never seen any heavenly people before." Chastened, Miss Moon doubled her efforts to be gracious.

On their way, a stop at a mossy spring revived the travelers. After visiting eleven villages and splashing across many streams, Lottie informed Mrs. Holmes that she was heading for their night's lodging. Mrs. Holmes, undaunted, graciously excused her less-tough companion and pressed on to yet another village. But Lottie did not find rest. Three boys and two young women settled on her kang to review catechism that they had learned on a previous visit. When they parted for supper they begged her, "Don't go to sleep. We will be back." By bedtime, she could hardly speak.[21]

Finding that one kang was "no bed of roses," Mrs. Holmes dusted it off and exclaimed, "How can civilized people live this way?" Lottie asked wonderingly, "Don't you think the Chinese are civilized?" "I don't mean the Chinese," she replied. "I mean ourselves!"[22] The next morning they set off in a snowstorm, eager for the comforts of home.

The New Lottie Moon Story

There Lottie immediately plunged into examining the students who welcomed her back.

Lottie also toured with Mrs. Crawford and even with women of the Presbyterian mission. A particular friend was Mrs. M. B. Capp, a widow of Lottie's age who was the sister of Mrs. C. W. Mateer.[23] When working with Mrs. Capp, Lottie preferred to teach the children in the stable yard while Mrs. Capp worked with the women indoors. Mrs. Capp traveled with a servant who cooked for them, but sometimes the women they visited would insist on preparing food. Lottie avoided eating Chinese food in the country. She had not mastered chopsticks, and Chinese food made her ill. However, she would eat it rather than embarrass her hostess.

Country trips involved much more than straight teaching. Curious women fired questions at her ceaselessly. "How many children do you have? What? No mother-in-law?" Sometimes the beleaguered missionary's patience snapped, and she would return the questions in rapid order. But she never outmaneuvered the Chinese. "Usually I am tolerably patient, but sometimes when I'm tired out, and when they begin to finger my clothes and ask dozens of personal questions, I feel ready to go wild. But they never feel acquainted unless they know all about one's father, mother, brothers, sisters, relatives, home, daily work, food, servants, what one's clothes cost. If you take out a needle, you must tell them it is a needle. 'Are you going to sew a piece of carpet?' Yes. 'Immediately?' Yes. 'Are you writing?' Obviously. 'To whom? Why?' " Miss Moon cried out for a machine to produce the answers.

One woman thus engaged called Miss Moon the hated curse, "foreign devil," and she did it as a matter of speech, probably not intending a particular insult. "Why do you curse me?" Lottie retorted. "If I am a devil, what are you? We are all descended from the same first great ancestor." The woman blushed in embarrassment and apologized.

The question of age always came. Lottie advised, "There is no chance to escape this dreadful question. Just screw your courage to the sticking place and say it out boldly. It will become easier every time."[24]

At times the missionaries could talk no longer. They turned to knitting, writing diaries, or reading. Nonetheless, their host family and friends by the dozens continuously stood by to gaze.

Miss Moon's conflicting feelings about direct evangelism in the interior were beginning to be resolved. During a very lengthy trip, she told herself, "I must conquer my unwillingness to talk and be fingered, and teach the children."

A few days afterward she was able to realize, "I have never gotten so near the people in my life as during this visit. I have never had so many opportunities to press home upon their consciences their duty to God and the claims of the Saviour to their love and devotion. I feel more and more that this work is of God." She was learning to turn hostile audiences into friends, to divert curiosity into Christian inquiry. She was delighted when she began to receive specific invitations to "preach" and to visit.

After many more days of living in Chinese homes she was able to rejoice over small pleasures. "Is it any wonder we feel like kings' daughters tonight?" she wrote from a room filled with cornstalks, tobacco, and farm supplies. "There are beautiful spiderwebs on the rafters and clean matting on the kang." Even on a trip that involved helpless exposure to drenching rain and freezing snow, she and her traveling partner could laugh, except when they were too tired to make a sound.

Reporting on an arduous tour, she said to Tupper, "I am always ashamed to dwell on physical hardships. But, this time I have departed from my usual reticence because I know that there are some who in their pleasant homes in America without any real knowledge of the facts, declare that the days of missionary hardships are over. To speak in the open air in a foreign tongue from six to eleven times a day is no trifle. The fatigue of travel is something. The inns are simply the acme of discomfort.

"If anyone fancies sleeping on brick beds in rooms with dirt floors and walls blackened by the smoke of many generations, the yard also being the stable yard and the stable itself being within three feet of your door, I wish to declare most emphatically that as a matter of taste, I differ. If anyone thinks he would like the constant contact with 'the great unwashed,' I must still say from experience, I find it unpleasant.

The New Lottie Moon Story

If anyone thinks that the constant risk of exposure to smallpox and other contagious disease against which the Chinese take no precaution whatever, is just the most charming thing in life, I shall continue to differ. In a word, let him try it! A few days of roughing it as we ladies do habitually will convince the most skeptical."

Then she berated the one million Southern Baptists for sending only one man and three women to witness to thirty million souls.[25]

In these rugged experiences, tempted to be resentful of the callousness of Southern Baptists while she was suffering, Lottie Moon endured real soul struggle. She turned to deeper study of the Bible and of religious books. She asked the Woman's Missionary Society at Cartersville to send her a subscription to a magazine on sanctification, *The Way of Holiness.*[26] And she took comfort and call from deepening understanding of the daily work of the man Jesus on earth: "Constantly wayfaring, no place of his own to lay his head, no privacy, no rest from the curious crowds, excessive publicity, no time even to eat bread . . . to the last degree trying and fatiguing to a refined and high-strung nature." This was the life she was being asked to lead, and she found sufficient sympathy and love to do so only by divine presence.[27]

On good days, especially when she had received a cheering letter from her beloved Dr. Tupper, she was more able to enjoy the rewarding aspects of her work. She came to love the scenery beyond the grim walls of Tengchow—the flashing blue sea, boundless fields of rippling green and gold grain, countless purple tablelands. The absence of fences and hedges freed her mind. She grew to love the little villages nestled in green hills, the pure air, the brilliant sunshine, the open sky. Here she could find God at work in the theater he prepared for the advent of his Son. At such times, gratitude would flood her emotions and her soul would sing praises to the Creator.

"As I wander from village to village, I feel it is no idle fancy that the Master walks beside me and I hear his voice saying gently, 'I am with you always, even unto the end,' " she said. In this simple land, she was finding herself able to walk in the footsteps of the One whom she had followed to China. She grew able to approach a village with a feeling of exaltation and thanksgiving for the trust of conveying the gospel.

"With a heart full of joy, it is no effort to speak to the people," she said. "You could not keep silent if you would. What does one care for comfortless inns, hard beds, hard fare, when all around is a world of glory, joy, and beauty?"

Her most intimate revelations of spiritual life betrayed a near mysticism—constant experience of the presence of Jesus Christ. She constantly read the devotional classics and adopted their truths—"Lord Jesus, thou art home and friend and fatherland to me."[28]

Prayer support from people at home became an urgent request. She wrote her Cartersville friends, "Your prayers help us bear up against the depressing influences around us."[29]

This spirit enabled her to build endurance for her travels. After a hard day, Mrs. Holmes could enthusiastically exclaim, "I like this sort of thing. It seems so romantic!" Miss Moon would be too weary to share Mrs. Holmes' boundless drama, but she was learning to find joy. And in the absence of joy she meditated on the words of St. Francis de Sales: "Go on joyously as much as you can, and if you do not always go on joyously, at best go on courageously and confidently."

At the same time, she could see no wisdom in a missionary rushing into an early grave. As early as December 1878 she was pleading for the Foreign Mission Board to establish a definite policy on furloughs for missionaries. As a student of missions methodology practiced in all denominations, she knew that many missionary-sending societies were adopting five-year and seven-year terms of service, broken with furloughs. However, Southern Baptists expected missionaries to stay out "for life." "It is as if you were saying to a soldier you were sending to the front, 'Do battle with the enemy. Mind, no furloughs! We expect you to fall on the field,' " she said.[30]

At times the Board had an understanding with a missionary that he or she might return in a certain number of years. If the Board became convinced that a valuable missionary was in danger of a breakdown after, say, twenty years, it might invite the veteran home to help stir up the churches. If a missionary fell upon a long-term but not an immediately fatal sickness, and if funds were available, he might return to the homeland—as in the recent case of the Moon sisters. But the absence of a formal policy placed a cloud over those who left the field. Miss Moon suggested that the Board institute a furlough after ten years of service. This was the first time she felt bold enough to try to remold mission policy.

She was undoubtedly moved by the condition of the Crawfords who had been on the firing line for twenty years with only the short trip to Japan in 1876. Repeatedly, the Board had been warned of Mr. Crawford's deterioration. Mrs. Crawford poured into her diary her terror as he began to have recurring "brain trouble." Numbness in his legs was becoming paralysis. "His thoughts are sluggish and his cheerfulness is suffering. He must take a trip for his health and mental recreation," she wrote.

On June 21, 1878, he fled from the scene, leaving the three women of the mission to manage the church merger dispute, schools, and itineracy all alone. Mrs. Crawford wrote in her diary, "Yesterday my dear husband left, perhaps for America. We all saw that a change was absolutely necessary. He goes expecting to remain a while in Japan, then to California, perhaps then to the east, he knows not where." The Board, hearing of his "stroke," approved his departure and agreed to pay half of his expenses.

The women got along fine in his absence, thanks to the service of Mr. Mateer in preaching twice a month in the Tengchow Baptist Church. However, the strain of that labor expended the last ounces of fortitude in Mrs. Crawford and Mrs. Holmes. In August 1880 Miss Moon was urging the Foreign Mission Board to bring Mrs. Holmes home. Sallie was panic-stricken about Landrum, fending for himself in America; and she, for all her energy, was at last burned out. On July 12, 1881, Mrs. Holmes left for America. Upon her arrival she could not locate her son. After advertising rewards for help in finding him, they were reunited, and she took him to Philadelphia to attend medical school. Following this trauma, for many years she was carried on the list of missionaries. But she was financially supported by a successful young Chinese man whom she had reared. She was never able to muster the stamina to return to the field which she had served so remarkably well.[31]

After Mr. Crawford had returned from his trip to the United States, serious disagreements between them about her methods of work, along with the departure of the strong Mrs. Holmes, brought Mrs. Crawford to her sickbed. She limped to the homeland November 11, 1881, and lay in hospitals in Richmond and New York for months before recovery. Eventually the Foreign Mission Board had to acknowledge the wisdom of Miss Moon's arguments for furloughs.

Miss Moon took to heart the lessons she had observed. She wrote, "Mission life takes the strength and energy out of us before we know it. We have to learn to be watchful and not overwork lest the time come too soon when we can work no more."[32] She quit driving herself at the merciless rate of Mrs. Holmes and Mrs. Crawford.

Although she had accommodated herself well to the problems of her calling, she had one persistent enemy—loneliness. For a woman brought up among hundreds of relatives and congenial neighbors, the daily circle of two Baptist women friends and a few Presbyterians was not sufficient. It was difficult for any of the persons in this situation to maintain a balanced perspective and optimistic attitude. Lottie deliberately tried to meet her needs by studying and exercising. French novels, literature of all denominations, modern and classic devotional books, Chinese literature, Greek poets, and popular literary magazines were regularly consumed. She took frequent walks to the sea, ten minutes from her door, and she liked to swim. In her yard she cultivated flowers and perhaps a few vegetables.

Personal loneliness gave her cries for additional missionaries a poignant note. She persistently asked for one or more single women to be assigned to the mission. She specified that they be "not young" and that they like children. Such missionaries would be able to help cope with the escalation of inquiries from Chinese women. And they would also give her company. "I am bored to death with living alone. I don't find my own society either agreeable or edifying," she told Tupper in 1880. Occasionally Tupper would notify her of a woman in the process of application. Hopes would rise, only to be dashed.[33]

In June 1879 hopes had risen in anticipation of the arrival of the Rev. J. H. Eager. He was single, and Miss Moon had apparently urged the

Board to find him a wife before he was exposed to the solitude of Teng-chow.

H. A. Tupper wrote back, "I have noted your generous inconsistency which I commend in your wishing for him what you have forbidden yourself! Please regard these last lines as if not written or let me make amends by repeating what I said in a recent speech, "I estimate a single woman in China is worth two married men' "[34]

Tupper had reason to believe that Miss Lottie was then in matrimonial discussions of her own, and she was deciding in the negative. There was only one known man in her life. He was the one who had interested her in a revised spelling method for the English language.

In September 1879 Lottie's letter to Tupper had an interesting P.S. "Hav yu eny rules for speling in the Fr. J? I ask bekaus I hav adopted the fonetic style of speling. But I shal not hav to spel that way, if your compositor snubs me by putting my letters in type in the old way. Please let me kno."[35]

Shortly thereafter she wrote, "Wi ar all in usual helth and antisipating kuntry work with plezur as sun as musketos abate. Yurz Sincerely, L. Moon. Don't you admir the nu speling?"

The "nu speling" was a project by the American Philological Society, of which Dr. Crawford Howell Toy was the president. Apparently Toy was writing Lottie more than linguistic theories. In the spring of 1879 he came under fire for the progressive theories of biblical interpretation and inspiration he was teaching at The Southern Baptist Theological Seminary. His dear friend and mentor, John A. Broadus, had warned him that he was on dangerously thin ice with his progressive course content, for the theories had not yet become widely known or understood among Southern Baptists. But Toy, in all sincerity, taught on, sure that truth would triumph.

A swell of adverse publicity during a fund-raising drive caused The Southern Baptist Theological Seminary trustees to ask for his resignation in May 1879, though a minority report condemned the move. Toy complied and his colleagues wept at the train station as he left Louisville.[36] The distinguished professor's many friends took the issue to the pages of the denominational press, where the controversy raged for months. Even his enemies did not question Toy's character or Christian commitment, but they did not want him teaching "liberal" theories to young preachers.

This development certainly gave a new twist to the correspondence between Miss Moon and Toy, which continued. In March 1880 she told H. A. Tupper, "What you say of our mutual friend is very pleasing to me. You are right in supposing that I 'think very highly of him' (this is not to go in the *Journal!*). Thank you for the nice, kind things you say to me personally. Would that I merited them"[37]

Lottie, now frantically anxious for Mr. Eager to arrive in China, informed the Mission Board that Eager needed an outfit allowance so that he could settle his affairs. Toy was her source for this information. And *"he"* later informed Lottie that Eager had a most suitable new wife. But Mrs. Eager preferred Italy as a field, so the Tengchow missionaries were disappointed.[38]

By this same time, Crawford Toy was at Harvard University as professor of Hebrew and Semitic languages.[39] Again, Lottie wrote Tupper: "You say sum veri nice things about 'our mutual friend' in which I agree. But I fancy he wd be both amused and amazed at the amount of 'humility' you ascribe to him. I trust he haz a bright future before him at Harvard. This is 'unofficial' please."[40]

At the Southern Baptist Convention of 1881, while the reaction to Toy's forced resignation still rumbled, the Foreign Mission Board appointed two popular young pastors as missionaries to China.[41] John Stout of South Carolina, who had been the instigator of women's missionary society work in that state, and T. P. Bell, a recent student of Dr. Toy's, were actually sought out by the Board. The Tengchow missionaries were elated to hear that Bell and his wife were appointed to their mission.[42]

Both men stood an examination by the Board members, but later a question was raised about their views of biblical inspiration. Both men let it be known that their views on the Scripture did not differ markedly from Dr. Toy's. Their appointments as missionaries were withdrawn. The Board did not wish to invite the inspiration controversy upon itself. However, H. A. Tupper was battered from all sides, even from missionaries. Most of the old-guard China missionaries insisted that even if the men did hold debatable views, they would never have occasion to get into hairsplitting theories in China.

Tupper wrote sadly intimate letters to Miss Moon. "I dislike to write you on this formal-looking sheet, for our letters are so free and easy and seem just as if you are talking to me . . . You have the power of making people *see* what you think—but you hate compliments! Now I want to come close to you and beg you to help me. Were I a woman, and I often wish I were, I'd say, 'Oh, what a dreadful time we have had about our missionaries-elect, Brothers Stout and Bell.' You see by the papers that they are not to go to China. This is a dreadful disappointment. But you will say, 'Is it not your own fault?' Now, my sweet sister, don't turn on the friend seeking your good offices. I know your love for Dr. Toy, which cannot be greater than mine for I love him with the love of a woman. But let me say that the Board does not hold to the view imparted to it [illegible] plenary verbal inspiration . . . (Stout) and Bell are the noblest among the noble. . . ."[43]

In September 1881 T. P. Crawford wrote astounding news to Tupper. The Tengchow mission, learning of the Bell situation, had met to regroup. Mrs. Holmes had been planning to hold on until T. P. Bell's arrival. The bad news of his not coming was the last straw for her, and she had immediately sailed. Mrs. Crawford also made plans to leave. All eyes looked to Miss Moon, who would have to take over all the schools. She coolly informed her colleagues, according to Crawford, that she would be leaving to "take the professor of Hebrew's chair at Harvard University in connection with Dr. Toy." The shocked group prevailed upon her to wait until spring 1882, after which time she would have heard from Tupper and Harvard.[44]

Crawford must surely have misunderstood the situation, as neither Harvard nor its associated women's school, Radcliffe, was to have women faculty for another forty years. Mrs. Crawford was probably more accurate when she told a friend of Miss Moon's, upon arrival in Richmond, that Lottie would be going to Harvard as Toy's wife. Lottie wrote her family to prepare for a springtime wedding.[45]

Tupper wrote her six weeks later, "The Harvard news was thoroughly appreciated by the writer," and he alluded to a matter of interest to her which would be received by the committee on China missions.

The wedding never took place. A gap of nearly two years cuts into the Tupper-Moon correspondence records, and it is impossible to determine what happened to what appeared to be a blossoming romance. Toy's family understood that there was an engagement which was broken because of religious differences.[46]

Missionaries of later years were to notice in Miss Moon's library many books on topics which had emerged in the Toy controversy. They understood that Miss Moon had made a serious study of these in connection with her friendship with Toy.[47]

But Toy's views already were well known to Miss Moon prior to the 1881 announcement, so there must have been other reasons. It is possible that her consideration of Harvard was indeed based upon career expectations. Although her Hebrew training was not formal enough to merit a teaching position at Harvard, she could have taught Greek or Romance languages. Toy might have overestimated his ability to shake Cambridge's traditions.

The most decisive factor was surely the China work. Mrs. Holmes and Mrs. Crawford were utterly unable to remain at their posts. Mr. Crawford was not performing well. There was nobody else but Lottie Moon in all North China to uphold twenty years of Southern Baptist investment. Lottie's sense of duty and commitment might have wavered in a siege of loneliness, but she would not have deserted under these circumstances.

A young relative later asked Aunt Lottie if she had ever been in love. The answer was, "Yes, but God had first claim on my life, and since the two conflicted, there could be no question about the result."[48]

That sort of commitment was reflected in the words read by young missionaries from the flyleaf of her Bible: "O, that I could consecrate myself, soul and body, to his service forever; O, that I could give myself up to him, so as never more to attempt to be my own or to have any will or affection improper for those conformed to him."

Miss Moon had now passed her fortieth birthday and had burned her

The New Lottie Moon Story

last bridge back to life in her native land. With perhaps a touch of mid-life crisis, she calculated carefully each step she took. She was of a mood to challenge tradition if necessary to find fulfillment in her work. She gave much study to the popular debates among missionaries and boards about methodology in China. A studious, careful woman like Lottie could not easily agree with all the ideas.

For *Woman's Work in China,* she wrote a serious paper about the "native dress" question. This was reprinted in the United States. She examined all sides of a controversial new trend for missionaries to adopt Chinese clothes and hairstyles. Her inconclusiveness satisfied nobody, probably not even herself. She thought that most Americans looked ridiculous to the Chinese if they tried to counterfeit themselves as Chinese.[49] She may have been influenced by the experience of C. W. Pruitt when he first tried Chinese dress. A Chinese man snickered at him and said, "See, the devil is pretending to be a man."[50] But Lottie thought the native costume might be useful deep in the interior. For the present she herself stuck to the most modest American clothing.

The status of women in missions was an underlying concern for Lottie. Influenced during Crawford's furlough in 1879, an editor was moved to plead for more men missionaries. He said, "The female missionaries are doing a good work, but they cannot be relied on to bear the brunt of conflict with heathenism. They are excellent helpers but not good pioneers." Lottie quickly picked this up and wrote a rebuttal to Tupper for publication. Tupper wrote back a lengthy assurance that he not only believed in women doing pioneer work, but that he was ardently promoting acceptance of the idea. "The interest which our women are exhibiting [in missions] is one of the striking features of our age. It is full of hope," he told Lottie. Her response was, "I am glad."[51]

The pressing plentiful opportunities to witness in the interior put Lottie's Southern Baptist traditions to the test. She fretted about speaking to groups of men inquirers. She and Mrs. Holmes refused admittance to some: "We are women. You must not come in." To others, she responsed differently. "At one village this morning, I had a long, earnest talk with, or rather to, a group of men," she said. "I sometimes feel very serious doubts about the prioriety of addressing a crowd, as we are sometimes almost forced to do, but to sit down quietly and talk in a conversational tone to thoroughly respectful men who listen in profound interest—I can only thank God that he gives me the opportunity to tell them of the Saviour."[52]

Lottie knew from her regular reading that the "woman's question" was by no means resolved back home. In fact, the denomination seemed to be polarizing on the subject. While more and more women were finding places of prominent importance through women's missions organizations (with strenuous encouragement by a major group of leading pastors), other men and women were becoming more vehemently opposed to nontraditionalism. Even within the circle of Lottie's missionary friends (presumably Presbyterian, for none of the Baptist women pioneers had this problem) there were women who criticized Lottie and others for venturing out of "woman's sphere." "It is comfortable to know that we are responsible to God and not to man. It is a small matter to be judged of man's judgment," wrote Miss Moon of such comment. The Presbyterian single women had no vote in their mission, and even a skilled woman doctor did not have the privilege of traveling about the field at will.

Miss Moon was still thinking in this vein when she wrote for *Woman's Work in China* on the plight of women missionaries. She seemed to identify herself with a sizable group of women who came to China to win the masses but found themselves trapped in teaching a rudimentary school, "the greatest folly of modern missions." She said, "Can we wonder at the mortal weariness and disgust, the sense of wasted powers and the conviction that her life is a failure, that comes over a woman when, instead of the ever-broadening activities she had planned, she finds herself tied down to the petty work of teaching a few girls."

Lottie wrote to prove that women missionaries could take care of themselves and also take care of unwitting men missionaries. She insisted that single women have the right to their own homes, own work, and equal voice in deciding mission business.[53]

When the Foreign Mission Board's committee on woman's work reported in 1885, it quoted Miss Moon's article from *Woman's Work in China.* It did not refer to her by name, but only as a "gifted missionary in China." The quote included her classification of single women missionaries into three categories: (1) Those who have serious grievances and want reform in the constitution of missions; (2) Those who are satisfied and willing to carry out their purposes by indirect influence; (3) Those who have their rights secured but who desire to see those rights extended to others. She added, "Simple justice demands that women should have equal rights with men in mission meetings and in the conduct of their work."

The Foreign Mission Board report, while generally being very progressive in tone, felt it necessary to add this disclaimer to her quote: "This is not endorsed by the committee but is reproduced to show what some others think."[54]

The disclaimer struck a raw nerve when it arrived in Miss Moon's hands. She fired off a smoldering letter to H. A. Tupper. "I wrote the article from deep and intense sympathy for my suffering sisters. I have belonged heretofore to the third class [referring to the classifications in her article] who are free. It seems to be the purpose of the committee to relegate me henceforth to the first class. I distinctly decline from being so relegated. Will you be so kind as to request the Board to appropriate the proper sum, say $550, to pay my return passage to Virginia? On arrival, I will send in my resignation in due form."[55]

Tupper allowed Miss Moon to cool off, and he must have sent her a message to oil the troubled waters. In the meantime she received letters from him showing clearly that the Board considered her a full partner in determining policy.[56] Her response, concerning conflict with T. P. Crawford, was back in her old vein of friendly counsel with Tupper. "I would like to ask of you a few questions on a subject which concerns me personally," she said, "Can you tell me or rather, will you tell me, if the China committee proposes to make any changes in the status of unmarried women in the missions? Here in Tengchow the ladies have always been admitted to mission meetings on equal terms with the gentlemen of the mission. Our meetings are held in a private parlor. They are simply a company of men and women who meet together to consult about matters in which all are equally concerned. To exclude the married ladies from these meetings might be unwise, but it would hardly be deemed unjust, as they would be represented by their husbands. To exclude the unmarried ladies would be a most glaring piece of injustice in my opinion. To such an exclusion I could never submit and retain my self-respect. I therefore rejoice in the fact that I belong to a mission in which all my rights were secured . . . . It was the deep feelings of the injustice and the unwisdom of this course [exclusion of women by other missions] that led me in *Woman's Work* to advocate a broader and juster view. I presume the China committee is laboring under a misapprehension of facts. Otherwise, I cannot see why they felt called upon to say that they 'do not endorse my position.' "[57]

Again she threatened resignation, but that step never became necessary. The Board, and certainly Tupper, were happy for her to function as an equal partner in China, as long as not much alarm was raised among the home constituents. Tupper had risked much ire on the woman's question, unflinchingly seeking the support of women in foreign missions. He often assured Lottie of his appreciation for women as missionaries.

A second factor pressing upon Lottie in the early 1880s was the problem of T. P. Crawford. Crawford was becoming an embittered, reactionary man. With much justification, he developed strong opinions opposed to paying Chinese to do Christian work. He rightly was eager for the Chinese themselves to support their own schools, preachers, evangelists, and students without any foreign money being involved beyond the support of the American missionary. The genuineness of his convictions was made somewhat suspect by his personal financial deals with Chinese, by his willingness to employ personal servants and teachers, and by his obvious jealousy of his wife's success.

The Presbyterian boys' school was quickly developing into a real college, and Mrs. Crawford's school was making parallel strides. Before Crawford's breakdown in 1878, he had informed his wife that her school might have to be disbanded in order to heal the "drift" in their marriage. Mrs. Crawford wrote in her diary, "I should deplore this— the very thought of it seems like amputating all my limbs. I hardly think it necessary." As soon as he returned from his furlough, he asked Mrs. Crawford to give up her huge medical practice. This she did, except for helping students and church members. Soon afterward, Mrs. Crawford left for her own surgery and furlough.[58]

Her husband accompanied her partway, for their adopted daughter was to be married at Chefoo, and he then remained in Shanghai a month. Miss Moon was the only Southern Baptist left in North China, and she felt the weight of the nation on her shoulders.[59] She combined her school with Mrs. Holmes's, and she took on the ministry—medical and otherwise—to the sick of the church. To make the job more convenient, she moved into Mrs. Holmes's thatched-roofed compound at the Little Cross Roads. This was to become her permanent home.

When Crawford returned, he took the scalpel to his wife's school. He instituted a scale of stiffening fees, and he began teaching English. Attendance immediately hit bottom. He also launched a psychological attack upon Miss Moon's philosophy of schoolwork. She did not begin charging her students tuition, though Crawford wanted her to. She did agree to begin teaching English. Crawford spent all of his time and energy on his school and the church, while Lottie stayed out of town doing country work in addition to her schoolwork.[60]

The tenseness of this situation eased when the veterans welcomed N. Weston Halcomb in January 1882 and Cicero Washington Pruitt in February. These two bachelors were the first additions to the mission since the Moon sisters had arrived a decade earlier. The joy of their coming rejuvenated Miss Moon, whom Pruitt saw to be "very energetic."[61]

The young men came committed to giving their all in interior work. They valued Miss Moon's instructions highly and dreaded to separate from her when they began their interior travels. With great excitement, Miss Moon welcomed a bride for Mr. Pruitt. She was Miss Ida Tiffany, a Presbyterian appointee who had sailed over with Mr. Pruitt. Miss Moon considered her an ideal missionary and helped train her in country work and Baptist ways.

However, conflict was quick to arise as Crawford began to impose his philosophy on the younger set. By 1883 Crawford was ready to junk his wife's school, but Pruitt and Halcomb saved it for her return. The mission outvoted Crawford and decided to enlarge schoolwork, including

C. W. Pruitt (FMB)

Anna Seward Pruitt (FMB)

Miss Moon's school, which was having to turn away applicants for the first time. Parents were suddenly interested in educating sons and daughters. Crawford took the opposition to heart and left for a month's vacation in Chefoo. The young people headed for the interior, and Miss Moon was again holding the fort alone in Tengchow.[62] She felt exuberant at the openness to the gospel in both personal witnessing and in schoolwork. She and the young men let the Board know that additional funds would soon be needed to enlarge the Moon school. Lottie felt that if she was going to run a school, she could manage one hundred pupils, as she had done in Cartersville, as easily as she could forty.[63]

After an absence of almost two years, Martha Foster Crawford returned to her post in Tengchow. She came with resolve to cooperate with her husband, even if that meant closing her school and all other concerns.[64] Her additional vote placed Miss Moon in the position of tie breaker as the old guard squared off against the young ones. Halcomb and Pruitt could see no harm in paying Chinese Christians for helping them open a new full-time station in Hwanghsien. This was a prosperous city about twenty miles inland which the women of the mission had prepared for harvest.

Lottie reacted to the conflict with great distaste. It brought into focus her own inner struggle about the best use of her life in China. She wanted to develop a major school for girls and saw the potential now for doing so. On the other hand, she felt the call of thousands of women outside, and she was gaining fortitude for itineracy. In one of her heart-to-heart letters to Tupper, she explained, "It does not pay a woman to give her life to teaching forty girls." If she did have a school, it must be of the highest quality and for a larger number. She wanted to force a showdown on foot-binding in the schools but feared the results. At length, she confided to her friend, "Under no circumstances do I wish to continue in schoolwork."[65]

Tupper heard this statement in light of T. P. Crawford's philosophy on schools, with which the Foreign Mission Board pointedly disagreed as a matter of policy. Many of the contributions from Southern Baptists were directed primarily toward the educational aspect of foreign missions, and the Board thought that their concern should be honored. As Lottie explained later, she did not oppose schools; she simply felt a call to do pure evangelism. In 1881 she had held the dying hand of her good Presbyterian colleague, M. B. Capp. Mrs. Capp died a victim to overwork in managing both school and evangelistic work. Lottie must have concluded that life was too short and the needs too great to spend time on anything but direct witnessing.[66]

She disbanded her school in late 1883 during a violent attack of contagious fever among the girls. She felt fairly certain that she would never reopen it, but hoped that the young hands would. She turned her efforts instead to city visiting.[67]

Her hope was to build up a "parish" of approximately three hundred families. As she began, she knew only fifty families who would welcome her calls. She dared not impose a visit on these too frequently, so she diligently applied her best persuasion on the walled compounds of Tengchow. By now she had a smooth style of personal evangelism. This she perfected under Mrs. Crawford's tutelage. Mrs. Crawford advised, "Get to the point. Introduce the gospel at the first interview." It was fairly easy to sustain a relationship based on curiosity about foreign matters, but this did not result in saved souls. A second lesson was to present the gospel without apology. "You're not infringing upon their rights," Mrs. Crawford said. "Speak to them as if you are delivering a message from heaven to them individually. Avoid abstract principles."[68]

Lottie, a polished conversationalist, excelled Mrs. Crawford in finding polite ways to start a direct witness. To a woman who admired the cleverness of the foreigners who made Lottie's glove, she said, "Yes, we are very clever, but we cannot make God." When the woman responded that Chinese often made gods, Lottie preached her sermon on idolatry.

Mrs. Crawford might not be so suave. She advised grasping control of the conversation early and getting right to the point. "Let me read you something from this book." Or, "Here are some very important things. Shall I not teach you?"

Some missionaries tried to introduce Christian distinctives surreptitiously, but the Baptist approach was to use the shock technique. Lottie learned from her early Chinese Christian friends to begin with the resurrection. Yet Lottie worked with a tenderness to human need. When she visited a woman whose treasured son had died, she offered sympathy first, then the message of heaven.[69]

As Miss Moon tried to find her own best ministry, she thought that others should also have that right. To a woman who was considering coming to Tengchow, she wrote a cordial letter of welcome. Her advice was to come on out, start language study, then decide what work to do. Although Lottie was hoping for someone to assume the girls' school, she did not impose it on anyone. At last her eleven-year campaign to get another single woman for Tengchow paid off. On January 22, 1884, Miss Mattie Roberts arrived. She lived with Miss Moon and was taught by her. Miss Roberts shared the pioneering spirit of the other young missionaries. Soon she and the eligible Mr. Halcomb married. The Pruitts and Halcombs set out to open the Hwanghsien station officially. Because of disagreements with Mr. Crawford about the paid assistants question, the Foreign Mission Board established two separate missions with two different treasurers. The happy picture of progress was marred when Mrs. Pruitt suddenly took ill with a typhoid-like fever. There was a Presbyterian doctor in residence in Tengchow, and he did his best, along with Miss Moon's nursing. But the patient died in her husband's arms on their second wedding anniversary.[70] Though the plans for Hwanghsien were temporarily halted, another young couple was on the way. Mr. and Mrs. E. E. Davault came in 1884. Of all their co-workers, only Miss Moon qualified for a testimonial to the Board back home, "She is an excellent worker."[71] The James M. Joiners arrived in 1885. No sooner had they made plans than the new Mrs. Halcomb, married less than a year, died and was laid beside Ida Pruitt on "Mount Hope," as the little foreign cemetery was called.[72]

The arrival of more newcomers meant further conflict with T. P. Crawford. When he failed to induce the Board to force the newcomers to bend toward him, he began to feel alienated. In April 1885 came the showdown among the mission, and Crawford decided to carry his battle to the home field.

Fearing the worst, Miss Moon told Crawford to his face what she thought of his pressure tactics. Then she reluctantly revealed the whole infected picture to H. A. Tupper. She explained that two years earlier, as the young couples had begun their work, Crawford planned to get the Board to change the rules under which the missionaries had come out. He tried and failed to get agreement from his colleagues. "While we are perfectly willing that he should carry out his views as far as himself and his wife are concerned, and also as far as he can induce others to accept them freely and without official pressure, we are not willing that these views should be forced upon us. Dr. Crawford insists that his plan would give perfect freedom to all parties. As the rest of us see it, it would make him, through the Board, dictator not only for life, but after he has passed from earthly existence. His plan included every cash [Chinese coinage] we should expend for mission work and extended even to the regulation of salaries. If that be freedom, give me slavery."[73]

Without Board approval and at his own expense, Crawford went through the United States preaching the doctrine of self-support. But Miss Moon had taken the precaution of informing the Board that he represented absolutely nobody but himself and his wife. She staunchly defended the right of the other members of the mission to set their own course of work, especially regarding schools. "It took Dr. Crawford twenty years to find out the folly of schools. He wished others to reach that point in as many months. Naturally, they declined when they saw as a result of the school, the best and most efficient members of our church."[74]

Miss Moon's disenchantment with Mr. Crawford, which she nurtured silently for nearly four years, did not extend to Mrs. Crawford. "Mrs. Crawford is a woman, I need not say, of excellent judgment and great tact," she reminded Tupper. But Lottie had grown weary of the old gentleman's tedious, dictatorial assumption of control over all mission affairs. In his absence the group freely met, elected a moderator, disposed of business, and dismissed in prayer. But when Crawford was present, he would harangue the group for two hours on his philosophy. When he saw that he could not influence them, he would not let meetings be held.

Tupper warmly appreciated Miss Moon's warning. In October and

The New Lottie Moon Story

November of 1885 Foreign Mission Board members heard Crawford's proposals—at length. The Board also asked veteran missionaries from other countries to be present and to evaluate his proposals. Crawford asked for self-support (or local finance by nationals) to be adopted as an inflexible policy in all mission work. As requested by Miss Moon, this the Board declined to do. Everyone acknowledged that self-support was the long-range objective, but a rigid change in policy might be a breach of faith with missionaries already on the field. Conditions varied across the world, and other missionaries did not wish to work under that system. Also, the Board preferred to think that God's grace could lift a Chinese or an African above the corrupting influences of money. Crawford, they explained, was at liberty to do his own work without paid assistants if he wished.[75]

Crawford also requested that every Baptist missionary in the world receive exactly the same appropriation. He wanted the systems called "missions" to be abolished, leaving each missionary a free agent. Confused by the inconsistency of his requests, the Board left these two ideas for further study. Then the Board specifically asked Crawford to return to his field and refrain from pressing his ideas before the churches of the Convention.

Crawford declined to cooperate. He kept the speaking circuit hot with his campaign, though he began running into bottlenecks constructed by friends of the Foreign Mission Board. He was refused a few strategic platforms, and he created great tension at the Southern Baptist Convention, which he insisted on attending. The host pastor at First Baptist Church, Montgomery, Alabama, courteously gave him a shot at his congregation, and Crawford aired his views at length before the Convention. He hung himself, and the issue was not brought to a consideration. He ultimately returned to China as an avowed enemy of the Foreign Mission Board. Instead of adopting his policies, the Board had responded by prohibiting its missionaries from entering into private business deals on the mission field and from drawing at will upon the mission treasury, both of which Crawford had done.

Meanwhile, the Tengchow mission had a burst of creativity without

Crawford. At last, the Hwanghsien mission was firmly established. Lottie dreamed with her colleagues that it would be the first link in a long chain of mission stations all across Shantung Province.[76] Already they foresaw that the next frontier should be P'ingtu, a village 120 miles inland from Tengchow. Mr. and Mrs. Pruitt and Mr. Halcomb had spied out the land there and found it promising. Mrs. Pruitt, on her deathbed, had fortified Miss Moon's curiosity about the place by telling of the eager, religiously inclined women who flocked after her during her brief visit.

Lottie made a brief visit to P'ingtu and agreed. "Such eager drinking in of the truth, such teachableness, I have never seen before," she wrote Tupper. "They are groping ignorantly after God."[77]

Lottie Moon stood on a new plateau of spiritual maturity and saw a clear summons to pioneer in the interior. To cement the sense of direction she felt, she took time to confer with Dr. and Mrs. Yates as they vacationed in Chefoo and to see Miss A. C. Safford.[78] She returned fortified for a new era.

She was able to write, "I am still a teacher, but my school is movable and my pupils are constantly changing."[79] Now she taught on the kang, sitting in fresh wheat on the threshing floor, under the trees, under the stars. She was free of her dependence on treaty port, free of dependence on homelike comforts, free of romantic thoughts of the United States, free of daily contact with T. P. Crawford.

Singing "Jesus Loves Me," carrying a supply of Bibles, catechisms, and Scripture portions, she felt armed for anything. Inspired by her new grasp of purpose, she felt able and fully willing to endure any physical hardship. "The food is not intolerable, as long as I keep well, although I do get tired of eggs three times a day," she told her old friends at Cartersville.[80]

On a strenuous day in the villages, her chair bearers lowered her to the ground for rest. A small boy came up to be rehearsed on the catechism. Then he ran off, to return with a bouquet of fragrant roses. This simple gift out of love and kindness won her completely for work in the interior. She turned toward P'ingtu.[81]

Notes———— See pp. 302-303 for Key to Sources.

1. Lottie Moon to Orianna Moon Andrews and Colie Moon, November 2, 1877, LMR.

2. Lottie Moon to H. A. Tupper, November 24, 1877, LMLF.

3. *Records of the General Conference of the Protestant Missionaries of China.*

4. Lottie Moon to H. A. Tupper, December 13, 1877, LMLF.

5. *FMJ,* March 1878; Lottie Moon to H. A. Tupper, December 24, 1877, LMLF.

6. Lottie Moon to H. A. Tupper, July 27 and October 10, 1878, LMLF.

7. MFCD.

8. *FMJ,* November 1877. See reviews by Basil Manly Jr. and "J. H.," *RH,* November 15, 1877. Review by C. H. Toy, *RH,* December 20, 1877. Miss Moon's defense is in *RH,* August 5, 1878.

9. *FMJ,* February 1878 and April 1878.

10. MFCD.

11. Ibid.

12. *HH,* April 1883.

13. Lottie Moon, July 28, 1878, Cartersville Minutes.

14. Series of letters about students from Lottie Moon to Emma Hampton, WMU.

15. Lottie Moon to Orianna Moon Andrews, April 29, 1981, LMR.

16. Numerous references in LMLF during 1878-79.

17. T. P. Crawford to H. A. Tupper, August 17, September 22, 1879, and January 1881, TPCLF. *FMJ,* August 1878; October 1880; and May 1881.

18. Discussion of the merger dominates Miss Moon's letters to H. A. Tupper in 1878, LMLF.

19. *RH,* April 11, 1878.

20. Ibid., August 4, 1881.

21. Lottie Moon to H. A. Tupper, November 11, 1878, LMLF.

22. *FMJ,* August 1880.

23. Series of articles in November 1879 issues of *WR* publish a diary of Lottie Moon's travels with Mrs. Capp.

24. *FMJ,* June 1880.

25. Lottie Moon to H. A. Tupper, November 11, 1878, LMLF.

26. Cartersville Minutes, 1879.

27. Lottie Moon to H. A. Tupper, November 11, 1878. Also published in *Woman's Work in China,* May 1879.

28. Lottie Moon quoting St. Bernard in letter to H. A. Tupper, ibid.

29. Lottie Moon, February 14, 1879, Cartersville Minutes.

30. Lottie Moon to H. A. Tupper, December 9, 1878, LMLF.

31. *WR*, January 12, 1882, and January 19, 1882; Pruitt, *Up from Zero*.

32. *FMJ*, August 1880.

33. Lottie Moon to H. A. Tupper, March 22, 1880, LMLF.

34. H. A. Tupper to Lottie Moon, June 30, 1879, Copy Book, FMB.

35. Lottie Moon to H. A. Tupper, September 8, 1879, LMLF.

36. Archibald Thomas Robertson, *Life and Letters of John Albert Broadus*, and John A. Broadus, *Memoir of Boyce*.

37. Lottie Moon to H. A. Tupper, March 22, 1880, LMLF.

38. Lottie Moon to H. A. Tupper, June 14, 1880, LMLF.

39. Biographical sequence for Crawford H. Toy is drawn from "Some Notes on the Toy Family," unpublished manuscript by Jane Toy Coolidge, and from "Crawford Howell Toy: Interpreter of the Old Testament," by Billy Grey Hurt.

40. Lottie Moon to H. A. Tupper, September 11, 1880, LMLF.

41. FMB Minutes.

42. Bell and Stout were not damaged seriously by this controversy. Unlike Toy, who joined a Northern Baptist church after going to Harvard, they remained stalwarts in the Southern Baptist Convention. Stout continued his leadership of "women's work." Upon his death, he had the distinguished honor of being pictured in the SBC annual and saluted for his work on behalf of women's involvement in missions. Bell became the assistant corresponding secretary of the FMB, the secretary of the Sunday School Board, and then editor of the *Christian Index*. For a sample of debate about the situation, see *RH*, April 28, July 28, August 4, and August 11, 1881.

43. H. A. Tupper to Lottie Moon, July 13, 1881, Copy Book, FMB.

44. T. P. Crawford to H. A. Tupper, September 12, 1881, TPCLF.

45. Lawrence, *Lottie Moon*. Mrs. Lawrence must have had sources not available in 1979, when relatives and Moon family papers did not reveal any information about the proposed wedding. Neither did a close examination of foreign missions records reveal any consideration in the 1870s and 1880s of Miss Moon or Dr. Toy going to Japan, as suggested by Mrs. Lawrence. If this happened, it must have been confined to the 1860s period when Toy was a candidate for Japan and Miss Moon was making her initial considerations of missions. Mrs. Lawrence's suggestions may be valid, but the chronology seems to be inaccurate.

46. Mrs. Jessie Johnson Harris, "My Mother, Julia Anna Toy Johnson," in John Lipscomb Johnson, *Autobiographical Notes*. "At one time Miss Lottie was engaged to Julie's brother Crawford. I have been told that religious differences caused this relationship to be broken, but this never changed the love and devotion of my mother." This same tradition is repeated by other nieces of Crawford Toy: Jane Toy Coolidge, Julia Frances Lipsey Steele, and Julia Toy Johnson Hewitt.

47. Dr. Gaston Recollections of Miss Moon, URL.

48. Lawrence, *Lottie Moon.*

49. *Woman's Work in China,* November 1881.

50. Anna Seward Pruitt, *The Day of Small Things.*

51. Lottie Moon to H. A. Tupper, May 10, 1879, and September 8, 1879, LMLF; H. A. Tupper to Lottie Moon, June 30, 1879, Copy Book, FMB.

52. *WR,* November 20, 1879.

53. *Woman's Work in China,* November 1883. The article earned Miss Moon some criticism in China, reflected in the November 1884 issue.

54. *FMJ,* May 1885.

55. Lottie Moon to H. A. Tupper, June 27, 1885, LMLF.

56. H. A. Tupper to Lottie Moon, June 5, 1885, Copy Book, FMB.

57. Lottie Moon to H. A. Tupper, July 17, 1885, LMLF.

58. MFCD.

59. Lottie Moon to Emma Hampton, September 22, 1881, WMU.

60. T. P. Crawford to H. A. Tupper, October 25, 1881, TPCLF.

61. *FMJ,* September 1882.

62. Ibid., June 1883.

63. *FMJ,* August 1883.

64. *FMJ,* December 1883.

65. Lottie Moon to H. A. Tupper, September 24, 1883, LMLF.

66. C. R. Mills, February 20, 1882, in Foreign Mission Correspondence, Presbyterian Historical Society. Lottie hoped that Pruitt and Halcomb would continue schools. See Pruitt, *The Day of Small Things.*

67. Lottie Moon to H. A. Tupper, February 11, 1884, LMLF.

68. Paper by Mrs. Crawford in *Woman's Work in China,* May 1880.

69. *FMJ,* September 1880.

70. Miss Moon wrote the obituary for *Woman's Work in the Far East,* May 1885. See also *RH,* December 11, 1884.

71. *WR,* June 11, 1885.

72. Miss Moon again wrote the sad situation for *Woman's Work in the Far East,* November 1885. See also *FMJ,* August 1885.

73. Lottie Moon to H. A. Tupper, April 4 and June 17, 1885, LMLF.

74. Ibid.

75. FMB Minutes. For some denominational reaction to Crawford, see *RH,* March 25 and April 29, 1886, and *WR,* April 8, 1886. Crawford was extensively reported.

76. Lottie Moon to H. A. Tupper, October 19, 1885, LMLF.

77. Lottie Moon to H. A. Tupper, November 17, 1885, LMLF.

78. *FMJ,* October 1885.

79. Lottie Moon, June 21, 1884, Cartersville Minutes.

80. Ibid.

81. *FMJ,* September 1884.

7
She Was
a Living Sacrifice

Miss Moon had never been more than fifty miles inland from Tengchow when she first journeyed to P'ingtu. Never had a Southern Baptist woman opened a new outpost in missions. But on Mr. Pruitt's suggestion, she boarded a shentze and swayed and jerked the 120-mile distance.

The exploratory trip to P'ingtu in the autumn of 1885 took four grueling days with three miserable nights in Chinese inns. Before this time Lottie had done everything possible to avoid staying in inns. They were rough affairs patronized only by muleteers and poor travelers who had no family connections with whom to lodge. Rude shelters were surrounded by sounds and smells of the stable yard. The innkeeper made his profit by feeding the traveling humans and animals. He did not clean, beautify, or furnish the hovels, so missionaries found them bug-infested and often had to fight off rats.

Moving so far inland meant that Miss Moon cut herself totally from foreign comforts, contacts, influence, and consular protection. It was a case of one very small woman engulfed in the Chinese culture.

But P'ingtu had its advantages. There was a prosperous walled city called P'ingtu, and it was surrounded by a large agricultural county by the same name. The people were more affluent than those in Teng-chow, thanks to fertile fields and a profitable bean oil trade. Yet they did not have Tengchow's snobbish ways. There was no resident foreigner in the area, and there were very few foreign visitors. P'ingtu was the twelfth largest population center in the world. Miss Moon could quickly draw a friendly crowd in these circumstances.[1]

The P'ingtu people were very religious, belonging to and tolerating many sects diligently seeking "the unknown God." Women of the region traveled great distances to worship at city temples. The spiritual harvest promised to be as prosperous as the agricultural, but no missionary had been able to establish himself there. Presbyterians had had early success in P'ingtu, but they were unable to keep a missionary in the remote place.[2]

Two Christians in the Tengchow Baptist Church were natives of the area and had introduced their relatives there to the gospel. One of these was Mr. Chao, the Crawfords' Christian servant. He escorted Miss Moon on her first trip through the beautiful harvest fields. Chao arranged lodging for her in a private home. With her own bedding, a supply of food, and Chao and family to assist her, she tested for herself the potential of P'ingtu.[3]

After adapting herself to the dialect, she was convinced that this place would meet her needs. Here she would be able to work unencumbered. She would be able to present the pure gospel without the financial inducement angle being involved. She would be able to explore completely her growing hunger for things spiritual. Indeed, she would have no alternative but divine relationships to sustain herself physically and emotionally.

After a month's groundwork, Miss Moon returned to Tengchow to prepare to establish residence in P'ingtu. On her own she had come to a conclusion that the leading Presbyterian of the area was able to articulate much later: "If experience teaches anything in China, it is that the Gospel succeeds much better in the country than in the cities. Preaching in a city chapel has a fine sound and looks like work. In point of fact, it is the easiest and least productive kind of missionary work."[4]

Crawford would probably have tried to discourage Lottie from P'ingtu, but he was still in the United States pushing his theories wherever he could get an audience. The United States consul strongly opposed women going inland, but C. W. Mateer said the objections were unfounded. Mrs. Crawford thought Lottie had a good idea, and she promised to visit P'ingtu herself as soon as possible. Pruitt wanted Lottie to go and was confident that she would survive.

Lottie prepared great quantities of warm underwear, bedding, a mattress, medicines, reading materials, Chinese literature, and staple foods. These were loaded on mules along with her cookstove and her little Chinese trunk which would serve as a table. She, in a shentze, headed the caravan that set out for P'ingtu in December 1885. Mr. Chao and his wife joined her to free her from housekeeping chores. She pledged to herself not to return to her house at the Little Cross Roads until the following summer.

The house she took in P'ingtu City's west suburb rented for twenty-four dollars a year. Mr. Chao had obtained it from an opium-eater relative, Chao Teh Shin. It was a row of four rooms. One room she designated as the kitchen and furnished with the cookstove. Another was to be the storeroom. One was the passageway. The other was an all-purpose room for living, sleeping, and receiving guests. This room had the traditional Chinese kang of mud bricks. The fire kindled under the kang was the only heat, so in Chinese fashion Lottie sat cross-legged on the kang by day and slept on it by night.

The house had a dirt floor, bare rafters supporting a thatched roof, and smoked walls. Lottie's one luxury was to have the walls papered and to have a paper ceiling placed across the rafters, as more prosperous Chinese sometimes did. She added local straw matting and rugs to the dirt floor, rolled out her mattress on the kang, propped up against her bedroll, and awaited callers.[5] They came.

First came the opium eater's wife. She needed employment, so she agreed to be the foreign woman's laundress. Another neighbor came to do business as a seamstress and became a good friend. A neighborhood man said he would draw water for her. Through these persons' influence, Miss Moon fairly quickly became accepted in the neighborhood.

Miss Moon wanted to establish a permanent presence in P'ingtu, so she did not make an immediate curiosity of herself by preaching in the streets. Instead, her strategy was to become a friend and neighbor. She would teach and consult on a neighborly basis.

When she went on the streets, she took Mrs. Chao. Through family connections she found many homes with which to exchange visits. Beginning with the Chao family and its connections, she soon had many homes in which she could work. Even in these she preferred only small family groups with whom she could deal personally and quietly.

To gain an entrée with children of the area, she baked and distributed cookies made by her Virginia tea cake recipe. At first the children and their parents rejected these in alarm, fearing that they might be poisoned. Then the delicious aroma overcame their fears, and the children came back for more. With them came their parents, bringing return gifts.

Although P'ingtu was hospitable enough, Lottie was still a foreigner or, as the people habitually said, "devil woman." Patiently and without anger, Lottie made it a firm rule to challenge those who reviled her. To adults she said, "Do not curse me. I am a human like you. We are brothers and sisters." To children she said, "To call me a devil is to show bad manners. You should call me teacher." And she visited their parents to secure a promise of politeness. By making an issue of the "devil woman" concept she was saying to the Chinese, "I am here to stay. I am human. We must treat each other with respect."

As the weather grew snowy, Lottie put on two complete suits of flannel under her American dress and shawl. Then, as she got uncontrollably cold, she made a deeper plunge into Chinese life-style. She had the neighbor woman sew her some Chinese clothes. Over her regular American skirt and waist, she placed a heavily wadded (or quilted) coat that extended below her knees. The sleeves were three times wider than American style, allowing mobility and a place to warm the hands. Over the wadded garment Lottie wore a robe of deep blue cotton, the common style and color of the average Chinese woman. The robe had enormous sleeves trimmed at the cuff with wide bands of black satin. Although Lottie found the modified Chinese outfit cumbersome and exhausting to wear because of its weight, she dared not take it off until warm weather. When riding, she found that it protected her from jolts.[6]

After her suspicions about adopting Chinese dress, she must have been chagrined to see its good effect on the people. Children stopped persecuting her on the streets. Women became more friendly. People no longer asked, "Are you a man or a woman?" With a suntan and with her curly black hair parted severely down the middle and slicked back into a twist, she could almost pass for a regular resident.

She ventured into villages of P'ingtu County by day, going out 122 times into thirty-three different places within a few months. Even the family of the local mandarin, the highest governmental official, summoned her to a visit. Miss Moon, always a strict Sunday-keeper, refused to go because it was her day of worship. So the curious mandarin rescheduled the visit for her convenience and sent a woman to escort her to the official residence.

Here Lottie was confronted with high-class polygamy. She recoiled as she stumbled into a corridor inhabited by an elderly woman, filthy with soot and opium smoking. The beggarly woman invited Lottie to sit beside her on the ragged frozen matting of her bed. Lottie learned that the pitiful creature was the mandarin's legal wife. Before she could make the woman's acquaintance, a servant swept her away. Miss Moon waited until the mandarin himself, in elegant robes, emerged from an inner apartment. Then she was invited in.

Contrasted with the wretched legal wife's squalor, the concubine's apartment was opulent. Comfortable couches were covered with rugs and blankets. While blind musicians played to entertain the foreign guest, the lady of the house had her morning smoke of opium and showed off her handsome son. It was producing this heir, while the legal wife's sons had died, which earned her the life of luxury instead of squalor.

In answer to the woman's probing, Miss Moon carefully explained the honorable intent of her presence in P'ingtu. Yes, women were permitted to join the followers of Jesus. No, they did not meet together with men, but in separate quarters. Lottie tried to explain a few points of doctrine, advised against smoking opium, and made a quick departure from the painful smoke and the more painful injustice of polygamy.[7]

Soon the entire countryside knew that a peaceable foreign woman was living in P'ingtu City preaching a new doctrine. Cordiality grew, and she had more invitations than she could accept. But she usually declined invitations to eat. Although she mastered chopsticks and could hold her own socially, the Chinese cooking usually made her ill. Instead, she had Mr. and Mrs. Chao prepare her food using the local produce. That included chicken, a little beef, eggs, cabbage, sweet potatoes, and small oranges. Although rice was not widely consumed in North China, it was available in P'ingtu and Miss Moon liked it. Tea was seldom drunk in the area. Miss Moon preferred coffee if she had it. She had brought along her own supply of American-style flour. So she was well fed.[8]

After a few weeks, she decided that her worst privation was in not hearing English spoken. To friends she wrote, "It has been one month today since I have heard anything but Chinese . . . There is not one person to whom I could speak English.[9]

During this long winter of 1885-86, Lottie Moon sought stability by putting down deeper spiritual roots. These were evident in the new tone of her letters, "I feel my weakness and inability to accomplish anything without the aid of the Holy Spirit. Make special prayer for the outpouring of the Holy Spirit in P'ingtu, that I may be clothed with power from on high by the indwelling of the Spirit in my heart," she asked.

In her Bible she wrote, "Words fail to express my love for this holy Book, my gratitude for its author, for His love and goodness. How shall I thank him for it?"[10]

When winter thawed and C. W. Pruitt came to check on his colleague, he was surprised to have a little Chinese-looking woman greet him. More surprising still, she would not come close to him, shake hands with him, or walk with him on the streets.[11] She explained her strategy: Demonstrate a Chinese-style Christian life, win the people to herself first, then to God. "We must go out and live among them, manifesting the gentle, loving spirit of our Lord," Miss Moon said. "We need to make friends before we can hope to make converts."[12]

Miss Moon was on to something, but she wisely did not burn herself out before she could put the ideas to work. She was desperately lonely and wanted to flee the one-hundred-degree summer temperature of P'ingtu. In June she set out for the Little Cross Roads house in Tengchow. This time she traveled by cart, a two-wheeled, mule-drawn, springless contraption. Lottie figured that bouncing in it over deep ruts was a good substitute for gymnastics.

En route she stopped in several villages to check on converts and inquirers. She looked in at Shangtswang, fifty miles from Tengchow, where the former North Street Church was now prospering under the leadership of N. W. Halcomb. She moved her church letter here from the Tengchow Church because it was the closest one to P'ingtu, because she felt the church needed her tithe, and because she was very fond of Halcomb. After her months of isolation from other Christians, communion service with this warm little congregation brought tears to her eyes. She felt that the Christian fellowship was akin to that of her days in Albemarle County.[13]

Back at the Little Cross Roads, she wanted to prop her feet up and read the accumulated mail of six months. But she had little opportunity for this. Mr. and Mrs. James M. Joiner had wilted under the rigors of interior living at Hwanghsien. They and their baby came to Miss Moon's house, where Mr. Joiner was required to rest for more than two months. "Heart paralysis" or "heat apoplexy" was the official diagnosis for physical problems of emotional origin.[14]

N. W. Halcomb was in Tengchow too, with problems of a different nature. The theological debates which had raged over the names of Toy, Stout, and Bell sent him into deep examination of his own beliefs. From what he could determine, his beliefs would not be acceptable to his supporters. Miss Moon agonized with Halcomb. She admired him and knew the mission needed him desperately. Every day for one month she studied with him and pleaded with him, bringing in all the power of her Bible studies in Greek and Hebrew and, perhaps, her own experiences with Toy. But as a man of great honor, Halcomb resigned from the Foreign Mission Board.[15]

Lottie frantically wrote to H. A. Tupper that Halcomb's worries were only temporary. She did not believe him unsuitable for foreign missions. She wanted Tupper to send a cable stopping the resignation, then to write Halcomb a comforting letter. But the resignation was accepted, and Halcomb went to work with the United States consulate

The New Lottie Moon Story

in Chefoo. He repaid the Foreign Mission Board for its investment in him. Soon he was acting United States consul.

Miss Moon strongly advised the Foreign Mission Board and her colleagues that a permanent station should be established at P'ingtu with resident families and single women. She suggested renting native houses and giving minimum refinements to them for missionary residences and chapels. Recognizing the refreshment she gained from coming out to her house at the Little Cross Roads, she proposed to set this house up as a retreat place for women missionaries appointed to the interior. She stressed in letters to Tupper that single appointees must be mature and serious, with no romantic expectations of missions. If the women were willing to endure hardships, they would be safe and useful there. If two women could work together, they would not be so lonely.[16] With her plans for expansion, with her self-sacrificing nature, and with many demands upon her from her co-workers, Lottie Moon began to assume the role of mother for North China.

Her plans for returning to P'ingtu were delayed when Enos E. Davault broke down in Hwanghsien. The Joiners, not yet well, hastened back to Hwanghsien, while the Davaults came out to be cared for by Mrs. Crawford. Miss Moon took the Davaults' house in Hwanghsien for the winter. Joiner's condition was precarious; Mrs. Joiner could not handle him alone; and someone had to watch over the little congregation.[17]

Joiner and Davault considered Miss Moon's ability to endure the interior life nothing short of heroic. They themselves were utterly destroyed by sights of dogs eating human corpses, by finding babies thrown beside the road to die, by going without Western companionship, by living in Chinese-style dwellings and on Chinese diet. They were also panic-stricken by worry over their children and children-to-be. In Hwanghsien they were a day's journey from medical aid.[18] When Mrs. Joiner and her baby became ill, Joiner begged Miss Moon to move over from Davault's house to care for them. Mrs. Davault had a baby November 2, 1886. She was by that time in Tengchow attending to her husband in the last stages of his illness.

Thus surrounded by illness, Miss Moon was remarkably calm and useful herself. Eventually she was able to get back to Tengchow to pack for P'ingtu. Here she met with T. P. Crawford, returned after nearly two years of struggle with, then against, the Foreign Mission Board.

When the mule train she engaged for her passage was late arriving, she stayed home to rest for a week. But the quiet was shattered by the loud wailing and celebration of a series of funerals in the neighborhood. She was relieved at last to board a mule cart bound for P'ingtu. The bottles and tins in her provision basket clattered madly, and the mountainous trail made Lottie feel that she was in a typhoon at sea. She spent a short night in a real bed at the Joiners' in Hwanghsien, then weathered Chinese inns without doors or windows until she arrived in P'ingtu in late April.[19]

She was cordially welcomed. Adults shushed their children who thought to call her "devil woman." Although Miss Moon was pleased with her opportunities and was in good health, she recognized that she needed a furlough from China. It would soon be ten years since she had seen the United States. Except for a few months before Mattie Roberts married Halcomb, she had been totally without a co-worker since Mrs. Holmes' departure in 1881. She was grimly surrounded by the horrors of mental and physical breakdown. She wrote H. A. Tupper for furlough permission. More importantly to the course of mission history, she launched a blitz appeal for laborers to join in the harvest. To societies who closely followed her work, she sent the word, "Pray ye therefore."[20]

Aware that other denominations had received great bursts of effectiveness from their women's organizations, and knowing that Southern Baptist women had many opponents in their move toward formal organization, she wrote powerful letters of encouragement to the women.

In May 1887, during the Southern Baptist Convention, women had their usual informal meeting under the encouragement of the mission boards. This time they passed a resolution to come to the 1888 meeting prepared to make a formal coalition of the various state central committees which had been fostered by the boards since 1872.

In the same *Foreign Mission Journal* that carried the report of this action, Miss Moon wrote of the progress of Methodist women. "They give freely and cheerfully. Now the painful question arises, 'What is the matter, that we Baptists give so little? Whose is the fault? Is it a fact that our women are lacking in the enthusiasm, the organizing power, and the executive ability that so conspicuously distinguishes our Methodist sisters?' "

She described the open doors for women in P'ingtu. She believed that strong women's organizations in Baptist churches would call out the women to come to China and would give them adequate backing. The editor of the *Journal* asked his readers to take note of Miss Moon's call, and her letter circulated widely.[21]

Repeatedly, in the leading Baptist publications and in every issue of the *Journal*, Miss Moon painted a glowing but realistic picture of opportunities in Shantung Province. Meanwhile, during two months in P'ingtu, she visited eighty heathen homes and taught daily in her own home. With only a small rest at noon, she worked from sunup to sunset and later. More than a dozen girls came each day to her home in school-like fashion to learn to read from religious literature. When her throat would crack and fits of coughing would stop her teaching, the girls would say, "No matter; bring out the book and we will study for ourselves."

By July she was back in Tengchow for summertime rest. The whole mission circle, including the Presbyterians, was trembling at the conditions of Joiner and Davault. The Presbyterians freely spoke of Davault's insanity.[22] The Baptists spoke only of his nervousness and his consumption which required constant vigilance. Everybody agreed that Joiner must get out of the country, and he was sent on a trip into Siberia.[23]

Miss Moon took the principles of the problem to her reading public. "When an army is in the field and a fight is coming on, it is wise to send the sick to the rear. In the army of the Lord, it is no mere idle boast to say that foreign missionaries constitute the van. Theirs is the post of honor; the post of danger. The time may have passed in China when a missionary has cause to fear personal violence. Yet there remains the climate with its subtle influence, sapping a man's vitality almost without his consciousness until he awakens to find himself a physical wreck."

Tungchow, July 19, 1887.

Rev. Dr. H. A. Tupper:

My dear Brother,

Please
thank the Board in my name
for the "cordial invitation" to return
to America, contained in your
letter of June 7th. I realize the
inexpediency of any missionary's going
home under existing circumstances,
if it can be avoided. I have decided
to try to hold on until next June (1888)
if I find that my health justifies it.
I have an intense horror of going home
"broken down", to be of no use to myself
or any body else. Keeping such a possibility in view & trying to avoid it, I
shall try to do the best work I can
in the coming year. My throat has
troubled me, at intervals, for some
years & for a short time last month
I lost my voice. If this should again

& the case for any length of time. It
seems to me it would be better to return
to America earlier than the time
above indicated, as, once there, I should
be no expense to the Board.)

I have felt very sorry for all your
trouble & anxiety about the late debt upon
the Board & rejoiced heartily that you
were able to make so very gratifying
a report to the Convention. We do so
long for some new missionaries, but
realize the fact that the Board can
only act as the churches furnish
the means. I am very especially anxious
that the work at Pingtu (Pingdoo) should
be pushed. Brethren Halcomb, Pruitt,
& Mrs. Pruitt in her short missionary
life, did no little work there. I have
sacrificed more in health & in comfort
for that region than for any other. I
believe that a good foundation has
been laid for a permanent station.

I do hope the Board will keep the
request of our mission to open a station
there as one of the possibilities of a
not very remote future. I always leave
P'ingtu with regret & go back & it with
joy. The affectionate kindness of the
people awaken a grateful affection for
them in my own heart. The opportunities
for work are simply boundless. The
children would beg me to go to their
homes as if it were a great favor.
Going out to make a visit by invitation,
I have had to refuse invitation after invitation as I would pass along the street.
I made about eighty visits in two months
& might have made many more but
for lack of time & strength. When not
visiting, girls were constantly at my
house learning. I suppose I taught some
fifty or sixty. These, in turn, frequently
each other, their older sisters at home,
or their younger brothers & sisters. I

could have spent my time pleasantly
& profitably in simply teaching these bright,
affectionate girls, but I had to remember that the work among the women
was of chief importance.

Perhaps you will accuse me of having
Pingtu "on the brain." I certainly have
it on my heart. Please do not put
this personal letter in "the Journal."

  With very cordial regards,
    Yours sincerely,
     L. Moon.

She graphically described the fierce sun blazing for fifteen hours a day, the physical hardships, the hostile, pressing crowd, the loathsome diseases, and most of all, the depressing consciousness of being hated. "In the missionary's surroundings there is everything to drag him down spiritually and mentally, and nothing to lift him up . . . overwhelming odds, the sense of responsibility," she wrote. Again she showed the example of other denominations and asked why Southern Baptists were so unmerciful to their missionaries. Why would they not send fresh reinforcements?[24]

It was not only sympathy for her co-workers she wanted; it was help for herself. In October Davault died horribly.[25] Though Mrs. Davault tried to stay at her post in Hwanghsien, she soon had to seek a better climate and moved south with her little son. The Joiners soon returned home permanently. The old guard took a census and found that of eight new missionaries added since Miss Moon's arrival, three were dead, three had broken down and left the field, and one had resigned over doctrine. Only C. W. Pruitt had survived and was in working condition. Mrs. Holmes had not been able to return. Mr. Crawford was present but steadily withdrawing. Mrs. Crawford was bravely carrying on. Miss Moon was standing strong but weakening.

In September 1887 an American man-of-war was ordered to Tengchow to show support for Americans who were threatened by rumors of war. Lottie Moon fled, not to the warship, not to America, but to P'ingtu, where she felt the protective leading of her Lord.

She poured into letters more anguished pleas for new missionaries. September 16 she wrote a letter which was to become immortal among Southern Baptists.[26] As early as 1881 the Woman's Missionary Society at Cartersville had taken offerings for Miss Moon on Christmas Day. These pious women who were unflinching in their commitment to missions thought this a fitting way to observe the Savior's birth. They and their families were invited to church on Christmas to lay their mite boxes on the altar.

Now Miss Moon heard that Methodist women had decided to observe the week before Christmas 1887 as a time of prayer and self-denial for missions. She passed on this idea to Southern Baptists, and it was published in the *Foreign Mission Journal* of December 1887.

"Need it be said why the week before Christmas is chosen? Is not the festive season, when families and friends exchange gifts in memory of The Gift laid on the altar of the world for the redemption of the human race, the most appropriate time to consecrate a portion from abounding riches and scant poverty to send forth the good tidings of great joy into all the earth?"

Then she advocated women's organizations to push this concept. "In seeking organization we do not need to adopt plans or methods unsuitable to the view or repugnant to the tastes of our brethren. What we want is not power, but simply combination in order to elicit the largest possible giving. Power of appointment and disbursing funds should be left, as heretofore, in the hands of the Foreign Mission Board. Separate organization is undesirable, and would do harm, but organization in subordination to the Board is the imperative need of the hour."

Lottie was many years ahead of her fellow Baptists in strongly advocating scriptural, freewill tithes and additional offerings. She would not permit women's groups working on her behalf to raise money by entertainments and gimmicks.

In her famous letter she said, "I wonder how many of us really believe that it is more blessed to give than to receive. A woman who accepts that statement of our Lord Jesus Christ as a fact, and not as 'impracticable idealism' will make giving a principle of her life. She will lay aside sacredly not less than one-tenth of her income or her earnings as the Lord's money, which she would no more dare to touch for personal use than she would steal. How many there are among our women, alas, who imagine that because 'Jesus paid it all,' they need pay nothing, forgetting that the prime object of their salvation was that they should follow in the footsteps of Jesus Christ!"

These strong words helped quell fears and opposition of some and helped bolster courage of others who were weighing the idea of a women's organization. Lottie was quoted to help shape the mountains of spoken and written debate throughout the spring of 1888. All eyes looked to the Southern Baptist Convention and the women's meeting of 1888, where the question would be addressed officially.[27]

Meanwhile, Lottie Moon heard from the Foreign Mission Board that her application for furlough was only reluctantly granted. She did not have to read much between the lines to see that Tupper was counting on her to maintain Southern Baptist interests in North China while the ranks were decimated.[28]

But Lottie had a horror of breaking down on the field and "being of no use to myself or to anybody else." And she was longing to see Virginia. The Viewmont house and property had been completely sold off early in 1886. With part of the proceeds she and Edmonia had jointly bought twenty acres of land just outside Scottsville. Edmonia, who was still sickly but sporadically teaching school in the area, had built a cottage for them. Both were counting heavily on Lottie's arrival in 1887. Edmonia wrote appealingly of the little four-room house with new Victorian furniture.[29]

With remarkable grit, Lottie resisted the lure of Virginia and assured Tupper that she would remain until the summer of 1888, if her throat held out. She then gave herself without reserve to P'ingtu.

Sha-ling, a little village ten miles from P'ingtu City, was showing remarkable interest in Christianity. There lived a man named Dan Ho-bang. On a visit to Hwanghsien he had heard from T. P. Crawford of Jesus, one who could remove sins from people. Upon returning to Sha-ling he learned that a woman living in the west suburb of P'ingtu was teaching the Jesus way. Mr. Dan sent three people to P'ingtu to invite Miss Moon to preach the Jesus way in his home. He graciously offered to pay chair bearers to bring her.

As soon as she could, she did go to Sha-ling and found two families there diligently seeking God and trying to lay up merit. Miss Moon taught them and was convinced that she had six likely converts. Many of the villagers were members of a devout vegetarian religion known as the Venerable Heaven Sect. They were open to religious teachings. She sent to Tengchow for help, and Mrs. Crawford came to teach Bible classes. The two women stayed in Mr. Dan's house and taught great crowds on the threshing floor nearby. Years later women would point lovingly to the millstones and say, "Here is where our dear Miss Moon sat to preach Jesus."

She helped the inquirers memorize vast portions of Scripture. She taught them hymns such as "The Father Surely Will Watch Over Me" and "Jesus Loves Me." She taught a prayer, explaining its meaning carefully, for it contained the nucleus of the Christian experience. "Oh Father, have mercy on me, forgive my sins, in the name of Jesus who died on the cross, Amen."

Although she was committed primarily to teaching the women, and next to dealing with the children, she could not keep the men from listening from adjoining rooms. In the case of Sha-ling, the men were the primary inquirers. Each evening and on Sunday she would conduct a service of worship. In a little low-ceilinged room, lit by wicks in saucers of bean oil, the worshipers would gather. A makeshift screen of grain stalks divided the crowd of men from women. With Miss Moon's direction, the semiheathen men would lead singing, read Scripture, rehearse the catechism, and pray. Miss Moon would sometimes comment on the Scripture. If Mrs. Crawford were present, she would be willing to deliver what amounted to a sermon.[30]

With such ready response to the gospel, Miss Moon was incredulous that Southern Baptist preachers and young women were not flocking to China. From P'ingtu she quickened the flow of appeals. Now she turned to shaming, chiding, flattering—any tactic to get the attention of the apathetic Baptists. In one appeal she concluded that the folks back home had all adopted the "new theology" the Baptist editors had been criticizing ever since the Toy episode. One had predicted that "new theology" would quench the missionary spirit.

"I conclude that the large majority of Southern Baptists have adopted this 'new theology,'" she wrote. "Else, why this strange indifference to missions? Why these scant contributions . . . . The needs of these people press upon my soul, and I cannot be silent. People talk vaguely about the heathen, picturing them as scarcely human, or at best, as ignorant barbarians. If they could live among them as I do, they would find in the men much to respect and admire; in the women and girls they would see many sweet and lovable traits of character . . . . Here I am working alone in a city of many thousand inhabitants with numberless villages. How many can I reach?"[31]

She told of how Presbyterian ministers were having to preach to

Baptist congregations. Did the brethren at home approve of that?

"We are told that Jesus went among the cities and villages preaching the gospel of the kingdom and it is added that when he saw the multitude as sheep without a shepherd, he was moved with compassion," she wrote later. She then portrayed the shepherdless sheep and villages of P'ingtu and urged, "Pray ye for laborers in the harvest."

Mrs. Crawford and Mr. Pruitt joined in her cry and they coined a new motto: "Thirty Seed-sowers for North China." For months this plea echoed around Southern Baptist channels. In her appeals, Lottie Moon emphasized compassion and love for the Chinese. "The missionary's first object is to convince them that he is human and that he is their sincere friend. By patience and gentleness and unwearied love, he wins upon them until there begins to be a diversion in sentiment."[32]

She told how patient love won her an invitation to visit a community of Buddhist nuns. Amid incense and ornaments she told them that burning incense cannot atone for sin, nor burning paper, nor knocking heads before Buddha. "Do these things make you happy when you do them?" she asked. The heads of the community answered, "We do not know why we do these things." They questioned her sincerely about Christian doctrine and gladly received books. This kind of visit renewed Miss Moon's zeal to keep the work afloat.[33]

The work in Sha-ling grew to include twenty families out of fifty in the village. Mr. Pruitt came to help with the men. Mrs. Crawford wrote, "P'ingtu is about to join the church en masse."[34]

Encouraged by her success as an interior missionary, Miss Moon grew even more Chinese in her life-style. She had a regular circuit of homes where she taught women doctrine and reading. She was no longer seriously depressed by sitting all day in barnyard conditions while teaching Scriptures and prayers. Nor was she too squeamish to eat a Chinese meal. With her chopsticks she picked around and consumed freshly poached eggs in boiling water and mein noodles (a kind of macaroni) which would not make her sick. To men who followed her respectfully along the road between her engagements with women, she "preached Jesus" as best she could.

Such walks were her only relief from fourteen-hour days of sitting on the kang or threshing floor with the women. Those who could crowd closest looked at books and pictures. Those too far away to see looked on longingly while braiding straw or sewing. Mothers would push their daughters forward, saying, "They will learn faster, then teach us when you are gone."[35]

In her appeals for workers she grew increasingly explicit about the high cost and rich rewards of interior work. "They must be men and women of absolute self-consecration, ready to come down and live among the natives, to wear the Chinese dress and live in Chinese houses, rejoicing to follow in the footsteps of Him who 'though he was rich, yet for our sakes became poor, that we, through his poverty, might be made rich.' We do not ask people to come out to live in costly foreign style . . . barely touching the heathen world with the tips of their fingers, but we ask them to come prepared to cast in their lot with the natives."[36]

With sincere sorrow, she left P'ingtu and the faithful group at Shaling to have her summertime rest. She promised to return in the autumn, bringing Mrs. Crawford. Although her extended target date for furlough had passed, she could not bring herself to leave for so long a time. Mr. Pruitt agreed with her decision. "It would be a pity for her to leave her work in P'ingtu," he said. "She is doing a noble thing."[37]

In Tengchow good news awaited her. An executive committee of Woman's Missionary Societies, soon to be called Woman's Missionary Union, Auxiliary to the Southern Baptist Convention, had been formed during the Convention at Richmond. Lottie was not pleased, however, when she learned that her beloved Virginia women had been kept from joining the Convention-wide organization because of opposition from the men of the state association in Virginia. Of all people, her old professors at Hollins and Albemarle Female Institute had led the opposition to an organization which they regarded as a threat to women's proper sphere. This was hard to understand. But it was good to know that Tupper had asked the women to undertake sponsorship of the Christmas offering Miss Moon had suggested. She dispatched encouragement to Miss Annie Armstrong, corresponding secretary of Woman's Missionary Union.

Work lay so heavily on her mind that Miss Moon could not sit quietly in Tengchow for vacation. So she accepted an invitation from Robert T. Bryan, missionary in Chinkiang, Central China. The married women of this mission had not learned Chinese, believing that their role was to work only in their homes with their own children. No single women had been appointed to this field. Bryan, who was an effective strategist, soon noticed that he could make no headway without "woman's work for woman." He sent for Miss Moon to help start it.

Under her guidance in the summer of 1888, more women began attending Dr. Bryan's chapel services. The missionary wives, for whom Miss Moon had no criticism, began to see how they might help. Later she wrote from Chinkiang, "I thought it would not be wrong to remain in a bright and pleasant society if I could at the same time, do good work as a missionary." The visit gave her personal comfort in being able to see her friend A. C. Safford, who was terminally ill with cancer, but who had spearheaded significant advances in Presbyterian women's work.

Dr. Yates joined Bryan in urging Miss Moon to desert Shantung and join their team. The tempting invitation lifted her spirits, but she declined. Instead she wrote Miss Armstrong and Tupper to hurry the helpers to P'ingtu so that she might train them in before leaving for furlough. She thought she could not endure for more than one more year. "I would I had a thousand lives that I might give them to the women of China!" she wrote. "As it is, I can only beg that other women and many of them be sent. Above all we need mature women. The Chinese have a high respect for such. It would not be proper in Chinese eyes for young women to go out in the independent way necessary in doing rough country work, in the interior. Besides, it seems to me too hard on the young ladies themselves. Of course, there may be exceptional cases."[38]

Pleading again with Tupper for rapid reinforcement, she made a radical proposal. "I have in the Hong Kong and Shanghai Bank a deposit that will amount to about one thousand pounds next March. It has occurred to me that the board might be willing to borrow it of me at six percent. I should probably leave it in their hands for many years, using only the interest annually."[39]

The New Lottie Moon Story

She thought of this proposal because the Foreign Mission Board was increasingly living on borrowed money. The Southern Baptist Convention each May would apportion the raising of funds among the state conventions. Expecting these funds to come in, the mission board would take short-term loans to maintain or expand the mission force. Funds would dribble in. Usually in the month of April, before the books closed prior to the next Convention, large amounts would come in and the books could be balanced. Sometimes there was a deficit.

When the Board did not accept Miss Moon's offer, she amended it. This time she offered one thousand dollars interest-free for one year, provided the money was used to send two women to P'ingtu. She was getting desperate. Whether the Board accepted this offer is not clear, but it was soon borrowing sums from Edmonia Moon.[40]

Her working vacation in central China delayed her plans for returning to P'ingtu. Early in October 1888, she was gathering her wits to return when two men of Sha-ling knocked at her gate. The women and girls of Sha-ling had grown anxious about her. These two faithful men had walked 120 miles, hoping to find her along the way. Not finding her, they bravely pressed on to her house.

As Lottie wrote Tupper of this touching experience, her anguish and exhaustion plainly showed through. Instead of writing her usual sculptured prose, she rambled, repeated herself, and splashed the pages with tears. "We are so weak—weak in numbers—none of us are strong. If we are not reinforced heavily, disaster will follow. Some of us may break down or die. Others will go in and reap the fruit of our labors of the past."[41]

C. W. Pruitt had brought cheer and new strength into the group earlier in 1888 when he took a new wife from the Presbyterian mission. As in his first marriage, the Foreign Mission Board "purchased" Anna Seward from the Presbyterians by reimbursing them for all expenses of her travel and outfit. With a wife, Pruitt moved to Hwanghsien to take up the property and work which by now had felled seven other missionaries. In moving, he resigned the work at Shangtswang, which he had taken over from Halcomb.[42] Now, in addition to P'ingtu, Miss Moon must take responsibility for the church at Shangtswang. "I shall virtually be the pastor," she wrote Tupper, with tears.[43]

Before she could answer the plea of the P'ingtu men, she spent three weeks in villages near Tengchow where she and Mrs. Holmes used to minister regularly. In mid-November 1888, she and Mrs. Crawford set out for P'ingtu. Mr. Pruitt promised to join them soon.

Tupper sized up the situation with alarm and wrote his beloved Miss Moon not to work herself to death. Feeling better in P'ingtu, she repeated her determination to work until reinforced. "While I do not a little work for men and boys, I do not feel bound to stay on their account," she said, but she would not desert the women. Regarding the effect of her communications, she said, "I fear you overrate my ability to arouse Southern Baptist women." She repeated her old goal of a line of women missionaries all across Shantung. "That seems to me a purpose worthy of the energies of Southern Baptist women," she said. "The speediest way to afford me rest is to send reinforcements immediately."[44]

At that very time, Woman's Missionary Union was taking the first Baptist Christmas offering for missions—an offering to send Miss Lottie Moon help in P'ingtu. The women had set a goal of $2,000. The infant organization moved fast to get word of this great project to the people. The Foreign Mission Board, which was pledged to bear the expense of WMU's work for foreign missions and divide miscellaneous expenses in half with the Home Mission Board, approved an expenditure of $100 for promotion of the offering. Annie Armstrong wrote by hand one-thousand letters to the various societies and wrapped seven-hundred packages of literature. She circulated three-thousand programs, one-thousand notices, thirty-thousand offering envelopes, and three-thousand circulars, all costing, with postage, $72.82. The results began to ring up in Richmond for a total of $3,315.26—enough to send three women to help Miss Moon.[45]

Already Miss Fannie Knight of North Carolina had applied to the Board to be sent to Miss Moon (or to Mrs. Crawford). She was quickly appointed, along with Mr. and Mrs. George P. Bostick. Two more young women volunteered for P'ingtu, but were not appointed until later in the year. They were Miss Laura Barton of Texas and Miss Mary J. Thornton of Alabama.

This cheering news gave Miss Moon courage to say that she would await their arrival and training before coming to America. She had spent the Christmas season of 1888 in Sha-ling. She taught the women and girls in a small inner room while men and boys sat in the adjoining chapel eavesdropping. None of these believers had yet been admitted to a church. Yet they had become aware of who was sponsoring Miss Moon in China. After praying in daily worship services for the arrival of a full-time missionary, they gave her letters to the Foreign Mission Board which Pruitt later forwarded with translation. Hearing the pitiful cries of these Sha-ling people, Miss Moon was moved to say, "If you cannot find ministers, send laymen to do the job."[46]

One of the letters, written by the head of the Venerable Heaven Sect, from which many of the inquirers had come, said, "I am a P'ingtu man. For more than ten years I have known of this doctrine, but did not inquire into it. On having an opportunity to inquire, immediately I truly believed. I am deeply in earnest in learning, but there is no pastor here to teach. I earnestly look to the Venerable Board to send out more teachers to P'ingtu . . . . The light of this mercy will shine everywhere and gratitude will be without limit. I am looking for it as if, when the earth is dry, rain is longed for."

The Sha-ling women wrote, "Send out more ladies to P'ingtu to teach these stupid women, to save these sinful women."

Pruitt told the Board what the P'ingtu people wrote of Lottie Moon: "It is an understood thing that religion is not confined to territory, but for its propagation men are necessary. For zeal in the propagation of religion, for pureness in giving instruction, we have never heard that there was the like of Miss Moon."

Pruitt devotedly added, "She is deservedly held in remarkably high esteem wherever in P'ingtu her face is known, and even farther, for her fame has gone abroad throughout the country."[47]

Hearing of the prospect of more workers, Miss Moon wrote Annie Armstrong: "Listen to no suggestions of delay. A two years' supply of clothing is all they need bring. They should have an abundance of heavy flannel underclothing. The climate in Shantung is colder in winter than it is in the same latitude in America. Please say to the new missionaries they are coming to a life of hardship and constant self-denial. They will be alone in the interior and will need to be strong and courageous. If the joy of the Lord be their strength, the blessedness of the work will more than compensate for the hardship. Let them come 'rejoicing to suffer' for the sake of the Lord and Master who freely gave his life for them."[48]

Miss Moon did not slacken in her bombardment of America for new workers. Now her appeals contained strong twists of irony. She told of teaching women and girls while men worked without a teacher. The men came to her and asked her to conduct general services. Once when they asked her to explain the parable of the prodigal son, she replied: "It was not the custom of the ancient church that women preach to men." Then she claimed lack of preparation, but they persisted. "I could not hinder their calling upon me to lead in prayer," she said. "Need I say that as I tried to lead their devotions, it was hard to keep back tears of pity for those sheep without a shepherd."[49]

Any explanation of how Miss Moon led such a triumph in P'ingtu when she was already at the frayed end of her strength can only be explained by her spiritual vitality. She hit rock bottom in the spring of 1889, when her health was poor. Completely disillusioned with human help, she gave up and admitted: "I hold not my life of any account as dear unto myself, that I may accomplish my course."[50] Soon after, with rest, her body and spirits renewed.

In her P'ingtu home she gathered servants and neighbors for morning and evening devotions. When trouble came, she fell immediately to her knees with students or inquirers to pray God's solution to the matter. The only thing she could not understand was why so few missionaries were coming. Each day she closed with a period of reflection in the "inner chamber" of her heart. Wrung out with the utter destitution of her surroundings, she reached to God until her soul was stirred; and she prayed fervently for laborers in the harvest. Then she took pen to ask the pastors of Virginia what was quenching the passion in their "inner chamber."[51]

In another letter she asked the ministers and laymen of Virginia, "How do you mean to remedy this abnormal state of affairs? For three years I have been working, mostly alone, in an interior city called

P'ingtu. I am expecting to spend the winter there alone. Not only women and girls are asking to be taught, but men are earnestly inquiring the way of life. As I am the only Baptist missionary within one hundred miles, these men must look to me this winter for instruction and guidance. I do not complain of the burden laid upon me by teaching heathen men in addition to my legitimate work among the women and girls. I merely come to you and state the facts.

"I write to call your attention to the fact that Virginia has only one representative in all China, and that one a woman," she said again. "What are you going to do, *yourselves in person?*"[52]

To the Virginia women she asked, "Send two of your choicest women—women who would be missed at home, whose going would make a gap in the church work and in the social circle, women full of zeal, faith, and consecration, no longer young."[53]

Miss Moon was rapidly becoming legendary. By the time of the first anniversary meeting of Woman's Missionary Union in 1889, her name was on many lips. The leaders of at least four state Woman's Missionary Unions could attribute their intense missions concern to Miss Moon. Mrs. John L. Johnson, Lottie's old school friend Julia Toy, was now the first president of the Mississippi WMU. She rose in the meeting to plead for Miss Moon's aid. "She is an invalid and should be at home but will not leave until someone comes to take her place. If I kept still in this meeting, I would not be a friend of Miss Moon."

Mrs. Stainback Wilson, the leader of women in Georgia, had helped raise the Moon House Fund, and she had led Georgia into the Union under Miss Moon's banner. Mrs. William E. Hatcher, the Jennie Snead of school days, was president of Virginia women. H. A. Tupper's daughter and Miss Moon's friend, Mrs. T. A. Hamilton, was president of Alabama women. All these key women carried the idea of a Christmas offering for China into another year and into permanency.

At the same meeting, Mrs. Davault, home on furlough, said, "I saw some men who had walked three hundred miles to see Miss Moon. They stayed at Tengchow three days to be taught, and Miss Moon accompanied them to their village. This shows how earnest they are. These men must have something."[54]

Men might resist her appeals, but at Christmastime women could not ignore the example of a woman who said, "As to your question about Christmas, when I am in the interior, it is just like any other day. Here (Tengchow), where there is a small foreign community, the day is observed. But I have not been here for several years at that season."[55]

In July 1889 Miss Fannie Knight arrived in Tengchow, and Miss Moon tenderly prepared her for her work. A teacher was engaged to help with study of the written language, while Miss Moon gradually introduced her to Chinese custom. Chinese clothes were fitted, a Chinese name was selected for her, and preparations were made for P'ingtu. At the same time, Mr. and Mrs. George P. Bostick were being trained by Mrs. Crawford. Soon Miss Laura Barton joined Miss Moon and was trained along with Miss Knight.

Miss Moon hurried back to P'ingtu in September. Miss Knight moved into the P'ingtu home with Miss Moon, leaving Miss Barton the work in Tengchow. The ladies invited C. W. Pruitt and G. P. Bostick to join in constituting a real church at Sha-ling. Pruitt baptized four men and two women, all from the families of Dan and Yuan. The immersion took place in a pool just outside of Sha-ling village.[56] Then with Miss Knight, they became the Sha-ling Baptist Church. This was the first church in P'ingtu County and the fourth Southern Baptist church in North China. Shortly thereafter, the four churches were formed into the Teng-lai Baptist Association, named for the Tengchow and Lai-chow prefectures in which they existed.

All of the converts, but especially the women, were laying their lives on the altar with their public baptism. After the ceremony, while the church was being organized, one of the young women impulsively threw her arms around Miss Moon and whispered, "How can I ever thank you aright for having come to bring me the good news of salvation?"[57]

Soon that young woman was married into a heathen household. Her friends urgently requested that Miss Moon go to encourage the girl on the eve of her wedding, which was Sunday. This she did; then she called all the church to meet with the bride early on Sunday. "Her face was radiant with a holy joy now that the time had come for her to

Part of the Tengchow Mission around 1890 (Seated left to right) Mrs. C. W. Pruitt, Mrs. George W. Bostick (1), Mrs. T. P. Crawford, Fannie Knight, Lottie Moon (Standing left to right) George W. Bostick, C. W. Pruitt

suffer for her Lord," Miss Moon wrote. After the bridegroom took her away to his house, the church continued its meeting, but one of the men sobbed uncontrollably. Miss Moon soon had the fearful congregation praying for their dear sister. The next morning Miss Moon received notice that the girl was "at peace."

The key part of the Chinese marriage ceremony was when the bride worshiped at the graves or ancestral tablets of the groom's family. Early in the bride's first conversation with her groom, she courageously let him know that she would not worship his ancestors, and with great modesty she told him why. After consultation with his mother, he informed the bride that she might have her wish. The bride likewise favorably impressed the dreaded mother-in-law. As she took her final departure to her new home, Miss Moon presented Christian books to her and prayed with her. The woman lived a triumphant life of witness among her unbelieving in-laws.

Teaching one young man who asked permission to call, Miss Moon was thrilled when he quickly responded to her teaching by laughing aloud. "I can't help believing. I can't help acting out my belief," he explained. These small triumphs kindled anew the strength of Miss Moon and readied Miss Knight as she learned the ropes.

But not all believers had immediate answers to their prayers for ease in Zion. A young woman was fearfully persecuted by her mother-in-law. She died in persecution but kept her faith.

One old man heard Miss Moon teaching as he hovered behind the women at the Sha-ling threshing floor. He came to her privately, and she gave him a New Testament. He was a diligent inquirer, but he was illiterate. He was brutally persecuted by his family, even locked up, but he always managed to find his way back to Miss Moon for encouragement and comfort. He asked a relative, Li Show-ting, a bright young Confucian scholar, to help him read the New Testament. The young man intended to scoff and to destroy the book, but its message gripped him. The young man, Li, also came to Miss Moon for instruction. She provided a book which softened his objections to Christianity. Recognizing in him unusual promise, she summoned Pruitt, and also Crawford, to deal with him. All these missionaries aided in the nurture of Li

Show-ting, but he always remembered that Miss Moon was his first teacher. In June 1890 he was accepted into the church after examination by Pruitt. Later he was ordained to become the greatest evangelist of North China, baptizing more than ten thousand converts.

During the Chinese New Year early in 1890 came the persecution which Miss Moon regarded as inevitable after significant Christian expansion. The Christians in P'ingtu had stopped worshiping their ancestral tablets, but they had not destroyed them. In connection with the New Year celebrations, their neighbors and families discovered that they were neglecting this rite so central to Chinese culture. Pastor Li was forced to flee Sha-ling to avoid death by his brothers, who fearfully beat him, dragged him by the hair, and tore his scalp from his head.

Old Mr. Dan, the original inquirer of Sha-ling, was tortured by a vicious mob of relatives. They bound his feet and hands behind him, strung him on a pole, and beat him before his ancestral tablets. He never recanted, but won over the unbelievers who observed. The Christians sent for Miss Moon. After prayer, she boarded a chair immediately. Normal reaction among missionaries of the region in times of persecution was to call in the United States consul. Treaty rights which protected the missionaries also were used to protect Chinese Christians.

Years before, Miss Moon had turned against treaty protection for Christians, for it tended to make them seek to live in treaty ports in the shadow of American missionaries. She thought that Christians should learn to bear the reproach of being Christian and maintain a witness in their homeplace.[58] Now she was faced with a great test of her conviction. She decided not to call for United States protection. Instead, she placed her own body between the persecutors and the Christians. Miss Moon told the leaders of the persecutors, "If you attempt to destroy this church, you will have to kill me first. Jesus gave himself for us Christians. Now I am ready to die for him." One of the vicious attackers took her seriously and prepared to kill her. The terrified converts warned her. She simply said, "Only believe, don't fear. Our Master, Jesus, always watches over us, and no matter what the persecution, Jesus will surely overcome it."[59]

She stayed beside the people as they were mistreated, giving them encouragement through Scripture and prayer. "Blessed are they who are persecuted for righteousness' sake," she taught them. Mr. Dan went to P'ingtu City until the storm of persecution blew past. There he conducted worship every Sunday and helped prepare the way for a church there.

Because Sha-ling Church learned to praise God in time of trouble, and because the Christians did not retaliate with legal action, it quickly grew to be the strongest and most evangelistic of the Shantung churches.

Mr. Dan, Mr. Li, and Mr. Yuan extended their witness to Li T'z Yuen, another P'ingtu village. When ten serious men inquirers were involved, Miss Moon and Miss Knight boarded a cart, drawn by two white mules, to visit. They established services for women, trained a leader, and sat back to watch a church develop. "The church in the house" was Miss Moon's first building block in P'ingtu. "God grant us faith and courage to keep 'hands off' and allow the new garden of the Lord's planting to ripen,"[59] she wrote. Her philosophy of church development was undoubtedly influenced by her neighbor, J. L. Nevius, famed Presbyterian mission strategist.

But there was no ordained pastor to handle baptisms, and the inquirers were coming in at a rate too great for the inexperienced believers to handle. Miss Knight and Miss Moon still wanted a resident male missionary and family to join them in P'ingtu. Not only did they need extra hands and an ordained helper, but they also needed the presence of other missionaries for morale boosts.

The two lone women became deeply attached to each other. Miss Knight considered Miss Moon to be the most courageous, useful, heroic, gentle of persons. "I think I might safely say that no missionary is making greater sacrifices than she," Fannie wrote to her family. Miss Moon, in return, viewed Fannie Knight as the answer to her prayers. The young woman was the one upon whom she could drop her mantle, knowing that the P'ingtu work would go on.[60]

Miss Moon appealed to the women of Virginia for help in securing more missionaries. She outlined the conditions at villages other than

Sha-ling. "The hard pioneer work has been done. Thanks be to God, there is now a wide-open door . . . . All the time I linger in this region, brief though it be, there rings in my ear the oft-repeated call from men and women in P'ingtu to go thither and teach them. I am trying honestly to do the work that could fill the hands of three or four women, and in addition must do much work that ought to be done by young men. The men are not here, nor as to that matter, the women either. I look to you, my sisters."[61]

Lottie was irked to hear people in comfortable pews theorizing about the proper role of women in the church, a topic which still claimed a large portion of Baptist gossip. Still smarting under the antiwoman stand of her Professors Hart and Cocke on the issue of Woman's Missionary Union, she wrote to them via the *Religious Herald*: "More than a year ago, in your collective wisdom, you advised the women of the Virginia Baptist churches as to what stand they should take with regard to foreign mission work. As a Virginia Baptist woman, I come to you now with a practical question."[62]

She outlined a typical occasion on which she and Mrs. Crawford were asked by men to teach them and to conduct worship. Should they oblige, or should they permit unbaptized and perhaps unconverted men to take the lead?

"You see our dilemma—to do men's work or to sit silent at religious services conducted by men just emerging from heathenism," she said. "I beg that brethren, ministerial and laymen, will take the matter into consideration and give me the benefit of their judgment." She asked Hart, Cocke, and other leading men to answer through the columns of the *Herald*. None dared answer, and Virginia WMU gained approval to join with the Southern Baptist Convention-wide WMU.

By August 1890 Miss Thornton had arrived to join Miss Moon, but Mrs. Bostick had died. It was hard to gain. Instead of taking her furlough, Miss Moon prepared to open up another P'ingtu village north of the city. Already she had regular work going on in four villages in addition to her home in the west suburb and in Sha-ling. Of these the P'ingtu City work was the hardest, but even it produced a woman convert in August of 1891. By now she had a huge following and was well known for her kindness.[63] Every Saturday morning after breakfast she ministered to forty beggars who appeared at her door in P'ingtu. To each she gave some cash, but she would lend money to nobody. The sick she visited and the poor she furnished with necessities, treating all equally. So the house-to-house teacher proceeded to leave a trail of believers who said of her, "How she loved us."

On November 25, 1890, Mr. and Mrs. T. J. League arrived in China, totally committed to the work of the interior. The mission soon voted that they should be the family for P'ingtu for which Miss Moon had prayed so many years. Miss Moon was jubilant. She could now look homeward.[64]

While Miss Moon had been faithfully concentrating on evangelism and church development, T. P. Crawford had been steadily plotting revenge against the Foreign Mission Board, still feeling hostile about his failure to make self-support a rule. Crawford had for several years ceased correspondence with the Board, and in 1889, at age sixty-nine, stopped taking his salary. Mrs. Crawford, however, continued normal relations with the Board and the constituency. Considering himself retired, and suffering from his old paralysis problem, Crawford went back to the United States. In 1889-90 Crawford traveled quietly in his homeland without making official contact with the Foreign Mission Board. He suffered a defeat at the Texas Baptist Convention in Houston and was politely ignored at the Southern Baptist Convention in Fort Worth.[65]

Back in China, as the gatekeeper for new missionaries arriving in Tengchow, he had ample time and inclination to influence them in favor of his beliefs. Mrs. Crawford, though vastly more pleasant than her husband, agreed with his self-support theories, which Miss Moon had admirably demonstrated in P'ingtu. Mr. and Mrs. Pruitt were also in favor of self-support, even opposing schools unless the Chinese could operate them without foreign supplement.[66]

But the newest arrivals—especially Bostick and League—soaked up Crawford's teachings without the years of perspective and tolerance which bracketed Moon and Pruitt. With most of the young missionaries in his camp, Crawford was able in late 1890 to get a vote for "Articles of

Agreement" under which the Shantung mission would operate. That Miss Moon would have agreed with them in principle is not surprising, but that she signed them as written is amazing. Probably she no longer had the fortitude to fight Crawford and had placed her mind on higher matters.

The "Articles" were sent by Bostick and League for publication in Baptist state papers. In essence they stated that the missionaries would be first of all evangelistic. In order to cut off "pecuniary expectation" they would hereafter use no mission money beyond personal and itinerating expenses. "We also deem it unwise for us to become pastors, school teachers, charity vendors, or meddlers in Chinese lawsuits," Bostick wrote.

They agreed to act together in opening and closing new stations, not opening one without a missionary of two or three years of experience living on the field. They also agreed not to purchase or build property for the mission but to rent.[67]

When the Board received the Articles of Agreement, danger signals went up; and T. P. Bell, now Tupper's assistant, wrote Miss Moon for an explanation of Crawford's intent. She wrote back one of her classic peacemaker letters. She thought Crawford had lost his feelings of resentment for the Board. She believed he was at peace with all his colleagues, although he took extreme positions. "I say this the more fully because I have always steadily opposed him whenever I saw in him any disposition to impose his views on any other mission or upon individuals of our own mission," she said. She attributed his poor judgment and harsh statements to his zeal, his absorption in other interests, and his preoccupation in helping others.

She explained her own position about self-support. "My study of the New Testament leads me more and more to feel that the Christian life is one of self-denial, and that we must lead our converts by example and precept to endure hardship. I do not think this ideal is best attained by bearing their pecuniary burdens for them and building their churches and establishing their schools, but by waiting patiently for the development that time will bring. I do not mean that I would refuse to aid native Christian schools or to subscribe to build churches or that I should fail to open my home or purse to a persecuted brother or one in any distress, but I should do it exactly as if I were in America, privately and not out of public funds."[68]

With that, she and the Pruitts sailed for America on the maiden voyage of *Empress of China*. Seasick and collapsed with headaches, she thought only of the land she had not seen for fourteen years. Edmonia awaited her in Scottsville, in the little four-room brown house called Bonheur.

Notes———— See pp. 302-303 for Key to Sources.

1. *FMJ*, February 1906.

2. *CR*, August 1870.

3. This compilation of the P'ingtu experience is drawn from several rather detailed accounts. At some points these accounts have been difficult to reconcile. One problem is that the eventual brilliant success of Baptist work in P'ingtu attracted many persons who wished to share in the credit. The person who really laid the foundation, Lottie Moon, did nothing to assure that history wrote her into the limelight. The person who did the second most work, C. W. Pruitt, was also reticent about his contribution. Rather than describe in detailed footnotes the judgments I have made, I will simply list the main sources of the P'ingtu story. Only when information comes from outside these will separate note be made.

a. Letters from Princeton S. Hsu, summer 1978, containing data secured from Mr. Wong Mien-Chaih of Taiwan, who knew Miss Moon in P'ingtu.

b. *A History of Chinese Baptist Churches* by Princeton S. Hsu.

c. "Account of Miss Moon's Work in P'ingtu" by Old Pastor Li, URL.

d. Letters to Una Roberts Lawrence from Florence Jones, June 28, 1923, URL.

e. *History of P'ingtu County Baptist Churches* by Tsui Yuan-Ting, translated from Chinese by C. L. Culpepper and Mr. Ku, his secretary.

f. "Beginnings in P'ingtu," undated and unsigned, but apparently written by Miss Moon without naming herself, item 208, LMLF.

4. C. W. Mateer, August 22, 1889, Foreign Mission correspondence, Presbyterian Historical Society.

5. Lottie Moon, January 11, 1886, Cartersville Minutes.

6. Lottie Moon, December 28, 1886, Cartersville Minutes.

7. *FMJ*, May 1886.

8. Lottie Moon, January 11, 1886, Cartersville Minutes.

9. Ibid.

10. Ibid.; notes from Miss Moon's Bible copied by W. W. Adams, URL.

11. Pruitt, *Up from Zero.*

12. Lottie Moon to H. A. Tupper, March 18, 1887, LMLF.

13. *FMJ*, June and July 1886.

14. *FMJ*, December 1886.

15. Lottie Moon to H. A. Tupper, July 27 and August 7, 1886, LMLF.

16. Ibid., August 7, 1886.

17. *FMJ*, June 1887. Also, Pruitt, *Up from Zero* and *The Day of Small Things.*

18. *WR*, May 20, 1886. "Nothing save zeal for the Master's work and the spirit of a heroine could induce a woman thus to throw herself in the midst of a people who revile her day by day," wrote Davault.

19. Lottie Moon, April 20, 1887, Cartersville Minutes.

20. Ibid.

21. *FMJ*, August 1887. For an example of its impact, see article by Mrs. Stainback Wilson, *CI*, 1888.

22. Julia Mateer, October 1, 1887, Foreign Mission Papers, Presbyterian Historical Society.

23. *RH*, September 29, 1887.

24. *FMJ*, October 1887.

25. *FMJ*, January 1888. Davault was the first graduate of The Southern Baptist Theological Seminary to serve as a foreign missionary.

26. Ibid., December 1887.

27. All Baptist state papers of 1887-88, *HH*, and Alma Hunt, *History of Woman's Missionary Union,* Revised Edition, should be consulted to study the forces which helped shape Woman's Missionary Union.

28. Foreign Mission Board Minutes, June and October, 1887.

29. Lottie Moon to H. A. Tupper, July 19, 1887. Lottie Moon to Edmonia Moon, December 31, 1886, LMLF.

30. *FMJ*, September 1888; *BB*, July 1889.

31. *FMJ*, January 1888.

32. Ibid., August 1888. Also *BB*, September 1888; *HH*, July and other issues 1888.

33. *FMJ*, July 1888.

34. *BB*, September 1888.

35. *HH*, July 1888. Mrs. Crawford makes the point in this issue that seed-sowing in P'ingtu was a work best done by women evangelists, rather than men, physicians, or teachers.

36. *FMJ*, October 1888.

37. C. W. Pruitt to H. A. Tupper, July 5, 1888, CWPLF.

38. Lottie Moon to H. A. Tupper, August 23, 27, 1888, LMLF.

39. Ibid., August 23, 1888.

40. Lottie Moon to H. A. Tupper, October 5, 1888, LMLF. FMB Minutes for this period reveal the loans from Edmonia Moon.

41. Lottie Moon to H. A. Tupper, October 5, 1888, LMLF.

42. FMB Minutes, 1888.

43. Moon to Tupper, October 5, 1888.

44. Lottie Moon to H. A. Tupper, January 8, 1889.

45. *FMJ*, March 1889. Hunt, *History of Woman's Missionary Union.*

46. Moon to Tupper, January 8, 1889.

47. C. W. Pruitt to H. A. Tupper, January 19, 1889.

48. Lottie Moon to Annie Armstrong, January 9, 1889; *FMJ*, April 1889; Lottie Moon to H. A. Tupper, February 9, 1889, LMLF.

49. *FMJ*, May 1889.

50. *FMJ*, December 1889.

51. *RH*, June 21, 1888.

52. Ibid., December 6, 1888.

53. Ibid., December 13, 1888.

54. *BB*, June 1889.

55. Lottie Moon to Miss Willie McCarthy, June 24, 1889, property of Second Ponce de Leon Baptist Church, Atlanta, Georgia. Copy provided to author by Luther Bootle.

56. *FMJ*, January 1890.

57. Ibid., August 1889.

58. Lottie Moon to H. A. Tupper, November 22, 1880, property of First Baptist Church, Newberry, South Carolina. Hyatt, *Our Ordered Lives Confess*, shows examples of how Christian treaty rights could be abused. Chefoo Consular Correspondence, National Archives, is filled with letters from missionaries interceding for Chinese in various lawsuits and invoking the treaty to protect Christians from persecution. Not one single letter of this nature from Lottie Moon can be found. However, she did on occasion threaten to take persecution matters to the consul, but each recorded example of such a threat shows Miss Moon's reluctance to confuse Christianity with American imperialism. For an account of Mr. Dan's persecution, see *FMJ*, September 1890.

59. Pastor Li recorded Miss Moon's ministerial heroism in persecution. Her only reference to her role was in the *FMJ*, July 1890. Her philosophy on church planting, illustrated by Li T'z Yuen is articulated in diary notes dated August, September, and October, 1890, URL.

60. Detailed quotations found in Lawrence, *Lottie Moon,* and diary notes (Ibid.) show that Miss Moon held Miss Knight in particular regard.

The New Lottie Moon Story

61. *RH*, January 17, 1889.

62. *RH*, May 9, 1889, and September 1, 1889. For background of the Hart-Cocke position about women's organizations which excited extensive debate related to the formation of Virginia WMU, see the *RH* for March, April, and May 1888. These men were on the committee which drafted the Baptist General Association of Virginia's anti-WMU stance.

63. *FMJ*, January and March 1891.

64. *FMJ*, May 1891. C. W. Pruitt to H. A. Tupper, July 1, 1891, CWPLF.

65. T. P. Crawford, *Evolution in My Mission Views* and *Fifty Years in China*. These books give details and Crawford's viewpoint of the split which was to come in 1893.

66. There is no doubt that Lottie Moon agreed philosophically that evangelistic outreach to the Chinese must not be tainted with material inducements. She agreed with Crawford that Southern Baptist money should not be used to set up programs and institutions that local Baptists could never hope to assume responsibility for. On the other hand, she was a peacemaker and was extremely generous. In contrast, Crawford was a troublemaker and a profitmaker. These differences made it possible for Lottie to be happy in her relationship with the denomination while Crawford was not.

67. *WR*, February 19, 1891.

68. Lottie Moon to T. P. Bell, June 30, 1891, LMLF.

8
She Was
a Benediction

ottie Moon wrote the Baptist women of Baltimore who were eager to see this legendary woman in 1891, "I have been so unmerciful to myself in China, that I must call a halt now and take a needed rest."[1]

And thus went the answer to all invitations for six months while her sister Edmonia soothed away the permanent headache. "For the sake of the work in China more than for my own sake, I desire complete recovery," she said.[2]

Ever a walker, Miss Moon trudged through the hills and forests of her youth. Her little cottage stood just a few miles down the road from Viewmont, which was now run-down and occupied by strangers. She was exactly one mile from Scottsville, where the river flowed, trains ran, and mail arrived. On her property was a bubbling creek. An elderly Negro couple worked as servants.

Edmonia was running the place like a miniature plantation with orchard, grazing lot, house for fattening chickens, vegetable garden, and a cow named Belle. In Lottie's room was a comfortable bed, a marble-topped dresser, and an open fireplace.[3]

Multitudes of kinfolks flocked in to see their cousin, but most of the immediate family was gone. Brother Isaac was the only one remaining, and he had moved to Radnor, Virginia. Her sister Orianna had died in 1883 with cancer of the womb. She and her husband had been operating a hospital in an old mansion in Scottsville, and she was buried in the town cemetery nearby. Lottie visited with Orie's sons in Roanoke, Virginia.

Lottie Moon, 1901 (Charlotte Churchill)

Mary (Mollie) had already died before Lottie's 1876 trip home, but now Lottie enjoyed seeing her daughter, Mamie, of Norfolk. Sarah Coleman Moon had married a Professor Myers, a music teacher, and had moved to Pittsburgh.[4]

Lottie was not too tired to correspond with H. A. Tupper or to invite him to confer with her in Scottsville. Within a month of her arrival, he was at her side to talk mission business. He feared the worst—that her absence from North China would unleash serious trouble with T. P. Crawford.[5]

When the Foreign Mission Board had amended the rules for missionaries after Crawford's 1886 trouble, several of the missionaries had declined to sign, including Mrs. Holmes (who was still considered on leave), Mr. Pruitt, and Miss Moon. Lottie, then expecting to be home within a year, had asked Tupper to wait until she could discuss the rules with him personally. Wisely, Tupper had not forced the issue. Apparently he was able to satisfy her concerns, and she was now belatedly ready to sign.

Alarmed at the clouds he saw darkening in China, Tupper wanted to know exactly who on the list of signers of the Articles of Agreement were friends of the Foreign Mission Board. He feared that Miss Moon was the only one.

Lottie assured the dear secretary that her love for the Board was unshaken and that Mr. Pruitt was also a friend of the Board, as well as the most scholarly, cordial, graceful, elegant, acceptable-to-the-Chinese man in North China. Unfortunately, Pruitt, not having Lottie's political savvy, spoke up to agree publicly with some of Crawford's friends who criticized mission policy. By now Crawfordites were uttering rhetoric of self-support in the same breath with hate for the Foreign Mission Board.[6]

One night Pruitt, in distress, detoured on a trip from where he was furloughing in Georgia, to pour out his soul to Miss Moon in Scottsville. The train arrived after the Moon sisters had retired for the evening. As he had only a short time, he sat on the porch while Lottie sat inside her bedroom in the dark, and they talked without seeing each other.[7]

With Miss Moon's great Chinese-style diplomacy, the breach

between Pruitt and the Board was healed. This was in her power to do because she could communicate directly with all the parties involved. But she could not scale the mounting differences between the Board and those back in North China. Soon after she and Pruitt had left Tengchow, more new recruits had arrived. These included Mr. and Mrs. W. D. Sears and W. D. King. They found no seasoned missionary in North China to balance the views thrust upon them by Crawford. Crawford explained that the Foreign Mission Board was an unnecessary evil. He insisted that it usurped scriptural authority of the churches to appoint, direct, and fund missionaries. It meddled with the personal affairs of missionaries. It wasted money. Crawford claimed that the Board was forcing subsidy for natives, although the missionaries in North China had worked without subsidy insofar as they wanted to. Crawford's drift merged with a kindred movement from Central China, where D. W. Herring disagreed with Board policy about the level of individual financial support and about freedom of missionaries to determine policy.[8]

In the absence of Miss Moon, and unchallenged by his peers in Tengchow and region, Crawford issued an inflammatory tract, *Churches to the Front.* He called for the end of the Foreign Mission Board as it was then functioning. This was published in February 1892.[9] The Board countered by dropping Crawford's name from the missionary list in April, but it retained Mrs. Crawford's name. Out of loyalty to her husband, but with sad good-byes and offers of fraternal cooperation, Mrs. Crawford resigned in July.[10] Gradually Herring, League, Bostick, and Miss Thornton (who married Bostick), and later Miss Knight and Mr. King—everybody left in North China but the Searses and Miss Barton—joined with Crawford in an independent movement which came to be known as the Gospel Mission.

Ensuing was a smoky, complicated dispute which drew off not only missionaries but whole churches and groups of churches. On the home scene, the Gospel Missionism was rooted in the Landmark controversy, and critics of organized SBC work had a heyday. The Landmark movement grew from the same time and place as T. P. Crawford. Its tenets of extreme independence of the local church and opposition to cooperative boards were a divisive factor in the SBC for as long as Crawford lived.

Miss Moon's role was to suffer, not in silence, with both H. A. Tupper and her friends in China, especially Mrs. Crawford. She was able to see the situation from all sides.

She agreed in theory with Crawford's philosophies but in practice with the Foreign Mission Board. At times she played the finest peacemaker role of her career. Tupper and the Board appreciated her in this role of which she said, "If, as you suggest, the noble office of peacemaker is in any measure to be mine, it can only be by frankest kindness on my part to my brethren and sisters in both missions, who differ from me in opinion. We are all equal, equally honest and sincere, and we all need kindness in the trials that are before us. The 'Gospel Mission' is now an accomplished fact and its members are entitled to the same social courtesies that Baptist missionaries extend to Presbyterians, Methodists, and to others."[11]

At other times she vociferously differed with the Board, but she always pledged herself to work with it. When it counterattacked Crawford with the announcement that his old enemy, J. B. Hartwell, would be reappointed to Tengchow, Lottie strongly advised against the move. She knew that with Hartwell would go Board subsidy of the Chinese, which she had come to oppose. More painfully, she recalled the Crawford-Hartwell feud of the 1870s. "His return means 'war to the knife' between the mission of the Board and that of the 'gospel' brethren. The very thought of it makes me heartsick," she said.[12]

She asked that the Shantung territory be divided so the two missions would not run into conflict about subsidy. For months there was uncertainty as both sides considered pulling out of Shantung. "For Southern Baptists and the 'gospel' brethren to turn their guns upon each other instead of fighting the common foe would be madness," she told Tupper. "I shall have to ask the Board to transfer me elsewhere if the fight is resolved upon. I have been in one terrible fight and I know that it would be renewed . . . life wouldn't be worth living."[13]

The more she thought of working with Hartwell the more she disliked the prospect, although she pledged high regard for him as a missionary anywhere else in the world. "Knowing as I do the circumstances of that past awful time . . . please request the Board to transfer me to Japan,"[14] she asked.

Tupper studied each of numerous letters from Miss Moon and responded to them in his usual intimate fashion. No other person in his vast correspondence received such lengthy, open, cordial letters. He was sensitive to her slightest criticism and he was terrified that she would jump ship. He did not reveal her several transfer requests to the Board members, but he nursed her along through 1893, until she felt able to make quick preparations for returning to China. Then he gently broke the news to her that her advice had delayed Hartwell's appointment for some time, but that he definitely would be going to China. "I know your judgments are carefully formed and I hardly dare to hope that your allegiance will be perfectly with the judgment of the Board, but I do hope . . . that you will, as a good and dear missionary of the Board, agree to submit to their action."[15]

In another letter he said, "I confess, my dear sister, that I feel disturbed at the thought that you may not approve, or may even disapprove, what the Board has done. I doubt if the Board has had a missionary more highly esteemed than yourself . . . If I had but one request in this world to make of you, my sister, it would be that, if possible, you keep in harmony as far as possible with the Board that honors you more than you know."[16]

Thus entreated, Miss Moon consented to stand by the North China mission and work with Hartwell. The Gospel Mission conflict was harrowing for the aged Tupper. Beset from all sides, and unable even to gain 100 percent support of Miss Moon, he resigned as corresponding secretary.

The continued troubling of this issue deeply colored Miss Moon's furlough; but after seven months of complete rest at Scottsville, she came out of hiding to help her denomination "weave longer ropes" for supporting missions. She signed on as a member of the Woman's Missionary Society at the Scottsville Baptist Church which her parents had founded and where Viewmont's rosewood and horsehair parlor furniture graced the platform. She helped the missionary society gain an edge on the more prestigious Ladies Aid Society of the church.[17]

In the spring of 1892 she made a tour southward en route to the Woman's Missionary Union annual meeting held in Atlanta in connection with the Southern Baptist Convention. She stopped at several churches, including the one in Macon where George Braxton Taylor, founder of the Sunbeam Band, the first Southern Baptist missions program for children, was pastor.[18]

She spent several days in Cartersville, Georgia, where the whole town turned out to welcome her. She spoke to a large meeting of women, and "her society" gave a fabulous reception for her. Former students, now grown middle-aged, gathered happily to see their petite teacher, now grown fat and fiftyish. While in Cartersville, she spoke on Sunday to the "colored" Baptist church and enjoyed several private visits.[19]

At the Southern Baptist Convention the Foreign Mission Board displayed an enormous crimson silk banner several yards in length. The Sha-ling Christians had sent it with this appeal for Miss Moon's immediate return. "We thank God that he gave his servants wisdom to choose and send so good a missionary as Miss Moon, whose heart is filled with love like that unto the Son of God."[20] If Miss Moon was personally recognized at the Convention, no record was made, although she would have been permitted a seat as an observer. (Very few women's presence had ever been acknowledged in a Convention.) She did meet with the Foreign Mission Board during the week.

At the Woman's Missionary Union meeting May 6, 8, 9, and 10, however, Miss Moon was the center of attention. She was introduced by President Fannie E. S. Heck as "our heroic missionary." The audience was breathless as Miss Moon stood in her Chinese robes to summarize nineteen years in China. She quoted with the view of a scholar from historical and current events to show that China was making rapid change into the modern age. "I must say the Chinese are fully equal in intellectuality to any," Miss Moon said.

"I have had as many as a dozen follow me crying 'kill! kill,' " she told the women, but times changed after the 1877-78 famine in Shantung. Describing vividly the open door now awaiting missionary expansion and church development, she invited the women to consider what they would do for China.[21] Her P'ingtu stories caused hearers to begin championing the work of missions in the interior.

Southern Baptists were engaged in raising missions money around the centennial of William Carey, the first Baptist missionary, and his initial journey to India. Every Baptist entity was encouraged to hold centennial meetings, which were actually missions rallies. Miss Moon did her bit for the cause by speaking in many churches and associational meetings, always traveling at personal expense. A typical stop was in the Baltimore area in April of 1893. She spoke in a half-dozen church missionary societies, then to the Maryland Woman's Baptist Foreign Mission Society.[22]

She left this engagement for three solid weeks of visits to country churches. She professed a decided preference for country churches. She was a country girl by upbringing; she worked in the country as a missionary; she preferred the values held by country folk to those dominant in industrial cities; and she was convinced that country churches held the key to mission expansion. With a touch of extrovertness, she told Tupper that she enjoyed being a "rare bird—a real live missionary" in churches that had never before seen one.[23]

In all these appearances she religiously followed the most conservative etiquette for a woman speaker. She made formal addresses only before women's groups. Men were not allowed to attend such meetings. She might fascinate men around the dinner table, but in a meeting with them she faded into the woodwork. When speaking she usually wore Chinese dress and displayed a few curios. When she spoke to the women during the Albemarle Baptist Association meeting in Scottsville, her meeting was held in the Presbyterian church. The men were in session at the Baptist church and were greatly disappointed that they could not drop in accidentally to hear her.[24] The memorable impact Miss Moon made on her hearers became evident in later years. Children throughout Virginia named their missionary hens Lottie Moon, then sold the hens' eggs to earn money for missions.[25]

One young woman who became a home missionary recalled Miss Moon's exact words many years later. In one of those Virginia country churches, sitting around informally with the women church members, she described her calling to missions—"as clear as a bell." "People talk of the hardships of missionary life. 'Tis true there are hardships. But I am so happy in the work that I never mind them." The women were deeply moved to hear this fellow-Virginian say, "China is my home." After three days of visiting in the home of her hostess, she left that family in a state of spiritual euphoria—as if she had been a living benediction.[26]

At the centennial meeting of Virginia Baptists in Richmond the ladies gathered at Second Baptist Church. Miss Moon spoke for foreign missions, while Miss Annie Armstrong of the WMU spoke for home missions. The throng of women was overcome by the thrill of hearing these two "greats" in one occasion, and at a missionary tea they pressed forward to grasp their hands. Miss Moon took this occasion to stress the Foreign Mission Board's call for one hundred new missionaries, and she told how other denominations were outstripping Southern Baptists in appointments.[27]

After she had grasped thousands of hands and answered as many questions, Miss Moon felt the need for a significant alteration in terminology. The "heathen Chinese" was a term she herself had often used in earlier days. She had outgrown the words and the negative concept that went with them. She loved and appreciated the Chinese and their culture, even as she wished them to become Christians. So "heathen" became a rude insult to her ears when uttered by the unknowing and uncaring.

"A returned missionary is pained by flippant remarks which have their root in ignorance," she said. She tried to point out that Chinese considered Americans barbaric devils with as much justification as Americans had in calling the Chinese heathens. Though of innocent origin as a synonym for *pagan*, the word *heathen* now held disdain.

"Isn't it time that we missionaries part company with those who roll this word *heathen* under their tongues as a sweet morsel of contempt? Shall we Christians at home or in mission fields be courteous in preaching the gladdest tidings on earth, or not?"

She reminded Americans that China was the most civilized nation on earth while Anglo-Saxons were sulking in the forests of northern Europe. "It is time that the followers of Jesus revise their language and learn to speak respectfully of non-Christian peoples," she insisted.[28]

With this shocking pronouncement she sought to reeducate the assembly of Woman's Missionary Union during the 1893 Southern Baptist Convention in Nashville. Her earnest and tender stories about courageous live or martyred Chinese women made a profound impression on the fifty-seven delegates and numerous guests. Her message of love and the successes of Sha-ling helped to counter the brutal hall-talk gurgling from the Gospel Mission situation.

Fannie Breedlove Davis of Texas spoke the feelings of many when she put her arm around Miss Moon and said, "You have been the inspiration of my life." Then to the women she said, "She has given her life. What must she think of us? Shall we come up next year with such a small sum?"[29]

At the WMU meeting she was fully at home with the sisters whom she felt she represented in China. In prayer, devotional exercises, formal addresses, or debate, her words carried weight. She spoke to favor the proposal that WMU seek to raise funds for support of all the women missionaries. She agreed that WMU should cooperate with the Sunday School Board in sponsoring a missionary day in Sunday School. Most surprising of all, Miss Moon endorsed using the Christmas offering of 1893 to further work not in China, but in Japan.[30]

All the nation was atwitter over the World's Fair in Chicago. She took her only niece, the teenage Mamie Shepherd, with her for a three-week tour to the fair in October.[31] Then she scurried home to pack excess baggage for her return to China. Leaving Scottsville on November 13, she met Eliza Yates in San Francisco and sailed on the *China* November 21. Hurriedly she dropped a line of welcome to Robert Josiah Willingham, who had been elected corresponding secretary of the Foreign Mission Board. Apparently without ever meeting this important figure in her life, she sailed.[32]

The voyage was a hot but interesting one, as the *China* put in at the Sandwich Islands (Hawaii). Lottie had left with a somewhat diminished attachment to home. Though pained by Edmonia's serious, chronic illness, she found little about her remaining relatives to identify with. Her nephews were not churchgoing men, a situation which "Aunt Lotte" tried to remedy by mail.[33] Her niece, born a Catholic, was soon to be married into a devout Baptist family which was personally involved in supporting Miss Moon. Lottie clearly saw herself as a woman of China, and one with the status of age and experience, not as a woman of America.

As soon as she was in China's embrace again, she donned her standard flowing blue robe with black satin trim atop an American skirt. She put on eighty-cent embroidered cloth slippers with pasteboard soles and did not vary the uniform until she headed back toward America ten years later. She was the only one of her American co-workers who consistently dressed in Chinese style, although some did when in the interior. "It covers a multitude of faults," she said of the long, loose sacque. "And it helps me get nearer to the people."[34]

She brought to China in her heart a tender letter from her beloved Mrs. Crawford. It was a "last will and testament" of woman's work around Tengchow. Mrs. Crawford left this work as Lottie Moon's heritage. "I was so glad to find that you have decided to come back here. It greatly lessens my sorrow at leaving these dear women for whom I have, figuratively, shed my heart's blood. You will have your own work in the Lung San Tien region, but I know you will not allow my Buh Go region to lie waste. Then, there are the Christians out at the deacon's village; and in the east, Chin Ta Sao, and also at Tsung Kia, Tu Wu, and other places. You will love and care for these as no one else can, for they are yours as well as mine."[35]

Thus Miss Moon's job description for her next term of service was placed on a different path from the previous work in the interior. But Lottie steadfastly sailed on to Chefoo and fought the familiar holiday season snowstorm overland to old Tengchow.

The Pruitts had preceded her and were back in their field of Hwanghsien. Hartwell had been in Tengchow since August. He had arrived with authority to purchase and occupy the Crawfords' house.[36] Crawford had built it during the American Civil War, had rebuilt it for the Moons, had obligated the Board to purchase it from him, and had been charging the Foreign Mission Board a steep rent for it ever since. In the face of Hartwell's arrival, the entire Gospel Mission group had evacuated to P'ingtu, where they spent the winter in residences the Foreign Mission Board had been using. Their plan was to open a new field farther inland, and they soon were far away in Taian-fu.[37]

Once Lottie had taken a close-up reading on the attitude and maneuvers of the Gospel Mission group, she was sorely irritated. To her well-placed connections in the homeland, she wrote letters explaining that these opponents of the Board and of paid agents were actually setting up their own. And she believed that some of the group were unfairly using Foreign Mission Board funds. Her faith in the Board had been completely vindicated. She was thankful to be rid of the bickering generated by Crawford.[38]

On the other hand, she sustained deep personal hurt at the disagreement with friends, especially Fannie Knight. Miss Knight was helping to house the Gospel group in P'ingtu, but she had not yet left the Board. All Miss Moon's hopes for peaceful reconciliation were penned to Miss Knight, who had carried out their P'ingtu work and had written faithfully. Miss Knight sent a warm letter of welcome as Miss Moon arrived in China, and Lottie responded with a revealingly warm letter which she called "a love letter . . . for yourself alone, for I am naturally very shy about expressing much of my feelings."

"Many greetings have I met since landing in China and especially many most cordial and affectionate in Shantung but none have sent such a glow of happiness as your dear letter, received while at breakfast this morning. You brave, noble, unselfish darling! My trust in you has not failed. I relied implicitly upon your promise that whether I lived or died, you would push the work at P'ingtu. Right nobly have you kept your word. It was our Lord's work, and you were only too glad and thankful to do it for his sake. Yet I cannot forget how you upheld my weary hands and cheered my sometimes almost fainting spirit during that first winter in P'ingtu together. Do you wonder then, my precious darling, that I turn to you with all and more than all the old time love and that if you are 'homesick' for me, I am longing with intense desire to look upon your dear face again? In China, you are my dearest and

(Upper) Shentze (Ruth Thornhill)
(Lower) Lottie Moon's House at P'ingtu (Anna Belle Crouch)

you know that I do not speak lightly words of affection. When I truly love, as I love you, it is with my whole heart.

"Yes, come to me, dear child, in the early spring. I had thought of doing some much needed work in this region before going to P'ingtu. You may help me in this and then in the summer I can go with you to P'ingtu."[39]

These plans and Miss Moon's hopes were dashed when Fannie Knight hastily married W. D. King and cast her lot with the Crawfordites as they moved out to Taian. Lottie had nothing else to say of Fannie, who died immediately after her wedding trip.[40]

The Gospel Mission spread the opinion that the Foreign Mission Board was wastefully overpaying its missionaries. In fact, some of the Gospel missionaries had reduced their salaries when still under the Foreign Mission Board.[41] In the face of this criticism and of a large debt, R. J. Willingham asked the missionaries if they would reduce their salaries by one-third. The answer was a unanimous willingness to compromise.

Lottie agreed to cut from six hundred dollars to five hundred dollars a year, but in the face of runaway inflation, would do no more. She was in the habit of maintaining open house for Chinese from the country who came to be trained, examined, and baptized into membership of the Tengchow Church. Also, she never turned away a beggar. She explained that Gospel Mission members refused this sort of generosity as a matter of principle, while she considered hospitality a Christian grace.[42] Miss Barton agreed with Miss Moon, saying that to eat meat once a day and to use soap in bathing should not be considered inappropriate luxuries for missionaries.[43] Their arguments convinced the Board, and the salary was set at five hundred dollars for each adult.

The Hartwells, the Pruitts, the Searses, Miss Barton, and Miss Moon now comprised the mission, with Miss Moon the senior member in China experience. Her past confidential fears about Mr. Hartwell were never again mentioned. She treated him as an honored colleague and gave herself graciously to helping Mrs. Hartwell, a third wife with young children, learn the language and find a work she could handle.

In the mission's first meeting after all had arrived, they squarely pounced on the bones of contention. Yes, they would reenter the school business. They agreed to open a boarding school for boys in Hwangh-sien under the Pruitts' direction. They put it on a paying basis except for a small teacher's salary from the Foreign Mission Board and a personal supplement.[44]

From the outset Miss Moon insisted that girls be given equal opportunity. By April Lottie had convinced everybody involved, including the Board. She quietly helped Mrs. Hartwell to set up the girls' boarding school in connection with her home, using a bilingual teacher.[45]

Lottie certainly had no objection to schools. If she had any qualms about the small Mission Board subsidy of these, she did not make an issue of it. Rather, she rejoiced that schools would rescue the children of Christian parents from the infant baptism taught in Presbyterian schools and the idolatry taught in Chinese schools.

The mission fully agreed that Miss Moon's own work would be evangelism in stone-hearted Tengchow and hundreds of surrounding villages. She might have claimed the fruitful, pleasant field at Sha-ling which she had developed, but she was willing to leave it to younger hands. Not until the Gospel Mission group had moved on did she visit P'ingtu. Then in May she subjected her fifty-three-year-old body to the four-day sentimental journey by shentze. She had personally bought property for the little church at Sha-ling. Now they proudly showed her the Chinese-style building they had put up for both school and church. Added to the forty members of the church, eleven more were baptized in her happy presence.[46] This was now the largest Baptist congregation in North China.

As the mother of the P'ingtu church, she was welcomed lovingly. Hartwell said her presence there was always a benediction. Perhaps it was the adulation of the Chinese which caused her to visit less and less frequently. Even before her furlough she had begun to withdraw from the field so as not to distract from the influence of her young co-workers.[47] Yet her love for the people never dimmed, and they considered her house in Tengchow as their house when business took them there.

After a two-month stay at P'ingtu and a round of her large countryside parish, Miss Moon declared a holiday for July. To have a month at home in the summer became a rule with her. She attended to her church duties in Tengchow, but she did no strenuous evangelistic work or travel. She lounged and read. In this July she studied Chinese with a scholar's curiosity.

Rested, she attacked the country work with a renewed zeal. There were more than one hundred villages within a day's reach. Between August and October she visited eighty-four of them.[48] Technically Miss Moon's job was "woman's work," but everybody knew that she had a way of harvesting the souls of men who eavesdropped on her work with women.

Her purpose was to teach Christian doctrine. To do this, she also taught the basics of reading. Her technique required sharp wits and flexibility. First she asked polite questions to find out the readiness of her audience. Often people remembered hymns or verses taught by her, Mrs. Holmes, or Mrs. Crawford years before. Then she flashed colorful pictures of Bible scenes, growing impatient while adults snatched them from children. Then she brought out simple books and tracts. On the same kang she might be teaching a bright, young girl and a dull, old grandmother, while a semiliterate man poked a hole in the paper window to tune in.

Throughout the visit she would work conversationally. Long ago she had given up sermonizing. The people would not sit still to hear such. But they would engage in dialogue, which Lottie adroitly turned to the subject at hand. To men and to others who could read, she gave books with a promise to return for discussion.

On a day's journey she would pack a lunch in her pocket. When she stopped to eat, people crowded against her and peppered her with questions. Boys observed who were "innocent of clothes as a babe just out of its bathtub—though they had never dreamed of such a necessity." She did not begrudge these hasty and tiring lunches, for with true evangelist's zeal, she always was calculating the lostness of her observers.

"At my age, I cannot expect many more years of work, so I must crowd the days as they fly by with eager toil for the master," she wrote a friend. But she was glad for sundown, when her chairbearers took her back to the Little Cross Roads house with its thatched roof, where she could sleep in her own small bed and thank God for peace and quiet.[49]

During that first year back on the field, China fell to war with Japan. Lottie, like other foreigners, was accused of being a Japanese spy, but she stood firmly on her reputation with the local people. Chinese officials wanted the missionaries to stay because their presence provided both real and imaginary security.

Rowdy soldiers with ancient guns were assigned to protect Tengchow from Japanese warships which paraded within sight. Lottie gave these men a wide berth, not caring to get into a showdown. When they shouted at her on the streets, "Beat the foreign devil," she took no notice. But when a neighborhood child dared to follow the soldiers' example, she took action. She commanded the sedan chair bearers to set her down and scurried in pursuit of the little boy. Trailing him into an inn, she demanded to see his mother. A crowd collected, with soldiers, and the mother appeared full of apologies. Holding her ground, Miss Moon fiercely explained that the child was following the poor example of the soldiers. "I tried to ignore them," Miss Moon said. "If I report them to the officials, they will of course be severely punished, for I have a proclamation of protection posted on my street gate. But if this continues, I will be forced to act." The soldiers retreated in silence, and she had no further trouble from the people.[50]

Amid the threatening climate, Miss Moon continued her country work, and she set up a new cry to the Foreign Mission Board for reinforcements. Hartwell had taken on the work of four men and he rapidly fell into a near-fatal illness. With apologies for bothering Secretary Willingham while he was preoccupied with a growing debt on the Board, she kept on the pressure for more men and for single women. Willingham, who did not know Miss Moon personally, curtly replied that every station in the world wanted reinforcements. She would have to wait her turn.[51] So she patiently undertook brief but informative letters to educate the new leader. And she doubled her efforts to cover the territory herself.

She was on her way home from Christmas in P'ingtu when she heard that the Japanese had bombarded Tengchow on January 16, 1895. By the time she passed through Hwanghsien, she was meeting refugees

(Upper) Lottie Moon's house at the Little Cross Roads (FMB)
(Lower left) James Boardman Hartwell (FMB)
(Lower right) Anna B. Hartwell (FMB)

fleeing the city. Old men trundled their valuables through the snow. Women of all ages hobbled on bound feet, the slush drenching their cloth shoes. Crying babies were freezing. On reaching Tengchow she comprehended the terror of the people. When she arrived at her own compound at the Little Cross Roads, she had her own moment of terror. A shell had demolished her wall and damaged her veranda and doorway. The missionaries were fleeing on the United States' warship, *Yorktown*.

Lottie arrived too late to join in her colleagues' frightened flight. Because of gunfire and ice they had had to climb down dangerous icy cliffs to get to the boat, and the Hartwells' luggage was left on shore.

With her co-workers gone to Chefoo Lottie pondered her vulnerable situation. She hastily tried to hire animal drivers to take her inland to P'ingtu, but even at robbers' rates they would not go. Meanwhile, she had time to gather her senses.

The gentry of Tengchow, who had not condescended to notice the foreigners in thirty years, came calling to ask her to remain at home to calm the people. In case of invasion, missionaries might fly American flags which would deter the enemy. So Miss Moon, the only foreigner in town, bravely lived in sight of the menacing Japanese ships, knowing that Chinese guns were unable to protect.[52] As in past times of danger, she rationally quelled her fear by thinking that God would protect her, keep her "immortal till her work was done."

The Tengchow Christians who had taken refuge at the Pruitts' schoolrooms in Hwangshien slowly returned to their homes. Miss Moon's neighbors dribbled back also. She keenly felt her responsibility to remain calm and hospitable at this time.

When Hartwell returned he opened the Tengchow Baptist Church for preaching services, and the crowds eagerly flocked in. For six weeks, he and Miss Moon dealt with unprecedented numbers of people eager to appreciate and hear them.[53]

Hartwell soon wore himself out, and Miss Moon suggested that his daughter, a missionary in Canton, be transferred to help him. Miss Anna Hartwell arrived in July 1895.

As soon as she caught the language she learned the countryside with

Miss Moon. Her aid relieved the strain on Miss Moon's throat, which was beginning to fail. Despite the war, Lottie visited 118 villages before September, and she set a goal of hitting 200 villages before the end of the year. But she reported to Willingham that she covered only sixty-nine villages in the last quarter. She apologized for being hindered by heavy rains and throat trouble. Willingham approvingly remarked in the *Foreign Mission Journal,* "What would she have done if the rain and poor throat had not hindered?"[54] To Miss Moon he wrote solicitously, "I fear you work yourself too hard."[55]

By year's end she was convinced that the day of harvest was coming fast. Not only had the mission grown in prestige during the war, but fifty-three baptisms and heavy financial contributions from the Chinese surpassed all previous dreams. During the annual meeting of the Baptist association, foot-binding and education were openly discussed, much to Miss Moon's pleasure. A new church in P'ingtu City, Miss Moon's old residence, was organized in 1895. Although Sears and Dr. H. A. Randle (an English physician-preacher who had joined with the Southern Baptists) did the baptizing in the P'ingtu area, they often gave Miss Moon and the other women credit for winning the converts.[56]

"I have never found mission work more enjoyable," Miss Moon exulted. She worked almost totally out of doors, except when regular pupils would invite her to their kangs. "To go out daily among a kindly people, amid enchanting views of nature, everywhere one turns catching lovely glimpses of sea or distant hills or quiet valleys, all this to me is most delightful. I constantly thank God that he has given me work that I love so much."[57]

Nevertheless, she was paying a high toll for her daily travels, and she began to measure out her strength carefully. Miss Anna Hartwell dropped by her house on a rainy day and found Miss Moon stretched out on the couch reading. "Isn't this jolly," Miss Moon laughed, using one of her favorite words. "Just jolly! I was ready to board my chair for the country when this rain came, so I decided the Heavenly Father had given me a holiday." Miss Anna hurriedly departed so her friend could rest completely.[58]

To her prayer supporters in Scottsville and Cartersville, she now often mentioned her throat troubles and the serious health problems that plagued both Presbyterian and Baptist missionaries. In late 1896 she diagnosed her aches as being partly neuralgia and partly nervous. She feared that she might have a nervous breakdown. So she gave herself the month off and stayed close to home.[59] The Pruitt children came to spend Christmas with American company, and she was cheered.[60]

Lottie considered that she lived a quiet life. She was living alone. According to Chinese customs, she did not go out to shop, but had clerks bring in goods for her choosing. She seldom entertained. Yet during monthly church business meetings, mission meetings, and associational meetings of all the churches, her compound would be flooded with guests. At such times she would have Chinese friends calling socially and for counsel.[61]

Among her missionary friends her home was known as a place of rest and refuge in sickness and weariness. Not only did they enjoy her well-ordered home and good meals, but they also treasured her up-to-date conversation. The best periodicals were always at hand. She read them all and formed her own interesting opinions. After a long siege of discussion about baptism in the *Christian Index*, she commented, "If our people were as orthodox on foreign missions as they are on baptism, wouldn't the money flow into the mission treasury? Wouldn't all the fields get needed reinforcements? The same Lord who said baptize said also disciple all the nations. Many remember one command and forget the other, yet they are equally binding."[62]

One visitor was Miss Lula Whilden, the single woman who had been appointed for South China when Edmonia Moon had come to North China. Probably Miss Lula was seeking rest, and the two classic pioneer women greatly enjoyed each other. Probably it was their only meeting.[63]

Other missionaries treasured her visits to them. Especially the children were jubilant when this favorite "aunt" arrived. C. W. Pruitt wrote after she visited and charmed his lonely children at Hwangshien, "It is a benediction to have her in the family."[64]

Always on the lookout for the safety and happiness of her co-workers, she began to press Willingham relentlessly for more help as soon as she sensed a pickup in contributions. Because she feared for Hartwell's life, she said, "The work is more than one man can do unless we could bid the sun stand still."

Her own health worries fostered statements such as this: "I've reflected much and sorrowfully on the fact that if the Lord shall call me from earth, there is no one here to take my work I am trying to do."[65]

Her work continued to take her into the country villages; but after the war, she found more open doors in the city itself. One day as she walked across the town, a strange woman stopped her asking cordially, "Isn't this Miss Moon?" Replying affirmatively, Lottie found herself ushered into the home of a woman who had heard the gospel many years earlier from the Crawfords. Now she was ready to hear more.

For her city visits, she was often accompanied by a Chinese Baptist woman. Other missionary women had a "Bible woman," (called "lady preacher" in Chinese) a regularly employed assistant who helped crash the cultural and language barriers. Miss Moon never seemed to have a personal Bible woman. After she passed middle age, propriety did not require that she have a companion. She did not need help with the language. She may have objected to paying women for doing the work which any Christian woman should engage in. Rare mentions of her Chinese co-workers indicate that they were volunteer church members. Or, perhaps, they were evangelists supported by the Woman's Missionary Society which Miss Moon helped to organize in the Tengchow Church in 1896. When she had a woman with whom to visit, they divided forces. One would work with women while the other dealt with children.[66]

Not all the changes in Tengchow were for good. Petty crime increased as the city steadily decayed. During 1896 and 1897 Miss Moon had so many thieves in her house that she was forced to appeal to the local mandarin. The first break-ins were in her kitchen. Then the main house was attacked, and her Chinese clothes were taken. At last a thief scaled her broken-glass-topped wall by grabbing overhanging tree limbs, and he scavenged her storeroom while she slept. This took her to the highest available official, who awarded her damages in court. Soon afterward she had the tree trimmed, her walls fortified, and a tile roof put on some of her buildings.[67]

The year 1897 found Hartwell so weakened that he and his wife went to San Francisco, where he was hospitalized for many months. Miss Anna took over her mother's school. Miss Moon was overloaded with responsibility. She was later to call it "one of the hardest years in our history."[68]

Serious disputes arose in the faculty of Mrs. Hartwell's school, and these extended into the church. Miss Moon became convinced that Anna Hartwell's Bible woman needed to be dealt with sternly, and Miss Hartwell reluctantly complied. Later Miss Moon decided that she had judged harshly and came to her young colleague with a wholehearted apology. "Oh, Miss Moon! Don't apologize to me. I am so much younger," Miss Anna responded with surprise.

"Why not?" Miss Moon replied. "I erred in judgment. You were right and I was wrong, yet I insisted, and you followed my advice. I want you to rescind the action and let the whole family know it was my doing, not yours." This display of honesty taught the young woman an important lesson about Miss Moon and about Christian living.[69]

Miss Moon taught a Sunday School class of young men. She met with them each Sunday under the bell tower of the Tengchow Church, having laboriously prepared her lesson. On Monday nights a class of illiterate men and boys came to her house to study the New Testament. Each month she conducted the meeting of the church's Woman's Missionary Society. The women encouraged each other in personal evangelism, they prayed together, and they contributed money to support both a man and a woman evangelist sent out by their small church.[70]

Yet her main work continued in the country. On a typical day she would visit at least two villages. Chairbearers would take her into the country immediately after breakfast. After a morning of teaching under a shade tree or in a friendly home, she would eat. If she were in a familiar home she might venture to ask a few minutes of privacy on the kang for rest after lunch. On one such day she could hardly drag herself up after the noontime rest. But she had an appointment in another village and the chair was waiting.

Emerging into the yard, she was crushed to find many women and children standing expectantly. "They wanted to hear you *kiang*," the hostess explained. Miss Moon berated herself for resting while people were eager to hear the good news, but tried to excuse herself by thinking, "I'm only human."[71]

After a day of cross-legged sitting on the kang she was glad for a few minutes' walk, while the chair bearers followed. A mile down the trail, she found her hostess working at the threshing floor and followed her to a rude and messy house of poverty. "Don't despise," the poor woman said apologetically. "I despise no one's surroundings," Miss Moon assured her.

The hostess cleared off a place on the cluttered kang, where the missionary settled herself. Women and girls crushed around her, while curious men were forced to wait in the stable yard.

The aged top mother-in-law of the house struggled down from the kang. Miss Moon, suspecting her intent, said, "You are old. Please sit down."

"No, I must get down to mind the baby," came the answer. And she went off to prepare the inevitable refreshments of poached eggs.

"Do you know why I came here today? I came to see the venerable aunt, and also to bring you a message from the true God," began Miss Moon.

"Aah, yes. Tell us. See—she has brought the book to *kiang* to us."

Holding up a New Testament, she continued, "This is God's own book. I have come to tell you his words. I dare not bring you my own words."

"What is your name?" the women wanted to know.

"My name is Mu."

"How old are you?"

"I am fifty-six years old."

"Ah. She has never committed any sins, obviously."

"No, none are without sin," Miss Moon said.

Then the gracious old lady appeared with the bowl of eggs floating in the poaching water. Miss Moon took a pair of chopsticks and began to choke down all the eggs and drink all the water. At the same time she continued talking. The women interrupted, "Is it possible that there can be a heaven for such as we?" Gladly Lottie described the way to heaven for suffering women who had never had hope cross their minds.

Winding up a country tour, she opened her little black lacquer travel desk to pen her contentment: "I bless the dear Lord for being with me on this tour. He keeps my heart first on himself, and so I have enjoyed the work today."[72]

Not all her ministerial duties were so peaceful. One of her women converts, Mrs. Wang, was a large landowner in Buh Ko. Her neighbors demanded a heavy land tax with which to finance theatrical performances as a thank offering to the gods. The woman refused and began to be persecuted by twenty-four men in the town council. She sent her servant to fetch Miss Moon for help.

In this case Miss Moon went armed with the treaty which guaranteed freedom of religion to Christians. She arrived on the day that four umpires came from a neighboring town to decide the case. Local Christians knew that these judges would rule on the side of idolatry.

Miss Moon stood by Mrs. Wang as counsel. She immediately took the offensive by asking the presiding officer, "Will you please be kind enough to read the twenty-ninth article of the treaty?"

He retaliated by saying that the foreigners and the Chinese were alike in their worship, both trying to lay up merit by good works.

"Fine laying up of merit," Miss Moon cut in. "Persecuting a widow!"

The man felt this thrust keenly. His breeding demanded veneration of widows.

Mrs. Wang stated her case while the men were silenced. Then they retaliated by saying that Christians shirked their community duties.

"I am willing to pay more than my share for repairing the town wall and bridges," Mrs. Wang countered. But the men wanted her to pay even more, else they would not protect her fields from thieves according to local agreement.

Miss Moon grew weary of their arguments and marched herself to the temple where the town council were gathered. Alarmed at her approach, they tried to deny their identity, but Miss Moon persisted.

"Mrs. Wang will have no face if she refuses to pay," said one.

"The people who oppress will have no face," Miss Moon retorted. She was making herself unwelcome, but she pressed on for an immediate settlement according to the treaty. It was halfheartedly given.

"This is not a small matter," she continued. "It is a matter in which two countries are concerned. The twenty-ninth article of the treaty says that Roman Catholics and Protestants who come to China to preach exhort men to do good, and that, if they establish churches, their converts are not to be persecuted. You may bring lawsuit, but two sides can play that game! Tomorrow is Sunday and I can't attend to business. But if necessary I shall return. If the matter is not settled here, it will go to Chefoo and Peking. Do you gentlemen understand?"

With a sullen affirmation from the men, Miss Moon ended the interview and marched out of town.

But she took no joy from her victory. If she had been a courtroom attorney in the United States, she would have been applauded. But she was not at all sure that this was the Christian way to meet persecution. In fact, it was exceptional for her to stand on treaty rights. "Maybe I should have just helped her bear the persecution," she thought as she journeyed. "But the treaty is clear. Even Paul asserted his rights as a Roman citizen."[73]

Missionary life in China had such complexities, and it also had its hazards. Miss Moon's vulnerable point was always her throat. For more than a month in 1897 her doctor, a Presbyterian missionary, advised her not to speak Chinese with its difficult tones or to travel in the country. So she entertained a profusion of Chinese houseguests. By the dozens came women inquirers and their babies. One row of rooms on Miss Moon's compound was furnished in Chinese style with kangs for the comfort of Chinese visitors. The walls were whitewashed, and the kangs were freshly matted. Simple meals were served at Miss Moon's expense. "They provide hospitality to me in the country, so I return to them," she explained.[74]

By early 1898 the dread of old age which had been hovering over Miss Moon settled heavily upon her. She wrote a young friend in Scottsville, "I begin to feel the effects of age. I have felt the uncertainty of life very keenly of late."[75]

Although death was no stranger to the little missionary community in Tengchow, the final days of Mrs. Calvin W. Mateer, one of the earliest Presbyterian missionaries, were especially hard on Miss Moon. They were nearly the same age and had shared many good times personally and professionally. Mrs. Mateer was an equal match for her remarkable husband. With seldom a rest the Mateers had raised their struggling boarding school to a splendid college for young men. She managed the school while Dr. Mateer did literary and engineering work. Late in 1897 she suddenly broke down completely, took to her bed, and never got up. For four months Lottie helped nurse her. With the few other women missionaries in Tengchow she took turns sitting up all night while Mrs. Mateer suffered. Her obituary in the *Chinese Recorder*, (where the grim realities of missionary life were not treated with cosmetics) said, "She died of physical problems, but also mental, the mental more potent." Speaking of the constant worries she had coped with for years, the paper referred to her final "long restless weariness" as a "vicarious penalty for those for whom she had worked."[76] Lottie thought a quick death would be preferable to Mrs. Mateer's anguished end, but this experience was a foretaste of her own final days!

Meanwhile, in Hwanghsien, all the missionaries were desperately ill. Two hours before a doctor arrived, the Pruitts' little son died. Forgetting her own sensitive throat, Miss Moon went immediately into the Pruitt home to nurse and amuse the surviving children.[77] With Hartwell still sick in the United States, with her throat constantly bothering her and her energy depleted, and with no prospect for new workers, she began counting her days.

Perhaps it was fear that her traveling evangelism days were limited that made her reenter her old field of schoolwork. Schools were growing immensely in popularity among Baptists. The boarding schools were large and flourishing. Because of the change in attitude in Tengchow, local children were becoming interested in mission schools. Early in 1898 Miss Moon began conducting a day school for the local students. It was coeducational—a real departure for China. Miss Moon used her old schoolrooms in the North Street property, a long walk from her house at the Little Cross Roads. She fitted them up at her own expense with tables and benches, books, and paper. "This school gives me much pleasure," she told Willingham.[78] She paid a teacher to conduct the daily memorization. After almost a year of operation, the school received a twenty-five-dollar allocation from the Foreign Mission Board. Miss Moon used this to pay herself back partially for her investment. "It's a Sunday School every day," she said of the little school. It featured the hymnbook *Peep of Day* and the Gospel of Matthew for curriculum, but she planned to add arithmetic and geography soon. This school was later named the Memorial School for Robert Barnham Whitehurst, and it was put on sound financial footing by the Sunbeam Band of Freemason Street Baptist Church in Norfolk.

The school cut slightly into Miss Moon's travel. She reserved Monday for examining the pupils and conferring with the teacher. She continued her men's Bible class on Monday nights, her Woman's Missionary Society meetings once a month, and occasional meetings with other missionaries. She was in the country Tuesday through Saturday. Sometimes she would stay overnight on these trips. In one promising village she rented rooms as a home away from home. Usually she would return by nightfall to sleep and eat at home. After the "incessant noise and publicity wearing on one's nerves home seemed like Heaven."[79]

Sundays were busy from sunup to sundown.[80] She arose at 6:15, bustled about in straightening the house for the English-speaking community's worship service, grabbed breakfast, and crammed for her Sunday School lesson. Before the church bell began ringing at 9:30, schoolboys who had walked over from the North Street neighborhood were peeking in her window. "Are you well, Miss?" They were invited to play on the porch until church time. A Presbyterian missionary preached in Hartwell's absence, while Miss Moon struggled to make the boys behave. The preacher rapped sharply on the desk to help.

After the Chinese service concluded, Presbyterians and Baptists from England and America, plus four English-speaking Chinese, gathered at Miss Moon's for worship in English. She invited them for dinner.

She had her usual brief lunchtime rest, then reviewed the Sunday School lesson for the young men's class at the church. Sunday School met at three o'clock. Back home, fifteen boys and girls answered roll call for a special class. The children were shooed away just before nightfall. Miss Moon rested with Baptist newspapers from the United States until her supper was served. Then she read from the Bible the fourteenth chapter of John—meditating on the verse, "Whatsoever ye shall ask in my name, that will I do." Writing in the diary occupied her until ten o'clock; then she went to bed.

Monday, her day for city work, held some special diversions. She translated telegrams and news stories for the *Shantung Times* as a favor to the vacationing foreign editor. Parting with the Chinese editor with many bows and smiles, she got ready for school recitations. By now she was allowing her boy students to learn classic Chinese primers as well as teaching them the Ten Commandments.

Housekeeping, even with servants, took some time. For example, she had to arrange delivery of coal by boat from Shanghai, to Chefoo, to Tengchow, then by mule from the Water City.

The rest of her week took her on the usual country tours. This time she stayed several nights in a traditional poor Chinese home with an earnest inquirer. Every meal she was served the local staple, "mein," a type of macaroni. It was sometimes embellished by salted onions and was always followed by the hot water in which it had been cooked.

Despite Hartwell's absence, more than one hundred baptisms took place in the churches associated with the Shantung Baptist mission during 1898. Miss Moon was delighted that many Chinese Christians as well as others were casting their approval with the "Heavenly Foot Society," an antifoot-binding movement. A majority of mission schoolgirls suddenly unbound their feet.

Early in 1899 sickness again haunted Lottie Moon. This time it was Miss Anna who felt ill. She had bronchitis, pneumonia, meningitis, and "congestion of the brain." Miss Moon constantly attended the young woman until her parents returned April 25 after a two-year absence.[81] The effect on the senior missionary was to make her more cautious about her own health. "Nervous troubles" were afflicting and felling three missionaries at the same time. Miss Moon attributed this nervousness—or emotional troubles that had long been the curse of the North China mission—to the climate. Certainly it was more likely the result of constant overwork coupled with hopelessness at being relieved.

That Lottie Moon remained comparatively free of such was a tribute to her own self-discipline. While others about her were falling apart, she shared her secret. "When I think myself threatened with nervous prostration, I quit work at once and take perfect rest. Not all people have the resolution to do this and, of course, not all are so situated that they can do it. I argue thus: I refuse to go any longer. I rest. I get well in a month or so and then take up my work . . . . As to the dryness, I feel it, but I use much water habitually. Besides a daily cold bath, I often thoroughly shampoo my head—sometimes every day. Most people are afraid of using water on the head as I do. They fear taking cold. I sometimes take a little cold in that way, but I argue that the taking cold is a smaller risk than the heat of the head which is so drying. A very hot head at night means loss of sleep and that simply wears one out."[82]

She was always willing to help nurse the sick, but she did not take unnecessary risks with her health. To Mrs. Hartwell's slight annoyance, Miss Moon refused to allow a Hartwell child who recently had whooping cough to come to her house on a social occasion.[83]

Miss Moon's correspondence with R. J. Willingham had usually been very routine. But late in 1899 he gave one of his rare displays of affection by saying, "I wonder if you know how much the brethren of the Board think of you and your work."[84] Probably much more to her liking was his announcement that new missionaries were under appointment. In mid-1899 Miss Moon welcomed Dr. and Mrs. J. W. Lowe, who were charmed by her entertaining reception. He was assigned to P'ingtu.[85]

Then, after eight years of pleading, Miss Moon got a single woman to be her co-worker. She was Miss Mattie Dutton, who arrived early in 1900. Miss Moon delightedly took the young Missouri woman into her home, set up a bedroom and study for her in one of the rows of rooms, and engaged a Chinese teacher for her. Miss Moon personally supervised while Miss Dutton "rang the four tones." Then she escorted her to the country to practice evangelistic work.[86]

These young faces helped the veterans psychologically as much as they did practically. A boost to morale was desperately needed. At the break between centuries came a breaking point between old and new China. Missionaries and their Chinese Christian families were suspended dangerously over the chasm.

Miss Moon, with her well-established contacts throughout the eastern part of Shantung Province, had her hand firmly on the popular grapevine. Prior to 1900 she became convinced that the Empress Dowager was encouraging not only antichristian but also antiforeign feeling and actions among the people. The missionaries kept the United States' consul at Chefoo, John Fowler, posted on their findings. For months they sensed growing danger but continued their work cautiously.

Fowler was unable to convince the United States' legation at Peking that the Chinese government was secretly stimulating the insurgents known as Boxers. Or at least, Miss Moon was convinced that this was the case.[87]

One of the early evidences of trouble brought Miss Moon to the rescue of her precious Christian friends. An antiforeign magistrate was bold enough to trump up false charges of robbery against some of the Baptist church members. He arrested thirteen Christian men between Laichow and P'ingtu. The accused had their queues (pigtails) tied to saddle horns of the cavalry horses; then the soldiers galloped the horses. The Christians either ran or were dragged by the hair over the miles to Laichowfu. Pastor Li hastened to get the missionaries to intervene to help rescue the Christians from certain death. In the meantime, the thirteen Christians were transferred to jail at P'ingtu. Hearing that her P'ingtu believers were in danger, Miss Moon was determined to stand by them. But she also heard that the Empress Dowager had given orders that missionaries and Christians were not to be protected. Frenzied bands of Boxers roamed the roads.

Over the grave warnings of her friends in Tengchow, Miss Moon planned her approach to P'ingtu. She obtained an enclosed sedan chair such as Chinese officials rode in. Then she dressed in a man's long Chinese robe and short coat like the officials wore. She added big rimmed glasses and slicked her hair back. On her head she wore a cap with an official's bright red button. She opened the front flap of her chair, sat with her arms folded on the crossbar, and looked royally from side to side. She successfully played this part all the way to P'ingtu. She found that the thirteen Christians had been released from jail but had been brutally tortured. She consoled and encouraged them. That she had risked her life to show love further immortalized her among the P'ingtu people.[88]

But almost before she knew it, her presence was not an aid but a further threat to the Chinese Christians. The Boxers were omnipresent, and the only hope of Chinese Christians was to cut identification with foreigners. Consul Fowler first begged the missionaries to come to Chefoo and then warned them not to travel without an armed guard. Although Tengchow Christians were not physically persecuted, they were ostracized. However, the situation in P'ingtu and in the country stations grew brutal. Missionary residences, churches, and schools in P'ingtu territory were demolished.[89]

Amid the unsettled conditions, missionaries quietly made their way to the nearest port, and a goodly group gathered in Tengchow in time for the hurried-up wedding of Jesse C. Owen, a Baptist missionary, to Rebecca Miller of the Presbyterian mission. Just hours after their marriage on July 1, 1900 in Lottie Moon's parlor, the consul firmly ordered all foreigners out of the province.

Miss Moon and her colleagues hastily boarded the Chinese gunboat *Hai-Chi*, commanded by the gracious Christian, Mr. Sah, an opponent of the Empress. He gave the missionaries deluxe staterooms and fabulous meals while protecting them from mutinous Boxers in the crew and Russian warships in the harbor. After several days, the U.S. *Yorktown* transferred the passengers to Chefoo.[90]

With her well-developed sense of Chinese affairs, Miss Moon predicted a long conflict; so she fled the refugee camp conditions in Chefoo on the first steamer for Shanghai. Conditions there were more peaceful. She and Miss Dutton visited with Dr. and Mrs. Bryan until they could book passage for Japan. If she had to leave China, there could be no more pleasant place of refuge than in Japan, the land of her first missionary dreams.

She and Miss Dutton were welcomed by Mr. and Mrs. J. S. McCollum, Southern Baptist missionaries in Fukuoka. After a short time in their house, the visiting women rented their own Japanese house. From July 1900 until April 1901 Lottie Moon was a missionary in Japan. She took a job teaching English in a commercial school. She was allowed to choose her own textbook, and her choice was the Bible. Soon her prize student was proficient enough to greet his teacher saying "Verily, verily I say unto you." She also taught private students in her home. Through

Lottie Moon with students at Japanese commercial school, where she taught English, 1901. (Charlotte Churchill)

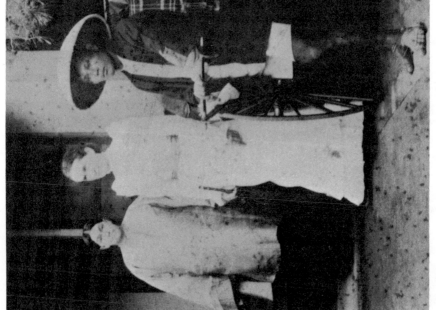

Lottie Moon (left), about 1908. Photo...

these personal contacts three Japanese young men became Christians. Miss Moon had her photograph made with them. She was also photographed with her whole class.[91]

Sitting for the camera was an unusual experience for Miss Moon. Although some of the missionaries in her area of China occasionally had cameras, she shied away from them. The nearest professional photographer was in Chefoo, and she would not bear the expense of having pictures made to satisfy the many casual requests she received. But the situation in Japan was different. Her admiring pupils undoubtedly wanted souvenirs of their experiences together, for many of the pupils corresponded with her for years. The Japanese-sized American woman in Chinese dress must have been quite an attraction.

Ever sympathetic to missionary families, Miss Moon became fond of the McCollums and their flock of children. She could not do evangelistic visiting because of the language barrier, and Mrs. McCollum was limited in visiting because of having to teach her children. So she and Miss Moon swapped roles. The McCollum children liked Miss Moon as a teacher, but one boy got a reprimand from his father for loudly commenting on the lady's strange custom of daily cold baths.[92]

Miss Moon considered the Japanese young men she taught to be lovable, bright, frank, and courteous. She left them with reluctance, prolonging her visit longer than was really necessary for the sake of safety in China. When she returned to Tengchow in April 1901, she made her plans for a vacation in Japan en route to her next furlough.[93]

Although Boxers occasionally troubled the waters, mission work was comparatively smooth sailing after 1901. Miss Moon pronounced her work more promising than ever before. Baptisms exceeded one hundred annually, even though churches were strict about admissions. The heroic examples of Chinese Christians who suffered and died rather than renounce their belief now bore fruit in thousands of friendly inquirers. Missionaries and Chinese church members in P'ingtu were entitled to huge indemnity payments for the damages wrought by the Boxers. They refused all such payments except when they were justly made by those who had actually done the evil. This policy won many friends for the faith.[94]

Miss Moon resumed her day school, her country and city visiting, and her Sunday services for the English-speaking community. A delayed celebration of the Owens' marriage took place on their first anniversary. All Baptist and Presbyterian missionaries dined festively and made toasts to the young couple. That same group of missionaries pooled their resources to build a picnic shelter at the beach. On July fourth they held a prayer meeting and tea party in the breezy house. Miss Moon enjoyed the restful out-of-doors but left the seabathing to the younger generation.[95]

She was now an old woman by her definition and an old saint by the definition of the Foreign Mission Board. Any time Willingham or other supporters of missions wanted to invoke the ultimate in missionary piety and wisdom, the name of Moon would be called in company with Graves (of South China) and Hartwell.

Her unceasing call for more missionaries was beginning to be heeded. She had held on in China long enough to raise a generation of young Southern Baptists who had received their missionary impressions from her story. Now they were coming to her aid. Miss Jessie Pettigrew, the first trained nurse appointed by the Foreign Mission Board, learned of God's call into missions in her mother's Sunbeam Band in Virginia. She had been reared on Lottie Moon stories and was moved by meeting Miss Moon on her 1892-93 furlough.[96] Along with Miss Mary Willeford, she was spending 1902 learning Chinese in Miss Moon's living room. Although the two young ladies slept in the Hartwell house, Miss Moon saw that they had proper teaching, and she offered them her study and dining room. Meanwhile, Miss Dutton had moved to P'ingtu, and Mr. and Mrs. Owen set up housekeeping in Miss Moon's guest rooms. The merry presence of these enthusiastic young people drove out the loneliness that haunted Miss Moon.

All the mission family was gladdened by the arrival of Dr. T. W. Ayers and his family. A successful journalist, Ayers had gone to medical school in middle age. God was preparing him to respond to a call to China which Ayers felt when he learned the tragic story of two Pruitt children dying without medical aid. Soon after Ayers reached Hwangshien, the mission met there, and Miss Moon stayed at his house. She met and loved his children. Ayers saw the need for a full hospital ministry, and Lottie shared his dream. The mission voted to ask the Foreign Mission Board for seven thousand dollars to build a hospital for Ayers—the first in Southern Baptist Convention history.[97]

A new station was opened in Laichowfu where Miss Moon had often worked. There was a promise of developing Christians as ministers and evangelists. The excitement of expansion on all fronts—schools, medicine, evangelism, new stations, relationships with the Chinese—delighted Miss Moon as she approached the furlough of 1902. She would have much to report to the Southern Baptist churches in her former home. Her own little day school had grown to include twenty-six males, several of whom were grown men, and thirteen girls. She was clamoring for funds to expand. She was upgrading the course of study although the simple Christian doctrinal books were the core. The school was now the nucleus of a new preaching point. Her Wednesday afternoon women's prayer meeting was gaining stature in the city. Street gates to homes of all social levels were cordially opened to her. She was an institution in Tengchow, and strangers called her name pleasantly as she trod the old millstone street.[98]

Yet the villages and the city were scarcely touched. When the mission got word of the appointment of two single women for North China, there was heated conflict about how best to divide them among the vast women's work. Miss Moon was adamant, and she could state her opinions forcefully, that the women were most needed in the still-rough country work. Mr. Hartwell wanted at least one of the women to work as a companion in the city with his daughter. Miss Moon thought that married women who had limited mobility should handle the city.

With these two stalwarts divided, the younger missionaries dared not take sides. The placement issue had to be turned back to the Foreign Mission Board, which ultimately asked the young ladies to make their own choices. Miss Moon could easily concur in this approach.[99]

Although she had looked forward to furlough, and she was entitled to one because of new Board policy which permitted a trip home every ten years, she was tempted to stay on the scene of action. But her own family was changing fast, and she reckoned that their days were limited.

Edmonia's poor health was driving her aimlessly from boarding house to boarding house all through North Carolina and Florida. The little home in Scottsville had been sold in 1897.

During 1900 the Foreign Mission Board had worked out a special annuity plan with Miss Edmonia. Woman's Missionary Union had recently instituted the idea of annuities for missions. The idea was for donors to give large sums to the mission boards, who would then pay a stipend to the donors for life. Edmonia placed $3,000 with the Board. The Board agreed to pay her $150 a year for life, then $150 to sister Lottie for her life if she should survive Edmonia. Letting the annual payment transfer to a survivor was a special concession made because of the Moon sisters' special ties to the Board. In the same period Edmonia was continuing to lend the Board small sums of money.[100]

Miss Lottie was eager to see her sister and also her brother, who had been near-fatally ill. There were great-nieces and nephews to meet, a few cousins left, and thousands of loyal women in the missionary societies, many of whom vied for the opportunity to contribute to this favored missionary's salary.[101]

In preparation for the voyage Miss Moon had to spend her 1902 summer rest period in Chefoo working with the tailor and shoemaker. It had been nine years since she had had American clothes, and she wanted to look adequate for the furlough occasion.

Ayers asked if his teenaged son, Harry, could return to America in Miss Moon's company. The bright young boy considered her his steadfast friend, spiritual guide, and intellectual counselor. In the absence of a proper school, he had found her library and her conversation a plenteous education. She had steeped him in Greek and Latin literature, demonstrated straight thinking, opened his eyes to a world view. With tact and wit she charmed him through what might have been tragic culture shock. He was smart enough to recognize greatness in her and to soak it up while he had the opportunity. She welcomed him as a travel escort. They stopped over in Japan for several days. New Year's Eve caught them at the McCollums' in Fukuoka. The foreign community gathered round for a festive party. At the stroke of midnight Miss Moon's rich melodious Virginia voice read Tennyson's "Ring Out, Wild Bells."

Harry Ayers grew to be a prominent newspaper publisher in Anniston, Alabama. His career as a journalist stood partly on the literary and moral gems Miss Moon planted in him, only one of the lives she incidentally touched along the way. He said, "To know her was not only a liberal education. It was a spiritual benediction."[102]

Notes——— See pp. 302-303 for Key to Sources.

1. Lottie Moon to H. A. Tupper, October 10, 1891, LMLF.

2. Ibid., November 3, 1891.

3. Edmonia Moon to Lottie Moon, December 31, 1886, LMLF. The map and description contained in this letter gave clues which enabled Mrs. W. Peyton (Mary Jane) Thurman, president of Virginia WMU, to locate the exact site of the house on property now owned by Edward Dorrier. In the fall of 1978, Mrs. Thurman took the author to the site exactly nine-tenths of a mile on Highway 20 toward Charlottesville from the three-story brick building in Scottsville. The Dorrier property is on the left. In Dorrier's pasture is a clump of trees on a knoll where the house undoubtedly stood. Mrs. Thurman made a complete abstract of the property in Albemarle County Courthouse, Charlottesville, beginning with Deed Book 86, page 454, May 20, 1886, and ending with Will Book 40, page 571, July 28, 1957.

4. Sarah Coleman Moon (Myers?) is assumed to have been dead by this time.

5. Lottie Moon to H. A. Tupper, November 6, 1891, LMLF.

6. Ibid., February 19, 1892, and March 21, 1892; also Anna S. Pruitt to Lottie Moon, February 15, 1892, LMLF. The series of articles by S. A. Goodwin in the *RH* beginning in December 1891 is an example of the criticism Crawford's supporters were mounting. Pruitt's letter of agreement in the *RH*, January 28, 1892, shows his mind at the time. By the issue of June 8, 1893, his words were more moderate. Miss Moon's feelings would probably have been similar.

7. Anna Seward Pruitt to URL, April 22, 192?, URL.

8. Susan Herring Jeffries, *Papa Wore No Halo.*

9. Crawford, *Evolution in My Mission Views; FMJ,* May 1892 and September 1893.

10. *FMJ,* November 1892.

11. Lottie Moon to H. A. Tupper, June 10, 1893, LMLF.

12. Ibid., February 4, 1893.

13. Ibid., February 6, 1893.

14. Ibid., February 7, 1893.

15. H. A. Tupper to Lottie Moon, April (?) 28, 1893, Copy Book, FMB.

16. Ibid., January or February 9, 1893. Other Tupper letters on this subject

are July 3, February 8, February 10, February 21, April 10, and others partially illegible. Pruitt did not share Miss Moon's opinion about Hartwell, but he had not worked in China during Hartwell's tenure there.

17. Lottie Moon to H. A. Tupper, November 16, 1891, LMLF; *RH*, January 28, 1892.

18. Diary of George Braxton Taylor, May 11, 1892, Virginia Baptist Historical Society.

19. Cartersville Minutes, 1892; *The Courant American*, May 5, 1892.

20. *RH*, May 12, 1892.

21. Ibid., May 19, 1892. *BB*, June-July, 1892.

22. *Twenty-First Annual Report of the Woman's Baptist Foreign Mission Society of Maryland*, 1893; Lottie Moon to H. A. Tupper, February 20, 1893, LMLF.

23. Lottie Moon to H. A. Tupper, April 13, 1893, LMLF.

24. M. B. Nicol to URL, September 14, 1925, URL.

25. Such references appear in women's columns of the various Baptist state papers and in early WMU publications found at WMU. See *RH*, May 4, 1899.

26. Katharine James to URL, February 3, 1923, URL.

27. *BB*, May 1893, and *RH*, April 6, 1893.

28. *FMJ*, May 1893.

29. *BB*, June-July 1893.

30. *WR*, June 15, 1893; *Minutes* of WMU, 1893; *FMJ*, June 1893.

31. Recollections of Lottie Moon by John Fitzgerald of Crewe, Virginia, provided by his daughter, Grayce Fitzgerald. John Fitzgerald was the nephew of Mrs. Isaac Moon, Lottie's sister-in-law, and he arranged for Lottie's burial.

32. Lottie Moon to R. J. Willingham, October 5, 1893, and September 5, 1893, LMLF.

33. Lottie Moon to William Luther Andrews, March 23, 1894, LMR; Lottie Moon to Mrs. Harrison, January 23, 1894, Virginia Baptist Historical Society.

34. Lottie Moon to Dear Cary, June 22, 1897, URL.

35. Crawford, *Fifty Years in China*.

36. Correspondence in JBHLF.

37. Crawford, *Fifty Years in China*.

38. Lottie Moon to Mr. Saunders, January 12, 1894, LMLF.

39. Lawrence, *Lottie Moon*. Also letter from Fannie Knight to Miss Moon, October 25, 1892, shared by Mrs. Russell Thomas.

40. *Woman's Work in the Far East*, November 1895.

41. *BB*, March 1890.

42. Lottie Moon to R. J. Willingham, February 28, 1894, LMLF.

43. Laura Barton to R. J. Willingham, March 3, 1894, Laura Barton Taylor Letter File, FMB.

44. C. W. Pruitt to R. J. Willingham, February 15, 1894, CWPLF; J. B. Hartwell to R. J. Willingham, July 10, 1894, JBHLF; Lottie Moon to R. J. Willingham, April 10, 1894, LMLF

45. Mrs. J. B. Hartwell to Anna, February 20, 1894, HFP.

46. Lottie Moon to Mrs. Harrison, October 22, 1894, Virginia Baptist Historical Society.

47. Anna S. Pruitt to Una Roberts Lawrence, April 22, 192?, URL.

48. *FMJ*, January 1895.

49. Lottie Moon, September 18, 1895, Cartersville Minutes.

50. *FMJ*, November 1895; Lottie Moon to R. J. Willingham, October 29, 1894, LMLF.

51. R. J. Willingham to Lottie Moon, January 11 or 19, 1895, Copy Book, FMB.

52. Lottie Moon, January 22, 1895, from a newspaper clipping at Virginia Baptist Historical Society; Lottie Moon, January 25, 1895, Cartersville Minutes; J. B. Hartwell to R. J. Willingham, January 24, 1895, JBHLF; J. B. Hartwell to Anna, January 20, 1895, HFP; Laura Barton to R. J. Willingham, March 16, 1895, Laura Barton Taylor Letter File, FMB.

53. *FMJ*, June 1895.

54. *The Mission Journal*, December 1895 *(FMJ)*.

55. R. J. Willingham to Lottie Moon, November 18, 1896, Copy Book, FMB.

56. *RH*, April 30, 1896; *FMJ*, December 1896.

57. *FMJ*, January 1895.

58. Anna Hartwell, *Royal Service*, December 1930.

59. Lottie Moon to Mrs. Harrison, January 16, 1896, Virginia Baptist Historical Society; Lottie Moon, March 24, 1897, Cartersville Minutes.

60. C. W. Pruitt to R. J. Willingham, December 24, 1896, CWPLF.

61. Lottie Moon to William Luther Andrews, November 7, 1895, LMR. Lottie Moon to Cary, June 22, 1897, URL.

62. Lottie Moon, March 24, 1897, Cartersville Minutes.

63. Ibid.

64. C. W. Pruitt to R. J. Willingham, March 26, 1896, CWPLF.

65. Lottie Moon to R. J. Willingham, March 9, 1896, LMLF.

66. Lottie Moon, February 25, 1898, March 24, 1897, Cartersville Minutes.

67. Lottie Moon to Mrs. Harrison, December 3, 1896, Virginia Baptist Historical Society.

68. Lottie Moon to R. J. Willingham, January 28, 1898, LMLF.

69. Anna Hartwell, *Royal Service*, December 1930.

70. Lottie Moon to Mrs. Harrison, February 24, 1898, Virginia Baptist Historical Society.

71. "Kiang" was the general word applied to pulpit ministry but also to other forms of religious proclamation. In early days the women missionaries often spoke of preaching. After Willingham took office they used the Chinese "kiang." Later they simply avoided mentioning their work in proclamation. Women in later times had many male co-workers and may not have had as much occasion to "preach" as the pioneer women.

72. *RH*, June 24, 1897. Quote was copied from Miss Moon's Bible by W. W. Adams, URL.

73. *RH*, October 7, 1897.

74. Lottie Moon to R. J. Willingham, July 1, 1897, LMLF.

75. Lottie Moon to Mrs. Harrison, February 24, 1898, Virginia Baptist Historical Society.

76. Ibid.; Lottie Moon to William Luther Andrews, April 28, 1899, LMR; *Chinese Recorder,* _____, 1898.

77. Pruitt, *Day of Small Things.*

78. Lottie Moon to R. J. Willingham, October 5, 1898, LMLF.

79. Lottie Moon, June 20, 1898, Cartersville Minutes. Lottie Moon to Woman's Missionary Society, First Baptist Church, Roanoke, Virginia, May 25, 1898.

80. *RH*, March 30, 1899.

81. Lottie Moon to William Luther Andrews, April 28, 1899, URL. Lottie Moon to Mrs. Harrison, June 2, 1899, Virginia Baptist Historical Society.

82. Moon to Harrison, ibid.

83. Mrs. J. B. Hartwell to Anna, May 22, 1900, HFP.

84. R. J. Willingham to Lottie Moon, December 29, 1899, Copy Book, FMB.

85. *FMJ*, December 1899.

86. Lottie Moon to R. J. Willingham, April 7, 1900, LMLF.

87. Lottie Moon to William Luther Andrews, June 28, 1900, letter provided by Mary Virginia Andrews.

88. C. L. Culpepper, in translation of *The History of P'ingtu County Baptist Churches,* and in personal letter to author, June 12, 1978, based on information he learned while a missionary in Shantung Province.

89. *FMJ*, August 1900.

90. Lottie Moon to William Luther Andrews, July 17, 1900, letter provided by Mary Virginia Andrews.

91. W. W. Adams, "Miss Lottie Moon, Some Recollections and Glimpses," 1947, WMU.

92. Mrs. J. S. McCollum to R. J. Willingham, January 21, 1901, J. S. McCollum Letter File, FMB. Also oral tradition recounted by descendants.

93. Lottie Moon to Mrs. Harrison, July 26, 1902; Lottie Moon to Russell, July 25, 1901, Virginia Baptist Historical Society.

94. Lottie Moon to Cousins, February 13, 1902, Virginia Baptist Historical Society.

95. J. B. Hartwell to Children, July 7, 1901, HFP.

96. Mrs. Minnie Pettigrew Voyles in interview with Mrs. Frank Ellis, 1978.

97. T. W. Ayers, *Healing in Missions.*

98. Lottie Moon to Cary, March 18, 1902, URL.

99. Lottie Moon to R. J. Willingham, November 7, 1901, LMLF.

100. R. J. Willingham to Edmonia Moon, May 23, 1900, and several other letters within a three-month period, found in Copy Book, FMB; FMB Minutes.

101. WMU Minutes, 1902.

102. Harry M. Ayers, "Lottie Moon As I Knew Her," *Royal Service,* December 1935.

9
She Was
a Tower of Strength

The people who met Lottie Moon for the first time in 1903-04 saw an elderly, dowdy, but energetic, magnetic Southern lady of the highest type. In her old-fashioned black skirt and cape, her high-necked blouse, and black bonnet, she looked the part of a unique visitor from another world. She was the perfect guest, ultimate listener, and enchanting conversationalist who could charm away the hours with endless insights.

People who had seen her through the two previous visits—1877 and 1893—noticed now that she had spread out with extra pounds, was graying slightly, had lost many of her teeth, and was raveling at the edges of her health and vitality.

Furlough meant a succession of parlors and porches where Lottie Moon sat to be admired by strangers who were listed as family and friends. She had a place to lay her head in Crewe, Virginia, where brother Isaac and wife were being cared for by a nephew, John Fitzgerald. Edmonia Moon came in from her vagabond search for health and took a little room nearby. The Crewe Baptist Church opened its arms to receive the honored visitor.

From this reunion headquarters, Miss Lottie trundled her trunk to homes of other relatives and to speaking engagements. In Norfolk she forged a strong bond with the Sunbeam Band and Freemason Street Baptist Church, which faithfully financed her school. There she also visited her only niece, Mamie, Mrs. James Herbert Cofer, whose husband was a member of Freemason Street Church.

In Roanoke, Virginia, she renewed ties with the sons of Orianna.

The New Lottie Moon Story

Luther Andrews made a place in his large family for Aunt Lottie while Isaac Andrews, next door, made a room for Aunt Eddie. A troop of great-nieces and nephews went with Lottie to speak in nearby churches.

In the green hills of Albemarle County she sniffed the elixir of youth at old family estates—Mount Ayr, Locust Shades, Snowden. Her cousins spared nothing to recreate the comforts of bygone days. Surveying the country scene, she remarked one day, "Oh, how I wish I could taste partridge again, like we used to have." The great Maltese cat sitting beside her sauntered out to hunt a plump bird which he soon laid at her feet.[1]

Bathing in the mountain creeks, driving winding roads, picnicking in the woods, repeating tales to the children, stretching out on first one spare bed and then another—these were the activities of a vacationer. But Lottie Moon did not find a Virginia home.[2]

"Lottie, dear, don't go back. It's time to retire. Stay here. I can't stand to see you go." Loving statements like these may have warmed the heart of one who had stood alone in another culture for thirty years. But they did not seriously tempt her.

"Oh, don't say that you don't want me to return. Nothing could make me stay. China is my joy and my delight. It is my home now," she would answer.[3]

So she made short work of 1903. She called at Richmond, where she stayed in a rooming house with a young cousin, Schuyler Moon. As ladies did not go to the Foreign Mission Board rooms to sit with the Board, the gentlemen appointed a welcoming committee to confer at her lodging. R. J. Willingham's house was nearby, and he extended hospitality.[4]

On the road, she spoke to many women's groups. As was the lingering habit of her day, she addressed only women. Among other men, Willingham was bold enough to slip into the back of the lecture rooms where she spoke. Some women would have pointedly paused until the intruders vanished, but Miss Lottie pretended she did not see.

She did not make an appearance at the annual meeting in Savannah of the Woman's Missionary Union, Auxiliary to Southern Baptist Convention; but she did speak to the WMU of Virginia at their meeting in Norfolk, sharing the platform with Annie Armstrong of WMU, SBC.[5]

Friends arranged for her to make an exciting trip to Charlottesville, where she attended the University of Virginia commencement festivities in 1903. She was the guest of a professor who gained admittance for her on two occasions when United States President Theodore Roosevelt spoke. Her hostess sent her in a carriage to Monticello, where a reception was held for the President. The glitter of the occasion did not impress the missionary, but she reveled in the sentimental journey through breathtaking scenery and the memories of her youth. She was surprised that Monticello was not as grand as she had recalled it from her childhood. "Later years dwarf one's early impressions," she commented.[6]

Along the visiting-speaking trail she stopped in Anniston, Alabama, where a dentist in the Ayers family took care of her need for teeth. Stopping with relatives in Chattanooga, she stirred up churches to contribute toward a hospital for Ayers.[7]

Miss Moon's messages continued the old theme: respect for the Chinese people, sympathy for them in their progress, concern for their idolatry, and pointed requests for more persons to work as missionaries. With some surprise, leading Baptists noted that the woman truly loved and sympathized with the Chinese beyond objective concern for their salvation. But for this trip, she added a new theme. "Why send missionaries to Africa if you will not go into the miserable homes of our colored brothers and sisters to uplift them?" she asked.[8]

With her sister-in-law, she visited the Negro population around Crewe, providing food, clothing, teaching, and compassion. "I have always found the colored people very accessible and ready to respond to kindness," she said. Her racial views had escaped the thirty-year erosion which had occurred in the South between black and white. Her antebellum affection for blacks remained, with only a touch of condescension. She was shocked at the callousness shown by whites toward their former household members and urged Southern white women to view the colored population as their personal mission field.

She encouraged anyone's disposition toward Christian witness and ministry. During her traditional visit to her friend, Mrs. W. E. Hatcher, in Fork Union, Virginia, she met a young woman from Atlanta, Mrs. James McF. Gaston. The woman was fascinated by the China allure of Lottie Moon, but she found herself doing most of the talking. Miss Moon warmly applauded her in her personal ministries to travelers in Atlanta. Later the young woman felt that she had talked too much, that she should have let Miss Moon talk. But she had not hindered the influence of Miss Moon, for she would shortly be joining her as a missionary in North China.[9]

On February 15, 1904, Lottie said good-bye to Virginia and all that it had held for her. Her farewells took into consideration the obvious decline of her brother and her sister. She did not expect to see them again.

On previous trips to the Pacific Coast, she had taken the northern and the central train routes. Now she chose the southern path and headed for New Orleans. There she boarded a sleeper bound for San Francisco. On February 27 she sailed on the *China,* sharing an economy stateroom with two strangers. After stops in Hawaii and tense calls in Japan, where war with Russia made sea travel risky, she soon touched her real home.[10]

At the Little Cross Roads, she put on her modest Chinese robes and settled with delight into her comfortable, ancient home. Old upholstered furniture, rocking chairs, Edmonia's little organ, a writing desk with a bookcase hutch, shelves on which to display trinkets, a little footstool, candlesticks—among these she could relax. Her loyal servants, paid from her personal salary, freed her from daily housework. She presided over her own table and maintained a schedule which even regimented time for rest and play. She returned to a work which she found full of amusement, excitement, soul reward, and challenge.

"Only in the pauses," she wrote an intimate friend, "would a choke of loneliness gurgle to the surface. I console myself by thinking that one can't have all the good things and that those I long for are in God's loving care. My life is too full for much of such longing." With characteristic reasonableness, she recognized that her heart was bound to China. "No one in Virginia really needs me," she wrote matter-of-factly.[11]

The killing days of pioneering were almost over in Shantung Province as well as in Richmond, where the Foreign Mission Board based its work. Miss Moon had been a pioneer in evolution of missions affairs on both sides of the Pacific. Now she was a tower of strength and wisdom by whom the rising generation could reckon.

China was tripping over its own feet in a rush to catch up with the twentieth century. During Miss Moon's thirty years there, China had telescoped two thousand years of modernization. The persistent push of missionaries had cracked the old educational system and was liberating the bound women. Within ten years, revolution would officially be the order of the day in China. The move among Sha-ling's leading citizens to replace an old pagan temple with a school building where Western subjects would be taught was a clear example of change.[12]

Southern Baptist missionaries were ready to adapt to their new opportunities. In the short months while Miss Moon was away, they had instituted major advances. A theological school was established in Tengchow under the grandfatherly hand of J. B. Hartwell and the scholarly hand of C. W. Pruitt. Within a few months, a training school for women church workers would also come into existence. A decided campaign was waged to develop an indigenous Chinese ministry and leadership.[13]

The Foreign Mission Board approved the building of the first Southern Baptist hospital. Financed largely by the First Baptist Church of Macon, Georgia, the Warren Memorial Hospital was being erected at Hwanghsien for the work of Dr. Ayers and Miss Pettigrew.[14]

The Chinese Baptists themselves formally organized to promote temperance, unbinding feet, evangelism, and Sunday School. On their own initiative they organized and supported schools.[15]

During this same period of Chinese modernization Southern Baptists and their Foreign Mission Board had buzzed through an intricate maze seeking a workable plan of missions. A theology of missions was becoming popularly accepted, and the writings of Miss Moon had helped to articulate it. The individual responsibility of every believer for the fate of untaught souls began to hang heavily over the Southern pulpits. A mission support and education emphasis in the local church, personified by Woman's Missionary Union which operated under the philosophy set down by Lottie Moon and Annie Armstrong, was producing missions involvement by steady pulse rather than by erratic impulse. The validity of the Foreign Mission Board itself had been tested in the Gospel Mission movement and had emerged with new luster.

Only a stable financial system was lacking, and the Christmas offering for foreign missions conducted by the women, along with their systematic emphasis on sacrificial giving, held promise of a better day. The Southern Baptist Convention formed a commitment to get would-be missionaries to the field, even on borrowed money. For each new arrival, appropriation was made for a comfortable American-style house.[16] The Convention was coming to a missions posture capable of bearing programs of massive proportions.

Miss Moon lost no time in adjusting her own career to this whirl of progress. While the demand of schools was at fever pitch, she returned to her original ambition for China—academic education. Schools restricted her somewhat to Tengchow, but she could still traverse the city and nearby countryside in short evangelistic trips.[17]

She called in her "teacher," Mr. Chiang, and got to work. Most missionaries, especially those involved in scholarly work, had a Chinese assistant who served as secretary. Chiang had been T. P. Crawford's personal assistant, and Miss Moon inherited him. Although Miss Moon continued to drill herself in Chinese studies under Chiang's direction, she would not spare the time necessary for perfection in the written language. Chiang helped her prepare lectures, printed materials, examinations, and correspondence. He was her go-between with the business world. He supervised workmen who built and repaired mission property. He bargained for purchases. He was her front man for evangelistic trips. In times past, when the self-support rule had been rigidly applied, Miss Moon paid her teacher out of her own pocket or did without. Now, in this more progressive day, the Foreign Mission Board contributed to his compensation.[18]

By April she was negotiating for the purchase of additional property on North Street, where her school for boys and girls was in session. As China became education hungry and her school improved in quality, grown men applied for admission. She organized other schools for girls.[19]

The students in the Memorial School not only studied six days a week, but also sat in Miss Moon's Sunday School and chapel services early Sunday morning. Then she walked them across the city for worship at the Tengchow Church on Monument Street. In the afternoon she taught yet another Sunday School at this church.

Also on the North Street site she opened a primary-level school for youngsters. The usual religious books were the basic curriculum, but to these she added a demanding course in geography, arithmetic, and Chinese classic literature.

The mission's girls' boarding school and the girls' school in P'ingtu ruled that feet must be unbound before admission. Lottie championed this rule as an ideal but was unwilling to enforce it in her own schools. She would turn away nobody. Girls who could not get into the more prestigious mission schools came to her.

"The school gives me great pleasure," she wrote. But she soon developed yet another ministry which touched her inmost heart. As soon as news of her return filtered through the villages, women hobbled on bound feet to her home at the Little Cross Roads. Some of them were her converts and her prospective converts from bygone travels. Others were baptismal candidates brought by Christian men who trusted Miss Moon's discreet and loving ways. All came seeking deeper instruction and spiritual comfort. These Miss Moon was delighted to give.

The row of Chinese-style guest rooms in her compound was steadily filled with as many as fifteen women and their children of all ages. Each stayed for many days, often a month. She taught these in the vacant moments of the day, prayed with them, led devotional services for them, rehearsed doctrine with them, played the organ for their singing. Believing that they needed ability to read if their Christian growth were to continue, she taught reading along with doctrine.

"The work has never been so satisfactory to me," she wrote Willingham. Yet she was going bankrupt feeding all those visitors. It never occurred to her to require payment for lodging and food or to ask the women to bring their own food. She considered them her guests. Often they had housed and fed her as she traveled the countryside. Virginia decency and Moon family custom required that hospitality be returned in China as much as it had been in the grand estates of Albemarle County. Never did Miss Moon hint that these women, some of them beggars, could be taking unfair advantage of her. To question their motives was not only beyond her hospitality, but was also foreign to her Christianity. The women came and stayed.

When their presence became too much of a financial drain, she did not throw them out; but she did appeal to Richmond for help. "It used to be a heavy burden financially," she wrote Willingham. "Now it is intolerable." She asked for a stipend for entertainment of inquirers. Willingham suggested that she get the request validated by her fellow-missionaries. This was difficult because others had neither her geo-graphical situation nor her attitude. Eventually, Willingham agreed to make her a special allowance, but she ceased to raise the issue. The end-less stream of guests was fed out of her own pocket. As the nearby Rus-sian-Japanese conflict drove prices out of the reach of common folk, Miss Moon simply put on a larger pot. She could not refuse old women and schoolchildren who were put out on the street. "It is delightful work," she wrote. In the first few months, three of the women guests professed faith in Jesus; but becoming a believer was not a requirement for sleeping on her spotless kangs or eating her millet."[20]

Also to the Little Cross Roads came transient missionaries. First to welcome her back was Mattie Dutton, who had fallen with a nervous breakdown at her post in P'ingtu. She stayed in Miss Moon's tender care for many weeks until Dr. Ayers ruled that she could not get better with-out distance from the field. Reluctantly, Miss Moon gave her up, for she considered her too valuable to lose. Miss Dutton never recovered enough to pass reentry.[21]

Other new missionaries were taking a firm grasp on the work. Miss Moon turned over an embryonic school to W. C. Newton, a new mis-sionary in Tengchow, and Jesse C. Owen was working the countryside with a school and with evangelism. They were entering doors Miss Moon had opened and were harvesting the fruit of her labors. "Our dear Miss Moon" had paved the road for Mary Willeford's school for training Bible women and women evangelists.[22]

The influx of new missionaries caused the Foreign Mission Board to require them to study the language for two years before undertaking any major responsibility. They also had to stand periodic examinations by other members of the mission. Some rebelled against this "dictatorial" attitude on the part of the Board, but not Miss Moon. She had seen too many married women unable to function and too many men broken down and discouraged by inability to cope. It was she who arranged teachers for newcomers, filled in and enriched language study with her scholarly view of the culture, and administered many of the examinations. At the same time, she believed in putting the newcomers to real mission work immediately. In the laboratory of Sunday School teaching and house-to-house visitation, the language came more quickly.[23]

One little shadow fell across her as she rose to grande dame status in North China. Someone in the Gospel Mission camp, which habitually criticized the Foreign Mission Board, its methods, and its personnel, put out the word in Georgia that Miss Moon was not teaching the Bible according to fundamental Southern Baptist tenets. Apparently the name of Toy, sufficient to cause panic in one realm of the Southern Baptist Convention, was invoked to cloud Miss Moon's good name. Two women took the accusation directly to R. J. Willingham, attributing it to Martha Foster Crawford.

Without disturbing Miss Moon, Willingham reacted in a low key, saying that never in thirty years had anyone hinted that Miss Moon's beliefs were in error. Mrs. Crawford was asked to explain. She said that Miss Moon had once declined to teach her catechism, but put the matter to rest by stating her confidence in Miss Moon and her regret that the Gospel Mission name had been involved.

Miss Moon retorted that Mrs. Crawford's catechism was taught cover to cover in her schools. She did not use the catechism in teaching country women as much as she used the book *Twenty Hymns,* containing prayers and the Ten Commandments. Both Miss Moon and Mrs. Crawford thought that any claims and past discussions were by now rusty with the passing of many years.

The New Lottie Moon Story

Willingham told the accusers, "Miss Moon may have differed with some ideas which Mrs. Crawford had, but that would not rule her out in the judgment of many people. Miss Moon may not have approved of all that was in Mrs. Crawford's catechism, but I have a number of catechisms of men where I did not approve of all that was in them." Lottie calmly wrote, "I have never taught contrary to the usual views of the Southern Baptists. I am trying in a very poor way, as I am aware, to lead the Chinese to the Lord Jesus. Deeply conscious of weakness and failure, I yield to none in devotion to the Lord." With that, the discussion ceased.[24]

The foreign community of Tengchow again erected its shelter at the beach in the summer of 1904. Their July 4 festivities there were rained out, but that did not disturb Miss Moon. She had gone ahead with her regular school examinations, as usual placing duty before pleasure. At other times she took afternoon walks to the beach and picnicked with the missionary circle.[25] The winter holidays of Thanksgiving and Christmas were also traditionally shared among the Presbyterian and Baptist missionaries.

"I am not equal to the rough country work," Miss Moon confessed in 1905, but she continued the village work to the south and west of Tengchow. Instead of taking lengthy trips, she answered the demands for more schools. The Memorial School now had fifty pupils enrolled. It was reaching the upper-class citizens she had long dreamed of penetrating. To upgrade school, she took expenses out of her own pocket until the Foreign Mission Board paid off its debt and could make allocations. She did not personally teach but served more as a principal. She cultivated friendships with the students. When one boy was baptized, she admitted, "The school is the joy of my heart."[26]

With her entry into the better city homes, she increased social and ministerial calls. For example, she arranged to welcome two new single women missionaries with a Chinese-style dinner hosted by three women of the official class. In return, the missionaries invited the Chinese official women to have an American-style dinner at their house.

Several new missionaries joined the North China team during 1905. Two of them, Ella Jeter and Ida Taylor, lived with Miss Moon for several months. With some awe, they undertook daily association with this legendary woman. That awe did not diminish as they became well acquainted. They began each day with devotions together. As Miss Moon read aloud from her Bible, the two young ladies cast glances at each other. Her reading did not match what their Bibles said. "What are you reading from?" one asked. "Oh, the Greek," Miss Moon replied, and continued her spontaneous translation. She demonstrated the same facility in reading freely from Greek into Chinese.[27]

Dr. and Mrs. Ayers' grown daughter, Lucy, came to join the mission family as soon as she graduated from college. This fun-loving young woman was salaried by the Foreign Mission Board, but not appointed as a missionary. She became a fast friend of the elder woman of the mission. Often she would ride over to Miss Moon's from Hwanghsien to break her hunger for social contact. To this young associate, part missionary and part adolescent, Miss Moon revealed a relaxed side. Together they explored Tengchow.

If Miss Moon noticed Lucy admiring a colorful curio, she would quickly purchase it for her as a gift. At the Little Cross Roads Lucy could share her small pleasures. "You see that I have rearranged the shelves. Can you guess why?" Miss Moon might ask. "To show off the Chinese things separately from the American?" would come Lucy's analysis. "Right you are!" Miss Moon would exclaim.

If the cook was away, Miss Moon would take Lucy across the courtyard to the kitchen to stir up cookies. Preparing tea, she might lovingly arrange and rearrange cookies on the plates. "Which side do you think is prettier?" she would wonder aloud. "Let's see. I'll first eat this brown spot, then save the prettiest part of the cookie till last."[28] Simple, almost childlike, was her delight in the ordinary when shared with a congenial friend. A woman who had held mind and spirit together with almost nothing was frugal with opportunities for pleasure.

Very seldom did this soft underside show. To most of her co-workers, new and old, she was a refuge of amazing strength, a place to turn in time of trouble and indecision. Even the Hartwells, who occasionally showed some resentment that Miss Moon was so beloved and well known, quoted her authority when major decisions were to be made.[29]

Ella Jeter, Lottie Moon, Jessie Pettigrew, 1907
(Ruth C. Thornhill)

Tengchow's standing as a city was crumbling into China's past. When the government abolished the old form of literary exams as a basis for civil employment, Tengchow's star ceased to shine. The Presbyterians almost abandoned the station; and Baptists would have too, except for Miss Moon's insistence. She would not give up on cold aristocrats who had never yet spoken to her—not when she had just won the first convert in her neighborhood![30]

But the mission did vote to move the booming theological school to Hwanghsien, a more prosperous and agreeable city. That relocation took Mr. Hartwell and his daughter (Mrs. Hartwell had died), the Pruitts, and the Newtons away. Miss Hartwell turned over the girls' boarding school to Miss Moon, who was left with all the responsibility for Tengchow. Her only co-workers were Misses Taylor and Jeter, who were still in training.

While coping with the constant complexities of the boarding school, she saw enrollment in her own two schools climb. Government schools were becoming more competitive, as they paid students for attendance. However, government schools required Confucian worship, so the mission was eager to counterattack with a Christian alternative.

Meanwhile, her own homeplace was alive with activity. Chinese women continued to seek shelter and instruction in her rooms. One was a schoolgirl from twenty years earlier, now fallen on hard times. "I feel very sorry for her and am glad for her to have a rest from household and farm cares for a few days," Miss Moon wrote, while the woman's children amused Lottie and drove everybody else crazy with noisy play.[31] The financial strain of entertainment eased when the Board restored salaries to six hundred dollars, a move the missionaries had requested in 1902.

Schoolwork was cutting into Miss Moon's evangelistic work more than she liked. She repeatedly claimed to prefer evangelistic visiting among all other work, and she took quick steps to turn over the boarding school to Miss Taylor. Misses Taylor and Jeter set up their own residence at the school and gradually assumed its control by the end of 1906.[32]

Meanwhile, Miss Moon had cause to be nervous about the return rise of Boxers. In other parts of China rebellion was rampant, and Tengchow was threatened with another serious siege of antiforeign, antichristian persecution. As the senior missionary in the area, she felt it necessary to break her perfect official silence on matters between church and state. She wrote to John Fowler, consul at Chefoo, with information she had discovered about a secret antiforeign group in Tengchow.[33]

As rumors grew more alarming, she thought of protective measures for the missionaries. Hwanghsien hospital had been left with a set of young missionaries, Miss Pettigrew and Mr. and Mrs. Edgar Morgan, when Dr. Ayers went on furlough. The skeleton Ayers used in teaching was left on display. Miss Moon was horrified at what the Boxers might do if they saw the skeleton. Rebellious Chinese had killed missionaries for as little as eating pickled onions, which they thought to be babies' eyes; the sight of broken baby dolls had been known to drive the suspicious into hysteria. She wrote a hurried and forceful order to get rid of the skeleton.

The young missionaries knew she meant business. That night, by dim lantern light, they took the skeleton into an unfinished room of the hospital. The three young people feverishly worked to move a stack of bricks. In the earth beneath they buried the skeleton, then replaced the bricks. They notified Miss Moon that no Boxer would ever find it.[34]

Fortunately, the dreaded trouble did not materialize in the regions of North China missionaries, and new progress was made in the churches. The mission voted for Mr. Pruitt to devote himself to the preparation of Bible and theological studies in Chinese. Miss Moon greatly favored this move and donated works to Pruitt from her own library.

The delight of early 1907 was the visit of Mrs. Crawford, Miss Moon's oldest colleague. The two had corresponded through the fourteen years since Mr. Crawford had led the Gospel Mission group to Taian, but they had seen each other only briefly during the exodus through Chefoo during the Boxer Rebellion. Now Mr. Crawford was dead, and his widow had returned to China to complete the work to which she had been clearly called. Possibly Mrs. Crawford was in Tengchow to clear the way for the Gospel Mission defectors to return to the Foreign Mission Board fold, as most of them eventually did on her recommendation. She rode into Tengchow on her specially-made wheelbarrow and stayed with Miss Moon. The seventy-seven-year-old visitor led a series of evangelistic meetings for women.[35]

During this period Miss Moon was joined in her evangelistic visiting by a Chinese Bible woman, Mrs. Kiang. She was one of Miss Moon's converts from the country and was now supported by the Woman's Missionary Society of the Tengchow Church. She made a helpful co-worker as Miss Moon gained entrance to the city homes. The two evangelists divided their audience according to age, with Miss Moon taking the older women.[36]

While Miss Pettigrew was visiting in Tengchow, she and Miss Jeter conspired to have a photograph taken of the famous Miss Moon. Miss Pettigrew's mother wanted a picture of Miss Moon, and of course there was none. A photographer was engaged, and Miss Moon was persuaded to cooperate. The young women brought out a chair and placed it in front of the flowers in the courtyard. Then they helped the tiny woman scoot back in the big chair. She was wearing a prim shirtwaist and black skirt of American style, as she was now sometimes inclined to do during hot weather. As the photographer took aim, the young women attempted to slip out of the picture. They were brought back by Miss Moon's sharp question, "And where are you going?" Thanks to Miss Pettigrew, Miss Jeter, and their families, the photo was widely copied and preserved. For many years it was the only published likeness of Miss Moon.[37]

When the July rainy season came, Lottie Moon declared her usual rest period. She was alone in the city for some weeks while the other missionaries were here and there across the province. With her little pet dog, she lazily read the days away, thankful for the steamy moisture. She wrote Edmonia that the dryness of the preceding months had been trying to her. Not only had she come to fear drought because of the famine which often followed, but also because the dryness kept her from sleeping. To fend off dryness, she drenched her hair in cold water or wrapped her head in a wet towel. Miss Moon was always a good Baptist, never afraid of water. When caught out in a rainstorm, she was always the last to raise her ever-present umbrella. Chinese took super-stitious offense at a person who opened an umbrella too early in a drizzle, and she always bowed to such custom. To her, umbrellas were primarily useful for shielding herself from the sun, for protecting her-self, for pounding the floor to emphasize a point, and for gaining a little visual privacy in a crowd.[38]

Late in October of 1907, the mission was twirling with excitement over the anticipated visit of secretary R. J. Willingham. No Foreign Mission Board official had ever toured the Orient. Willingham may have been lured in this direction by the expectation of visiting his mis-sionary son in Japan.

The meeting of the association, now renamed Shantung Baptist Asso-ciation because of the spreading work, was scheduled to coincide with his appearance. It was to be in Tengchow, but an outbreak of meningi-tis in the schools forced the meeting to Hwanghsien at the last minute. Miss Moon traveled there for the exciting occasion.

Soon after the meningitis scare, Tengchow was struck by an outbreak of bubonic plague. Fear of it hung over the city during Christmas, when Lottie quietly opened cards and remembrances at home. She engaged a man to give her yard a thorough cleaning in order to deter plague-carrying rats; then she fled to Hwanghsien for three weeks.[39]

Foreign Mission Board appointments to North China continued to climb. New appointees bypassed Tengchow and went to more produc-tive fields toward the interior. Miss Moon laughed with a touch of irony when she read early in 1908 that the Board had passed a rule requiring two men missionaries in every station. "I am painfully aware that there is no man in Tengchow to bear the burdens that rightfully should fall on masculine shoulders," she wrote.[40]

Miss Taylor had responsibility for the girls' boarding school and assisted to some extent with evangelistic and church work. But the heaviest workload in Tengchow was Miss Moon's. She now ran three or four day schools with students in excess of sixty, counseled a steady stream of visitors, taught the women who now came in somewhat organized classes to her homeplace, oversaw two Sunday Schools in dif-ferent ends of the city, and kept the church going between the monthly calls of a missionary pastor. All this she did not consider her main work, which was still to visit women systematically in the city and in a rim of country villages. It was fear that the Presbyterians would take over their productive village work that caused Miss Moon to write sternly to Richmond.

J. B. Hartwell, on furlough in the United States, wrote the same cautions to Willingham. Ayers had alerted him that Miss Moon needed help and Hartwell said, "Misses Moon and Taylor hold the fort for the native Christians. There is not even a native pastor. Miss Moon, our oldest lady missionary in Shantung, loved and honored by both natives and foreigners for the noble, persistent, and successful work she has been doing all these long years, is now like myself, older than she was thirty-five years or more ago. I feel that this is a crying need, an imperative need."[41]

But she was not to receive help yet. In fact, she was to receive a further burden. Miss Taylor had been for some months losing her health in the strain of work. On her way home from an exhausting country tour, already ill and vulnerable, she collapsed in her shentze and wrapped a wet towel around her head, as taught by Miss Moon. When the mules paused, a strange old man thrust into her shentze a child covered with smallpox. This exposure, added to other exposures and to unbroken exhaustion, brought Miss Taylor nearly to her death in early the summer of 1908. She was diagnosed as having three different forms of smallpox all at once.

There was nobody to care for her but Miss Moon. For three weeks, day and night, the sixty-eight-year-old trouper fought almost alone for Miss Taylor's life. "It was beautiful to see Miss Moon, with her silvered hair, assume the burden of nursing," Newton wrote, as the self-forgetting feat passed into the memory book of North China missions. Florence Jones, a new missionary nurse studying Chinese in Hwangh-sien answered Miss Moon's call for help. In six-hour shifts they tended the unconscious form, pulling sheets from the bleeding sores, washing the blinded eyes, trickling nourishment down the inflamed throat.

Lottie knew that she herself had overdone and needed to rest. As she was scrubbing her hair and disinfecting herself, she quipped to Miss

Jones, "I'd rather go home than to heaven!"[43] She left Miss Jones to complete the cure. Miss Taylor, a virtual invalid for many months, eventually had to leave her post. To Willingham, Miss Moon sent a stiff letter asking the Board not to allow missionaries to come to the field without a smallpox vaccination.[44] Returning to her home, Lottie was in quarantine for weeks, her loneliness proving more a strain than the physical work of nursing.

In the fall, she alone reopened all the Tengchow schools. The Foreign Mission Board granted two thousand dollars for improving the girls' boarding school building, and she led in operating the school until help arrived in February 1909.

The closer China moved to Western-style modernization, the greater came the demand for learning the English language. Miss Moon began teaching English personally in the Memorial School. This move brought a constant stream of requests from men wishing to study. She had a struggle to keep these from eating up her wisely guarded time for rest. One man who taught English himself pestered her for lessons every Saturday. He brought books in fine print that hurt Lottie's eyes, then wanted to sit uncomfortably close beside her while she checked his reading. "I would not come so close to any man!" she confided to Eddie. "I suppose he thinks I would look over the little books that I detest with a foreigner, but I would not unless he were my brother." Another man pressed for English lessons two afernoons a week. She declined with explanation that she must have her afternoons open for evangelistic visiting. So he watched her street door faithfully. If she did not go out, he knocked persistently. She firmly continued to decline and stopped teaching English altogether as soon as possible.[45]

With great relief and pleasure, Miss Moon began welcoming a new succession of workers late in 1908. In October came Dr. and Mrs. James McFadden Gaston. Dr. Gaston had been an active Presbyterian in Atlanta when he heard a Baptist pastor speak of Miss Lottie Moon with such reverence and fervor that he was moved to pray for her frequently from that time. For ten years he remembered her story as he became a Baptist and a missions volunteer. Then Mrs. Gaston had the opportunity for a personal visit with Miss Moon in Fork Union, Virginia, during the 1903-04 furlough.[46]

As the doctor arrived in China, his first wish was to see this woman who had figured into his calling to China. The Gastons arrived by the little steamer which now ran along the coastline between Chefoo and Tengchow. Miss Moon sent a bright schoolboy with a memorized speech in English to escort the new missionaries to the Little Cross Roads. She stood on her veranda with outstretched arms to welcome the couple and invited them to spend their first weeks of orientation with her. They were then to move on to Laichowfu to open the third Southern Baptist hospital in North China.[47]

Miss Moon by now was accomplished at reducing the entry shock for new missionaries. She tucked them into spotless, comfortable beds with good mosquito nets; fed them gigantic Virginia biscuits and four-course meals, properly served on patched and repatched table linens. She drilled them in customs and introduced them to the language.[48]

Dr. Gaston figured that her age was seventy-five. (The years in China had faded the bloom of youth more rapidly than the calendar had.) But he judged her to be in very good health with good hearing and eyesight. Considering her age, which was actually sixty-eight, he was amazed at her dawn-to-dark work schedule. He saw her orchestrating schools, teaching, proclaiming the gospel. But, he sensed that she was maneuvering more and more of her work into her own compound to avoid the rigors of travel.[49]

Dr. and Mrs. Gaston were particularly impressed with the standing Miss Moon had achieved in the community. "Law Moo Guniang"—Old Miss Moon, or Revered Miss Moon—everybody seemed to know her. Within sight was her dream of reaching the scholarly class in Tengchow. Gaston knew that she had rare qualifications for this task.

No sooner had the Gastons been weaned and sent on to Laichowfu than another greenhorn arrived. Wayne Womack Adams, a tall young bachelor, came to China because the story of Miss Moon alone in Tengchow had been told in the halls of The Southern Baptist Theological Seminary. Now he was here to become a permanent part of her Tengchow scene. He spent his first night in her American-style guest room. At dawn he spotted in the next row of rooms an old beggar woman, one of Miss Moon's permanent guests. For nearly a year he semiboarded with Miss Moon. He had his own residence, which Miss Moon had prepared a short distance from her home, but he took his meals at the Little Cross Roads, splitting the cost with her. He recognized from the start that he was getting much more than good cooking in this arrangement. He was also getting an education. Miss Moon selected a Chinese name for Mr. Adams and immediately "invited" a teacher to work with him.[50]

On Adams's first Sunday at Tengchow Church, W. C. Newton came over from Hwanghsien to preach. Unexpectedly, he called on the newcomer for announcements in church. "I'll ask Miss Moon," he said, and dutifully sped around the curtain that divided the men's seating from the women's. Miss Moon sensed that he was coming and headed him off with her trusty open umbrella. "Mr. Adams, this will not do. The first rule of life in China is that men do not enter where women are." She never mentioned the incident again. After she dropped a clue for a new missionary, she never nagged. Adams survived the humiliation and in this fashion learned quickly to honor Chinese custom.

He wrote glowing letters to his fiancée, Miss Floy White, who was completing her studies at Woman's Missionary Union Training School. He told her of a class of thirteen non-Christian women living and studying for three weeks in Miss Moon's Chinese guest rooms. Some of these would have been regular school students had it not been for their parents' refusal to unbind their feet. One of this class asked for baptism before the course ended. Miss Moon's diplomacy was demonstrated when she prevented a Christian girl student from being sold as a concubine. She did it with "skill and firmness," Adams told Miss White.

Their dinner-table conversation was always stimulating. Miss Moon not only read the daily newspaper from Shanghai, but she studied it carefully, comparing all the dispatches until she formed her own opinions to discuss with Adams. They ate by the light of kerosene lanterns. If Miss Moon did not have a complicated evening schedule, she would invite the young man to linger for talk in the living room, where she burned tallow candles—the most inexpensive form of lighting. But Adams was a good guest. When he heard the cook complete the kitchen cleanup, he made his exit so the house and wall could be properly locked for the night.

One evening the house next door, unoccupied, caught fire. Flames spread to the roof of a building in Miss Moon's compound. Adams went to the rescue while neighbors stood back and expressed their hostile belief that the foreigners were getting what they deserved. Christian people came to help, as did men from the mandarin's court. When the fire on Miss Moon's side of the wall was put out—with slight damage—Adams and the Christians went to the aid of the neighboring property. This move impressed the bystanders favorably, especially when they understood that the fire had originated on Chinese property.[51]

About this time Miss Moon experienced an outbreak of neighbor children calling her and other foreigners "devil." If she couldn't get an opening to neighbor homes on a positive note, she would make an entrance on a negative note. This she did, to ask the neighbors to teach their children mannerly obedience to the law which forbade use of this curse.

At Christmastime the Tengchow missionaries were invited to celebrate with the families at Hwanghsien. Adams was hungry for a home-style observance. Miss Moon was also pleased with the invitation and had her transportation waiting at the gate when a problem arose. She sent Adams ahead while she stayed home alone to attend to duty. Although the foreign community at Tengchow usually ate roast goose together on Thanksgiving and Christmas, Lottie Moon never allowed these to distract her from emergencies in her work.

At Miss Moon's hands, Adams made a quick adjustment to China. He told the Foreign Mission Board, "I like the Chinese people. In fact I admire them far beyond what I expected. I don't know how I would ever have gotten along these six months without the kind and most helpful counsel of Miss Lottie Moon. She is one of the nobility and we all love her. And how the Chinese love her is beautiful to see."[52]

When Adams reported for mealtime on January 11, 1909, he found Miss Moon strangely disturbed. He knew that something was troubling her but was too polite to ask what. She did not discuss her personal affairs with others, and he would not risk offending. Not until years later did he understand the cause of gloom that made the old hands tremble and the eyes cloudy.

The New Lottie Moon Story

Her nephew, Luther Andrews, had written of Edmonia Moon's death. This beloved little sister had moved to Starke, Florida, approximately two years earlier. She had attended but not joined the local Baptist congregation, appreciating their missionary society. She had purchased a lot and built a tiny board and batten cottage. Her very few close acquaintances considered her a near-pauper who was sick and moody. In many ways her life was still in China, being lived through her sister. Every week for thirty-one years she wrote Lottie cheerful letters which were answered frequently. She corresponded occasionally with relatives in Virginia. Rarely she would dispatch a question or tidbit of advice to the Foreign Mission Board, which continued to take small loans from her. Her introverted life seemed filled with regrets and with an unfulfilled search for holiness. "Surely God has not put us here to exist—to suffer and to enjoy; but he has a work for each one," she wrote longingly in 1887. On November 19, 1908, lying in bed with woolen covers pulled over her, she put a gun to her head and died. Just days before, she had written a chatty letter to her relatives, full of proud reports on Sister Lottie's heroic deeds in China.[53]

With Edmonia went Lottie's closest relative and dearest love on earth. Already she had lost her brother, Isaac, and oldest nephew, Tom Moon, whom she had loved with little contact since before the Civil War. Lottie Moon was progressively being cut off from the stakes which held her to this world.

Now all the correspondence from her nephews in Roanoke concerned business and tragedy. Edmonia had been embalmed without permission, and the nephews wished to sue to avoid payment. Lottie preferred to pay. Edmonia had been given a tearless funeral after her nephew had ordered her body switched from a fine coffin to a cheap wooden one. Lottie's response was stoic. No emotion at all was betrayed to those in America. Emotion was betrayed but not shared with those in China. The news was not as great a shock as it might have been, she wrote Luther, because she had missed letters from Eddie for three mails.[54]

Although Lottie was Edmonia's heir, and she should have come into a small inheritance, she was persuaded to turn it over to the executor,

Floy White Adams (FMB)

W. W. Adams (FMB)

Tengchow Mission about 1908-10 (Standing left to right) William Carey Newton, James Boardman

Isaac Andrews, to settle his costs. She tersely wrote the Foreign Mission Board that the annuity which had been paid quarterly to Edmonia would now be payable to her. She wanted the first few quarters' checks to go to the Roanoke nephews.[55]

Miss Moon turned her remaining strength into the work, and she swallowed her sorrows in order to speak happiness to others. As hostility became more open in the streets of Tengchow, she was able to turn it to friendliness. North China reported 16 churches, 56 schools with more than 1,000 students, 42 native men evangelists, 14 women evangelists, and more than 2,000 church members. Among the schools were Miss Moon's Memorial School for boys and men, a boys' school taught in classic style in the country, and a rapidly growing girls' school.[56] But a lid was about to be clamped on this progress, as enlargement outstripped funds. The Foreign Mission Board closed its financial year in 1909 with a debt of $32,000.[57]

In the excitement of a Convention, the Baptists would vote a budget for advancement of work. Then by a most informal system, paid agents in each state convention were to raise an apportioned amount of the total budget. It was a risky system. Churches of the era had no consistent plan for designating money to foreign missions. Only a personal visit from a foreign mission agent or Board member would cause a church to take a collection for missions. If the agent of another Baptist cause had recently harvested in that church, the mission collection would be small. Tithing and systematic giving on a personal level were being promoted by WMU, but had not come into vogue. Contributions increased every year, but not at the same rate that the Board had been authorizing expenditures. Expecting the funds to come in, the Board would borrow money, such as it had done from Edmonia Moon. During the month of April, with the help of some of the Baptist newspapers, the Board tried to whip the constituents into a heated frenzy of emergency giving. Sometimes it cleared the debts before the SBC met in May. This year it did not. The burden of this debt crushed on Miss Moon and her colleagues with much more damage than it did on the typical Southern Baptist. As soon as she settled affairs about Edmonia's estate, she turned the quarterly annuity payment over to the Foreign Mission Board for debt clearance.[58]

Jane Lide (FMB)

As predicted, the Gospel Mission system was breaking up. The death of Mrs. Crawford ended its cohesivensss. The supporting churches were too stingy, Miss Moon told Willingham. She urged that the Board assume support of the missionaries and the field they had opened in West Shantung. The Board welcomed back a number of missionaries and further increased its need for funds.[59]

The Board was already committed to sending out a group of young women who had just completed their work at the WMU Training School. While a group of them were praying one day at the school, asking God's guidance for their future work, Mrs. Maude R. McLure, the principal, called them for a conference. She had received a plea from the Foreign Mission Board for helpers to work with Miss Moon in China. The girls readily took this as an answer to their prayer. In May 1909 Jane Lide and Jewell Legett were appointed, as was Floy White, who was pledged to marry W. W. Adams in China. With Mr. and Mrs. J. V. Turner, they landed in Tengchow in October.[60]

Miss Moon had been preparing eagerly for the arrival of the future Mrs. Adams, and the entire North China mission welcomed the rare circumstance of a wedding. Miss Moon ordered that it be a proper Christian occasion as an example to the Chinese. She helped Adams prepare his house with red decorations befitting a Chinese bride. He went off to escort his beloved from Japan, while Miss Moon completed wedding plans.

She had sedan chairs waiting at the beach for the new arrivals, and she took the bride-to-be into her own house and gave up her own bed. For a week she pampered Miss White and assisted with her preparations. In Chinese propriety, the bride remained behind closed doors and did not see her future home. Miss Moon strictly chaperoned the brief visits between the lovers. On October 28, 1909, the wedding party and guests gathered, many of them staying in Presbyterian missionary homes.

At 4:30 Miss Moon flurried into her courtyard, having been busy with the wedding dinner at the Adams' home. There she beheld the wedding party. Adams had come for the bride with a beautiful new sedan chair—his gift to her. He was ready to escort her away. Standing nearby were two bridesmaids, Jewell Legett and Janie Lide. They were wearing their very best, newest, WMU Training School commencement dresses. Miss Moon's face dropped at the sight of the maids. "You're not going out of my house in those clothes!" she exclaimed.

"But Miss Moon, they're all we have," the girls said. The stylish tight dresses outlined girlish young figures perfectly. Miss Moon stood aghast while the wedding party sailed out of her gate, through a throng of Chinese onlookers, to the Adams house.

Only later did the young ladies understand Miss Moon's embarrassment. The dresses made them look immoral to Chinese eyes. The Chinese carefully disguised the female form under loose cloaks which Miss Moon had come to favor. A few years earlier she had instructed Miss Pettigrew never again to wear a certain modest, but form-fitting, pink dress. The mortified young lady, sure that she was forever disgraced for having worn the dress while playing the organ at church, packed it deeply into her trunk. For years it lay there until she had worn out every other dress. Fearfully she put the offending frock on for a mission meeting. Miss Moon, who by this time had been to America for a furlough, greeted her by saying, "Oh, my dear, how sweet you look!"[61]

Dresses were forgotten as Dr. Ayers gave the bride away. Dr. T. O. Hearn of P'ingtu, a native of Miss Floy's home state of Alabama, performed the ceremony. S. E. Stephens of Laichowfu was best man. The WMU Training School graduates, including Alice Huey of Laichow, sang the benediction from the ninety-first Psalm, which they had learned at Training School.

Miss Moon, Miss Taylor, and Mrs. Mary L. King, who had recently joined from the Gospel Mission group, had prepared the seated dinner for twenty guests. Soup, fish, and salad; goose and vegetables; tea and coffee; dessert and candies—it was an elegant meal lasting until late evening. The young people thought that Miss Moon did not approve of some of the rougher teasing in the toasts, but later they realized that she left the party early simply because she was exhausted.

Miss Moon had lost her boarder, but she had gained a valuable co-worker in Floy Adams. The young woman soon took over one of Miss Moon's boys' schools. The elder stateswoman insisted that the couple hire a young man as a cook. He smoked opium, but Miss Moon thought he could be reformed. She was right; he later became a preacher. Miss Moon trained Mrs. Adams in the proprieties of a witnessing visit—how to bow, sit on the kang, direct the conversation, and use the printed props. The Adamses adored Miss Moon and suspected that she tenderly saw in them the fulfillment of her own sacrificed marriage. She was their only guest for their first anniversary celebration.

Miss Moon also was training Janie Lide, who was to take Miss Taylor's place at the boarding school. She tried to plant in these new women the ultimate missionary capacity—to identify with the people of China. She drilled harshly—some thought too harshly—on details of grammar, dress, and manners. Some appreciated her purpose in rigidly enforcing etiquette.

"It is comparatively easy to give oneself to mission work, but it is not easy to give oneself to an alien people. Yet, the latter is much better and truer work than the former. It includes the former and goes beyond it. It is the difference between the letter and the spirit," she taught from experience.[62]

Miss Moon poured all her skill into Janie Lide, who had admired the elder missionary from her childhood. She steadily exposed her to village life and taught her the tricks of the visitation trade. One day she ordered her chair bearers to put her down, then ordered Jane's chair down. "What is it, Miss Moon?" Jane asked. "It's good-bye," Miss Moon quipped, and settled back in her chair. With a word to the bearers, Lottie was off; and Jane was left to cope with a rowdy group of village children jabbering questions, examining her hands, peeking under her dress, and giving her the classic foreigner's introduction to the country. As Miss Moon had predicted, Janie laughed and had a good time.

Another day, Miss Moon assigned to Janie half the women in a large group and dispatched her to the far end of the hall to teach them. While Miss Moon taught her own group, she listened to Miss Lide's progress. Afterward, the elder woman called Miss Lide aside, with serious face. "Well, we will not be working together any longer," she began. "Oh, Miss Moon. What did I do?" Jane anxiously asked. "You did beautifully, my dear. With so many people needing the gospel, it is wasteful for us to work together. From now on you will work independently of me."[63]

As a trainer of "baby missionaries" she could be at the same time abrupt and patient, determined and flexible. Having suffered to establish certain methods of work, she was willing to let the younger generation make its own mistakes in strategy.[64] She awed some women missionaries into silence—those who did not intend to be more than housekeepers for their husband.[65] But the willing ones she encouraged and personally trained. She coached Mrs. Turner in "Jesus Loves Me" in Chinese, then applauded her halting success in teaching a family. When two little girls of the family enrolled in school, Mrs. Turner was given all the credit.[66]

With her open door she soothed out the shock of homesickness. She taught the wives how to achieve American cooking with an illiterate Chinese cook and unknown ingredients. She protected the young ones from being crushed by responsibilities beyond their readiness. In Mr. Adams's case she said, "I will not let him take responsibility that will break him down prematurely."[67]

She gave advice for physical survival. She warned the foolish young not to eat the tempting local apricots, then cured the dysentery of the disobedient. She ordered them to walk with slow Chinese dignity, then showed them how to discipline every minute to make haste slowly. She fussed if they forgot to wear their pith helmets outside, then toughened them to preach in the sun for hours on end. To Miss Legett's question about the tomatoes ripening in her dining room window, she said, "I eat one every day and sleep fifteen minutes after lunch. Try it!"[68]

Most importantly, she contagiously lived out her respect for the Chinese people. "When in China, I give the road. I am a guest here." "We invite a teacher. We do not employ one." W. C. Newton always recalled, "She taught me to appreciate Chinese custom."[69]

To one she said, "Write. Write at least a half-hour each day. Write constantly to America of the need of these dear people for Christ."[70]

And through it all she showed her own humanity, her need for forgiveness, and her capacity to forgive. "I can't control my own temper and I am not prepared to control others," she told Miss Lide, and thus passed to her capable young hands the prestigious girls' boarding school. One young missionary said, "She was so free of malice and self-seeking, and her piety was so deep and strong."[71]

Miss Moon radiated such strength and stamina that her young co-workers placed her on an ever rising pedestal. Mrs. T. O. Hearn visited her for three days and could only call the experience an inspiration. She recognized Miss Moon as a pioneer who seemed miraculously translated into the modern age. "She lives alone and works every day," Mrs. Hearn wrote. "Aside from her school work, she does country work, which is the hardest work a missionary has to do.

"Her home and manner of living is plain and it seemed to me un-suited to a lady of such rare intellect, education, and refinement—like a diamond in a setting of silver. And yet, as I noted with interest the gentle dignity with which she performed her daily duties, and the plea-sure she took, I realized that although she is a woman of rare attain-ments and would be an ornament to society in America, she is not out of place in China. The love of Christ which fills her heart makes her well fitted to live among her less enlightened sisters and lead them out of their narrow groove into the broader life of light and happiness in a Savior's love."[72]

When Mrs. Hearn worked Miss Moon's old field of P'ingtu, where seven churches now were prospering, she stumbled across old women who had been singing Miss Moon's hymns and repeating Bible verses for twenty years, waiting for someone to return to baptize them. "We reap what others have sown," she recognized.[73]

When the Shantung Baptist Association met in 1910, and the mission met in conjunction, Miss Moon joined the group traveling to Chefoo. The rewards of that meeting must have thrilled the one who had worked hardest for them. A large crowd of second-and third-generation Christians participated. Nine new missionaries were introduced, and two of them were already speaking Chinese. It was a pivotal meeting, and all eyes turned to J. B. Hartwell, feeble, frail, the elder statesman. He recounted historic times. However, Miss Moon, with the same number of years in China and only five fewer years of age, was regarded as a yet active part of the future.[74]

Dr. Gaston presided over the mission meeting. Miss Moon quietly listened to the debates. When she had formed her opinion on the question, her eyes would dance sharply, and Gaston would recognize her. She rose to debate with objective skill and took part efficiently in committee work. The tense topic of the meeting was whether to cooperate in an interdenominational university. Gaston admired the logical way she presented her views in favor of limited cooperation. Her position was an unpopular one and she lost the argument gracefully when the group ruled out cooperation.[75]

Though her co-workers hardly noticed, Miss Moon was slowing down. The Gastons came to her for relaxation in the summer. They sat in rocking chairs and steamer chairs on the veranda, Mrs. Gaston listening in while her husband and Miss Moon covered all history, biography, and current events in their conversations. The Gastons thought they were drawing strength from her, but she was undoubtedly drawing more from them.[76] Her eyes were no longer able to work by candlelight. To keep pace was a challenge, but she still covered eighteen nearby country villages, visited every afternoon, and monitored the work of young missionaries.

The successful Memorial School now had a faculty of three excellent teachers and a select upper-class clientele. Over much opposition she insisted on teaching the Chinese classics along with the Christian and Western academic courses. She retained as her own special pets five different schools for girls, three of which met in her compound simultaneously. "I love them more than I can tell you," Miss Moon said of the schoolgirls. "It is a delight to have them in my home place. These are my jewels." With the Memorial School for men and boys, her forty-year dream of superior education was being realized. With the girls' schools she saw the hope for Chinese women of the future. The sweet dregs of her life were being tasted in her own courtyard, which was overrun with children.[77]

She had always had a special communications link with children, perhaps because she was so near their size. When the Newton children had opportunity to choose the guest whom they wished to invite for Christmas, "Aunt Lottie" was their immediate candidate. This woman, when past age sixty-five, sat on the floor with them, carried them on her back playing horse, told fascinating stories, and brought presents. Even if she did tend to say, "Speak up, child," and frown sternly, she made the children feel importantly loved.[78]

A child who picked flowers from her ever-blooming yard was slightly corrected, then told to pick all he wanted. Children who peered inquisitively at the window were invited in for a visit. The cook freely doled out cookies from a bottomless jar. Pet dogs roamed at will among the playmates. This merriment touched her chords of delight. Her only sorrow was to see so many of the girls trying to run with bound feet.

Crepe myrtle and other trees shaded her yards. One was a perfect climbing tree with a swing hanging from its branches. One day a favorite boy fell from the tree and was picked up dead. Her heart was crushed. Her ministries and apologies to the boy's mother were directed as well to her own self. The tree was butchered, never again to tempt the young. But the Little Cross Roads house was still a playground.[79]

The children of her nieces and nephews appealed to her as well. As "the pauses" came more frequently, she wondered about them and hoped to see them someday. Her furlough was due early in 1913—"if I should live"—but she persisted in delaying the date of departure. She would be needed to keep the schools until Miss Taylor returned. She would not want to miss this event or that.

She had struck up a frequent correspondence with a grandniece whom she had never seen, the granddaughter of her brother Tom. Mattie Moon lived in McAlester, Oklahoma. As Lottie Moon tried to figure how she would pass a year in a strange land among virtual strangers, she calculated that she would board a few months in Mc-Alester, stay awhile in Roanoke, then journey on to see sister-in-law Mag in Crewe. Although she wrote about furlough, her heart was not in it. She showed much more expectation in the fantasy she was promoting with Luther Andrews. She hoped he would bring his children on a long visit to China.[80]

It was appropriate that Miss Moon's pioneer career should last through the great revolution in which the old Manchu dynasty was deposed in favor of a republic. Although decidedly a revolutionist herself, Miss Moon kept a strict image of neutrality in conservative Teng-chow, where the aristocracy and official class were imperialists. As hostilities broke out, so did the plague. Her schools had to close, and Lottie paid the twelve-dollar fee for an inoculation. She was placed in a lonely month-long quarantine which isolated her from cheering influences.[81] The plague and the war drove prices up unmercifully. Miss Moon wrote the Foreign Mission Board to send the annuity payments for certain quarters to her. "In times of famine and revolution one sometimes feels the need for money more than usually," she simply said.[82]

Famine broke out in Central China. It did not immediately appear in Shantung, but the effect rippled prices. Miss Moon was unusually sensitive to the descriptions of famine she read in the Shanghai papers. Her letters to America graphically and urgently pleaded for contributions to relieve the suffering. To her nephew, Isaac, she wrote as if she were at the moment actually seeing the scene, "Fancy people dying on the streets and by the roadside simply for lack of food. I was thinking a good deal about the famine in Anhui when suddenly the plague swooped down on us here. Last night, a Shanghai paper, no, not last-night, but recently, sent my thoughts back to the famine . . . . Possibly,

The New Lottie Moon Story

if I should live until then, I may see you in 1913."[83]

To Luther she wrote prophetically, "How can we bear to sit down to our bountiful tables and know of such things and not bestir ourselves to help? I hope you know that missionaries not only give their money, but give their lives to help the famine stricken. Hardly ever did I know of a famine that did not claim its victims among missionaries."[84]

While plague and famine in China snapped at her usual cheerful spirits, the Foreign Mission Board debt dashed her optimism. The Convention year began in June 1911 with an unprecedented, overwhelming debt of $89,000. This was equal to almost one-fifth of the total budget of foreign missions.

Lottie Moon was not the only missionary horrified at this staggering amount. C. W. Pruitt wrote to R. J. Willingham, "We are weighted down by the debt and are praying daily." Missionaries commonly made jokes to each other about the perils of living on borrowed money.[85]

Willingham, who now had 273 missionaries to correspond with, no longer had time to write chatty, cheery letters to Miss Moon. She heard from him rarely in form letters urging frugality and threatening retrenchment in face of the debt.

In his first letter to her in more than two years, he said, "The last few months have been quite hard on us. It is difficult to know how to plan. Our indebtedness has been so great it will take over $600,000 to carry out the work which we had already planned for and to meet the debt. Last year our receipts were only $500,000. We are trying to be very careful."[86]

In another personal word to Miss Moon, he said, "I wish we could sit and talk awhile." Then he pounded in the harsh truth: "We are in an embarrassing position on account of our debt. We do not know what to do."[87]

For a woman with very limited means, the decision was agonizing. Should she give her resources to relieve the suffering of the people she loved? Or should she give to the cause of her life, so that her co-workers might be able to remain on the field? For a few months, she chose the latter course in disposing of her annuity payments.

While these problems without solutions roared privately through her mind, she went bravely ahead with her work. Her Tengchow Church called its first native pastor. She now managed seven schools.[88] In the fall of 1911 women from three Woman's Missionary Societies met in Miss Moon's living room to organize the Woman's Missionary Union of North China. She was elected the president, but famine and flood would prevent a meeting in 1912, when she would have presided.[89]

The WMU organizational meeting took place during the meeting of the Shantung Association—renamed the North China Baptist Association as the work had spread. During the meeting her beloved Pastor Li of P'ingtu reported that he was baptizing more than 250 persons a year into the seven churches for which he was pastor. He also told that the P'ingtu Christians were suffering from famine. Floods had wiped out their crops, and many of the church members were living on sweet potato vines, roots, and ground leaves. Missionaries in P'ingtu were busy doing relief work to which other localities contributed. The report from P'ingtu struck deeply into Miss Moon's soul.

The present realities of war kept her on edge. A schoolboy reported to her house one day with his queue cut off. This was the sign of the revolutionists. The child thought it would please his beloved foreign teacher. Miss Moon was horrified and scolded him firmly. "Go home and attach that queue to your head before you come back," she commanded. She did not regard his show of sympathy safe for himself or for her in Tengchow.[90]

Some of the Christians joined the revolutionaries who plundered the temple of the pagan god of the city. When Miss Moon heard that some of the temple relics were in the home of a Baptist family, she was furious. She marched herself to the culprits, demanded the loot, and issued a forthright rebuke. "This is religious persecution—the very thing Christians have objected to and have been subjected to. Such behavior is not Christian!" She intended to take the booty to the city council for restoration to the temple, but Mr. Adams handled that upsetting detail for her. To every non-Christian acquaintance she made apologies and explained that religious persecution was not the Christian way.[91]

When the military tried to provide guns and ammunition to the missionaries, Miss Moon was horrified, hid her face behind her hands, and banished the weapons.[92] Fighting grew intense around the Baptist stations in January 1912. The consul urged the evacuation of all foreigners. The entire mission force left Hwanghsien for Chefoo. However, when Miss Moon learned of the fighting in Hwanghsien, her first thought was not to flee, but to go to the aid of people there. Nobody ever knew how she managed to arrive at Hwanghsien unscathed, but for ten days she took command of the hospital. The Chinese medical personnel rallied when they saw her courage. The frightened women calmed down and went to work caring for the wounded and sick who crowded the hospital. Miss Moon personally did what she could to relieve the suffering, mainly carrying cups of tea to the patients and to the overworked staff.

When Dr. Ayers and other missionaries took lives in hand to return to Hwanghsien, they were shocked to find Miss Moon calmly presiding. When she saw that the rightful chiefs were back, she packed up and announced that she would be returning to Tengchow. "But, Miss Moon," the men exclaimed, "they are shooting out there. It is not safe!" When she refused to linger, the missionaries sent word to the opposing generals that Miss Moon would be passing through the battle lines at an appointed hour. As her chair passed escorted by a young missionary, Carey Daniel, firing ceased. She made the twenty-mile trip without incident. Coming back, Daniel encountered dangerous fire. Later in the week Ayers not only was under fire, but also threatened by bandits along the same route.[93]

One soldier she dealt with personally. As she and Jane Lide walked for pleasure one day, they took the path outside the city wall. It was flanked on one side by the ancient stones and on the other side by a low moat. Suddenly a mounted soldier rudely galloped toward them on the path. "Don't worry, Jane," Miss Moon comforted. "I'll teach him some manners." When the soldier bore down on them and would have trounced them into the moat, Miss Moon suddenly thrust open her umbrella in the horse's face. The horse shied, and the soldier found himself in the moat, looking very surprised.[94]

By May Miss Moon was jubilant that China was a republic with a Christian calendar and a declaration of religious liberty. She wrote high praises of Sun Yat-sen, and she also approved of President Yuan.

Yuan was the governor of Shantung who had protected the missionaries during the Boxer trouble. Early in his career as a minor official, he had innocently wandered into the women's section of the Tengchow Church. Miss Moon, with her trusty umbrella, had ejected him from the forbidden territory with an explanation that Baptists maintained good Chinese decency for women. Thereafter, he was a friend to the Baptists; and he praised their high moral principles during the indemnity settlement after the Boxer Rebellion.[95]

The year 1912 began with the death of J. B. Hartwell, Miss Lottie's only contemporary in China. In his dying hours family and friends stood by to see him speak out of his deep sleep as if greeting people who had preceded him to heaven. When he greeted a Chinese deacon, and then a missionary of South China, they believed that he was simply suffering hallucinations. But after Hartwell was buried, they learned that those he greeted really had recently died.[96]

Missionaries were awestruck at this story, but Miss Moon's reaction must have far exceeded others'. Still another pioneer of China, Rosewell Graves, was soon taken to his Maker, and E. Z. Simmons, also a hero of South China, followed. Lottie Moon was in a dying company, and she knew it.

By now Miss Moon had totally lost her objectivity as a foreign missionary. She was no longer an aloof emissary who arrived to give the heathen glad tidings. She could no longer divide people into "us" and "them." The Chinese people and Lottie Moon were one. She took on their struggles one by one as they appeared at her door. The "school" of women was now a hostel for beggars. She not only doled out pittances to those who asked, but she took them into her home.

Among her company of feeble women was one who had attempted suicide in the face of her inability to get food. She had thrown herself over a bridge into a stony dry riverbed, but was slow to die. She lay helplessly as the sun parched her wounds. Miss Moon heard of the scene and went at once to rescue her. Soon the pitiful creature was lying on one of Miss Moon's freshly clean Chinese kangs. The repulsive body protested as gentle hands untangled the snarled hair, cleansed the gummy eyes, treated the inflamed wounds, and scrubbed the grimy fingernails. Food came, and with it a small foreign woman speaking words of comfort. For weeks she lived in this luxury as Lottie Moon spoke to her of one God who sent his Son to suffer so that poor women might be uplifted. Gradually the sufferer's anguished face grew peaceful. Perhaps she had understood the message.

The missionary who saw Miss Moon laboring with this miserable wretch could not help thinking, "Wasted alabaster?" Was Lottie Moon, the talented, brilliant Miss Lottie, a wasted gift poured out on such a specimen? Or was she the very personification of the Savior?[97]

In the summer of 1912 there grew among the mission families a concern about Miss Moon. A gentle conspiracy was hatched. Various children of the mission family were sent to spend days with or near Miss Moon. On these vacations the children were to run errands and keep Miss Moon cheered up. One boy from the Gospel Mission, remembering tedious lectures delivered by Mrs. Crawford, was reluctant to deal with another elderly woman. However, he found Miss Moon full of fun and modern ideas. The little Newton girls enjoyed their stay, but they reported that Miss Moon's eyes were too weak to see the bugs crawling in the cereal. Her fine cook was growing old and looked rather emanciated.[98] Yet Miss Moon was still on the job; missionaries were very busy; and who would think that the strongest woman in North China history might seriously need help?

Indeed, Miss Moon continued to be the scribe for conveying mission decisions to Richmond, which she did succinctly and forcefully. In midsummer she informed Willingham of the Tengchow group's plans for using two new single women who were expected to be appointed. She gave exhaustive reports of her schoolwork and country travels. "In my recent country work I have experienced the perplexities incidental to working alone. The Chinese girls who used to be extremely timid and shrinking are now wide awake and alert . . . . The girls came to my lodging so persistently, that I could not get away for visits and when the women came to me, I could but give them a divided attention. These things should not be!" Always she pleaded for more workers.[99]

Before summertime was over, the Gastons dropped by for a visit and found things all right. To Mrs. Gaston she said, "If I know my own heart's desire and prayer to God for these people, it is that they might be saved."

Privately, her anguish mounted. Her bankbook reflected her concerns—large bills for coal, contributions to the famine relief fund, small loans to other missionaries and to some of the Chinese, books for the schools which always cost more than the Board allowed, rent for a chapel where schoolchildren went to worship. And finally, late in the summer of 1912, a strange note for a bankbook: "I pray that no missionary will ever be as lonely as I have been."[100]

In the fall of 1912 the denominational press from the previous spring caught up with her. She read about the intense struggle to clear the Foreign Mission Board debt. "Perhaps there are no people who watch for the result of our campaign with more profound interest than our missionaries," said one paper. "If our people at home could realize what it means to the missionary when he feels that his brethren at home are not sustaining him . . . ." The writer obviously was aiming at the home audience. He could not have realized how profoundly his words would affect a missionary on the field. Such emotional appeals helped, but the Board debt was not wiped out. It was only reduced to $56,000.[101]

The turmoil of the campaign took a big emotional toll on the key circle of foreign mission supporters at home. The *Religious Herald* editor frankly said, "The greatest care ought to be taken not to inflict unnecessary distress upon the people who are keenly and generously interested in the affairs . . . . Our Boards must look to such restriction of their expenditures as will make such a stressful campaign as that which has just closed unnecessary . . . . In the management of our common work, we are having too many crises."[102]

When Mrs. Adams appeared at Miss Moon's wearing a warm fur, she was greeted with a none-too-graceful, "Don't you know the Board is in debt?"[103]

The news that Pastor Li had baptized in 1911-12 nearly 500 P'ingtu people seemed to have no effect on Miss Moon. She thought rather of their having to live on bark and sweet potato vines. Assurances that

The New Lottie Moon Story

missionaries were caring for these people were not enough to stop her helpless spin of worry. Instead of giving her annuity payment to the Board debt, she kept it for the famine sufferers. As usual, she believed that she was going to have to be strong alone. If nobody else could find a solution, she would have to try. She would let the burden fall on her and pray for God's help.

But this time the burden was too heavy, and her body was too weak. The tower of strength crumpled under the misery of others. In her complete distress she could only cry, "My God, my God, why hast thou forsaken me?"

She sent for Mr. Adams, who was a short distance in the country. He came hurriedly. She made out a new will and asked him to be executor. She told him that she was totally out of money. As she thrust a few financial papers at him, he quickly calculated that she did have a small amount of money in the bank, certainly plenty to last until her salary was issued again. He tried to show her. Then he offered her a loan. Nothing could reassure her.

On Miss Moon's reading table lay the mail. A letter from Richmond said that no more missionaries would come to Tengchow until the debt was gone. The *Religious Herald* was open to the obituary of an old friend. She stared blankly beyond these at sights too horrible for anyone else to see.

Miss Lide and Mr. Adams agreed that she must get out of her house, away from the constant depression of her "adopted sisters." Miss Lide took steps to close the house, dismissed the old cook, and packed Miss Moon's clothes. When the time came to leave, her abject tears cancelled the plan. Mrs. Turner took meals to her, and that is when the mission learned the true state of affairs. Miss Moon had ceased to eat so that her impoverished Chinese might be fed.[104]

After about two weeks of uncertainty, the frightened young missionaries called the nearest medical help, nurse Jessie Pettigrew, who came promptly.

Miss Moon did not recognize her friend at first, but Miss Pettigrew's best professional manner slowly chipped away the deep silence. She found at the base of Miss Moon's ear an enormous carbuncle-like growth which was eating deep into the head. Miss Pettigrew treated and dressed the sore. "Tell me what is the matter, please, Miss Moon."

"It is troubles in my mind," she replied, "I am such a sinner. I have been so awful. So unworthy." She told Miss Pettigrew that she was a pauper; all her money had been given away.

This strange talk unnerved the nurse, so she prescribed the standard North China cure—a change of scenery. Only by promising Miss Moon that no cost was involved did she convince her to visit Hwanghsien. At close range then, Miss Pettigrew observed a woman who dozed listlessly by day, tore her hair by night, and never ate.

An ancient Chinese custom that lodged in Miss Moon's mind now became an obsession. She recalled that useless old people were once walled into sepulchers or caves with a few day's food supply and left to die. This was the fate she felt she deserved.[105]

Miss Pettigrew notified Dr. Gaston in Laichowfu, and he dashed immediately to Miss Moon's side, collected her into a shentze, and took her to his home. He devotedly cared for her, keeping her distress and terror private. Miss Cynthia Miller, a missionary nurse, aided him. Soon she was reflecting Miss Moon's agony over the Board's desperate finances. Miss Miller was planning a furlough, and she decided she would take secular employment in America to avoid vacationing on the Board's borrowed money. "It is hard for one to hear her and not become depressed. It seems impossible to divert her from the Board's finances," she told Dr. Willingham. And she quoted Miss Moon: "Just think of Mr. Newton's seven little children, all starving to death."

From across Shantung came missionaries to decide what to do. With hope that the scenes of America would heal the shattered personality, they prepared her to travel. Miss Miller would take an early furlough to accompany her.

While she prepared to depart, Miss Moon was bundled to the home of Dr. T. O. Hearn in P'ingtu. Nurse Florence Jones and the Hearns constantly attended her, trying to turn back the pall of malnutrition. Miss Moon was an unwilling patient. In rational moments, she wanted her old place on a P'ingtu kang, teaching the women. In other moments, she cried out against all human frailty.

The New Lottie Moon Story

Leave China? In time of need and duty? This was the cruelest of all twists, and from the depths of Miss Moon's soul welled a cry of anguish that pierced every missionary heart in North China. But the medical missionaries hastened to move her to the new port city of Tsingtao, where she could be cared for more discreetly and effectively until the time to sail.

At 2 o'clock in the morning Dr. Hearn and Miss Jones packed a shentze with pillows and prepared Miss Moon for the long day's journey to the coast. Firmly, but tenderly, Hearn tucked her in, only to have her bounce up. "Just lay down, dear Miss Moon. Lay down now," he comforted. Suddenly the characteristic Lottie was back, with sparkling eyes. "I will not lay down, sir, but I will lie down," she quipped.

The tearful mission family watched from the balcony as the mule litter cortege solemnly rocked out of P'ingtu. The eerie lantern light fell for a moment across Lottie Moon's tortured face, etching a memory none could forget.[106]

Notes——— See pp. 302-303 for Key to Sources.

1. Interview with Elizabeth Tompkins, 1978; Cary Tompkins to Francis, September 18, 1925, URL.

2. Mrs. Frank Russell Moon to Fannie, URL.

3. Interview of Mrs. W. E. Hatcher by Una Roberts Lawrence, handwritten notes, URL.

4. Foreign Mission Board Minutes; Richmond *City Directory,* 1903.

5. *RH,* October 22, 1903; November 19, 1903. Willingham episode recorded by W. W. Adams, "Miss Lottie Moon, Some Recollections and Glimpses," WMU.

6. Cary Tompkins to Frances Knight, September 18, 1925, URL; Lottie Moon to Bettie Fowlkes, September 20, 1905, Virginia Baptist Historical Society. Miss Moon refers to the presidential visit having occurred during her 1893 furlough. Her mind must have been wandering during this letter full of reminiscence.

7. Interview with Lucy Ayers Pitman, 1978; interview with Mrs. Charles Goode, 1979; Elizabeth Landress Dalton, *Twenty Years and More,* dates Lottie's visit to Chattanooga incorrectly. The author surmises that 1904 must have been the proper year.

8. Lottie Moon to Bettie Fowlkes, September 20, 1905; interview of Mrs. W. E. Hatcher by Una Roberts Lawrence; Fannie E. S. Heck in *FMJ*, November 1910.

9. Mrs. J. McF. Gaston, "Miss Moon As We Knew Her," WMU.

10. Lottie Moon to Annie, February 11, 1904, Virginia Baptist Historical Society.

11. Lottie Moon to Bettie Fowlkes, September 20, 1905.

12. *FMJ*, April 1904.

13. *FMJ*, January 1905; Lottie Moon to Annie (Mrs. Frank Russell) Moon, July 7, 1904, URL.

14. Ayers, *Healing in Missions.*

15. *FMJ*, July 1906.

16. Correspondence of C. W. Pruitt, mission treasurer, and R. J. Willingham reveals the more prosperous and progressive approach to mission expenditures.

17. *FMJ*, September 1905; June 1905; November 1905—all show Lottie Moon's school reports.

18. Lottie Moon to R. J. Willingham, November 14, 1904; January 21, 1905, LMLF.

19. Ibid., September 22, 1904.

20. Ibid., 2, 1904.

20. Ibid., and May 10, 1904; R. J. Willingham to Lottie Moon, June 13, 1904, Copy Book, FMB.

21. T. W. Ayers to R. J. Willingham, August 12, 1904, T. W. Ayers Letter File, FMB.

22. *FMJ*, July 1903.

23. C. W. Pruitt to R. J. Willingham, November 25, 1904, CWPLF, shows a negative reaction to language requirements.

24. Lottie Moon to R. J. Willingham, November 14, 1904, and December 14, 1904, LMLF. R. J. Willingham to Mrs. Stainback Wilson, September 2, 1904; to Mrs. G. C. Kerr, September 19, 1904; to Martha Foster Crawford, December 12, 1904; to Lottie Moon, December 12, 1904; to Mrs. G. C. Kerr, December 14, 1904, Copy Book, FMB.

25. Lottie Moon to Annie (Mrs. Frank Russell) Moon, July 7, 1904, URL.

26. *FMJ*, September 1905; Lottie Moon to R. J. Willingham, September 8, 1905, LMLF.

27. Ruth Thornhill to author; Lottie Moon to R. J. Willingham, November 2, 1905, LMLF.

28. Interview with Lucy Ayers Pitman, 1978.

29. See JBHLF for this period.

30. Lottie Moon to R. J. Willingham, May 7, 1906, LMLF.

31. Lottie Moon to Cary, May 26, 1906, URL.

32. Lottie Moon to R. J. Willingham, December 18, 1906, LMLF; Lottie Moon to Cary, May 26, 1906, URL.

33. Lottie Moon to John Fowler, March 12, 1906, and March 15, 1906, Consular Records, Chefoo, China, National Archives. This is the only occasion in consular correspondence records that Lottie Moon wrote personally to the consul. Yet she surely knew Fowler and had business with him. Lottie Moon to Annie, March 26, 1906, provided by Mrs. J. S. Andrews.

34. Taped recollection of Mrs. Edgar Morgan, June 23, 1977.

35. Lottie Moon to R. J. Willingham, May 31, 1907, LMLF; *Kind Words,* January 1908.

36. Lottie Moon to Annie, March 23, 1907, Virginia Baptist Historical Society; *FMJ,* August 1907.

37. Minnie Pettigrew Voyles in interview with Mrs. Frank Ellis, 1978; Lottie Moon to R. J. Willingham, May 29, 1907, LMLF.

38. Lottie Moon to Edmonia Moon, July 9, 1905, provided by Mary Virginia Andrews. Letter fragments from Lottie Moon provided by Orie Andrews Davis.

39. FMB Minutes; Lottie Moon to Edmonia Moon, December 31, 1907, provided by Orie Andrews Davis. Lottie Moon to Miss Shepherd, January 3, 1908, LMLF; *FMJ,* January 1908.

40. Lottie Moon to R. J. Willingham, May 16, 1908, LMLF.

41. J. B. Hartwell to R. J. Willingham, July 25, 1908, JBHLF.

42. *FMJ,* November 1908; Lottie Moon to R. J. Willingham, July 10, 1908, LMLF; Lottie Moon to Elizabeth, July 7, 1908, Virginia Baptist Historical Society; fragment of letter from Lottie Moon, provided by Mrs. J. S. Andrews; *RH,* January 5, 1911; recollections of Florence Jones recorded by Anna Belle Crouch.

43. Taped recollection of Mrs. Edgar Morgan, June 23, 1977.

44. Lottie Moon to R. J. Willingham, July 10, 1908, LMLF. Vaccination had been Foreign Mission Board policy since 1905, and Willingham thought Miss Taylor had been vaccinated. Lottie suggested that it had failed to take effect.

45. Lottie Moon to Edmonia Moon, November 4, 1908, provided by Mary Virginia Andrews.

46. Dr. Gaston's Recollections of Miss Moon, URL.

47. Letter fragment apparently written by Mrs. J. McF. Gaston, LMR.

48. Mrs. J. McF. Gaston, "Miss Moon As We Knew Her," WMU.

49. Dr. Gaston's Recollections of Miss Moon, URL.

50. The Adams episodes are drawn from writings of both Mr. and Mrs. W. W. Adams in "Miss Moon As We Knew Her"; letter to Una Roberts Lawrence

from W. W. Adams, July 21, 1925, URL; "Miss Lottie Moon, Some Recollections and Glimpses," unpublished notes by W. W. Adams written for WMU; unpublished manuscripts and notes by Mr. and Mrs. W. W. Adams at Samford University Library; and notes on interview with Mrs. Adams by the author, 1967.

51. Lottie Moon to William Luther Andrews, undated letter, URL.

52. W. W. Adams to R. J. Willingham, May 21, 1909, W. W. Adams Letter File, FMB.

53. Mrs. Robert Alexis Green, Starke, Florida, in letter to the author, December 12, 1978. Mrs. Green interviewed Edmonia Moon's neighbor, Hugh Brownlee; a local merchant, Jack Quigley, who sold the coffin for Edmonia; and the undertaker's son, Dewitt Jones. They are the sources of scant information about Edmonia's life and death in Starke. Edmonia's house still stands on the corner of South Church Street, across the street from the funeral home. She was buried in Crosby Cemetery. Her grave may have been marked with a cross bearing the name "Lucy," or it may have been left unmarked. The purchase of property by Edmonia from the Brownlees, her will, actions by Isaac Andrews as executor, and the sale of the property by Isaac and Annie Andrews are recorded in the Bradford County Courthouse, Starke. Also, Edmonia's will is recorded in Albemarle County Courthouse, Will Book 31, December 9, 1908. A sample of Edmonia's regard for Lottie is seen in a letter from Edmonia to Annie, owned by Charlotte Churchill. Quote is from *RH*, June 2, 1887.

54. Lottie Moon to William Luther Andrews, January 4, 1904, and Lottie Moon to Isaac Andrews, March 6, 1909, provided by Mrs. J. S. Andrews; wills and deeds in Starke.

55. Lottie Moon to R. J. Willingham, January 12, 1909, and July 6, 1909, LMLF.

56. *FMJ*, May 1909.

57. *RH*, May 6, 1909.

58. Lottie Moon to R. J. Willingham, July 12, 1911, LMLF.

59. *FMJ*, September, 1908; C. W. Pruitt to R. J. Willingham, September 1, 1911, CWPLF; Lottie Moon to R. J. Willingham, September 18, 1909, and following, LMLF.

60. Interview with Jewell Legett Daniel, 1978, and personal papers given by Mrs. Daniel to the author. She is the source of details about the Adams wedding, and these are repeated in Adams Papers at Samford University and in the author's notes of interviews with Mrs. Adams.

61. Mrs. Minnie Pettigrew Voyles in interview with Mrs. Frank Ellis.

62. Miss Moon reached these conclusions in her own struggle to love the Chinese, and she recorded them in letters to friends.

63. Jewell Legett Daniel interview.

64. Mrs. C. W. Pruitt, "Miss Moon As We Knew Her."

65. Lucy Ayers Pitman, interview with author.

66. *FMJ*, February 1910.

67. Lottie Moon to R. J. Willingham, July 6, 1909, LMLF.

68. Jewell Legett Daniel interview.

69. Without fail, the recollections of "Baby Missionaries" of this era take particular note of Miss Moon's remarkable love for Chinese culture. She apparently came to grips with cultural identity to a far greater extent than any of her contemporaries and regarded such adjustment as essential to missionary effectiveness. See Pruitt, "Miss Moon As We Knew Her."

70. Jewell Legett Daniel interview.

71. Ibid.; Eliza S. Broadus, "The Heavenly Book Visitor," WMU.

72. *FMJ*, December 1909.

73. Mrs. T. O. Hearn to R. J. Willingham, March 28, 1910, T. O. Hearn Letter File, FMB.

74. Anna Pruitt to R. J. Willingham, July 8, 1910, CWPLF; North China Mission Minutes, FMB.

75. Dr. Gaston's Recollections of Miss Moon, URL.

76. Ibid.

77. Lottie Moon to Mrs. J. McF. Gaston, June 7, 1911, URL; Lottie Moon to Cary, July 9, 1910, URL; SBC Annual, 1911.

78. Adams recollections; interviews with Rachel Newton Dickson, 1978 and 1979.

79. Anna Hartwell, *Royal Service,* December 1930; Eliza Broadus, "The Heavenly Book Visitor," WMU.

80. Letters of Lottie Moon to her niece, Martha Moon, November 28, 1910, and May 3, 1911, provided by Louise Haddock and available in LMLF; Lottie Moon letter fragment, apparently to William Luther Andrews, owned by Charlotte Churchill.

81. Lottie Moon to Cary, April 12, 1908, and March 6, 1911, URL; Lottie Moon to Isaac, February 21, 1911, provided by Mrs. J. S. Andrews.

82. Lottie Moon to R. J. Willingham, December 23, 1911, LMLF.

83. Lottie Moon to Isaac, February 22, 1911.

84. Lottie Moon to William Luther Andrews, March 24, 1911, LMLF.

85. C. W. Pruitt to R. J. Willingham, October 6, 1911, CWPLF.

86. R. J. Willingham to Lottie Moon, August 7, 1911, Copy Book, FMB.

87. Ibid., August 15, 1911.

88. *FMJ*, August 1910.

89. Blanche Syndor White, *Saved to Serve: A Brief History of the Development of Woman's Missionary Unions in Other Lands.*

90. W. W. Adams, "Miss Lottie Moon, Some Recollections and Glimpses."

91. Ibid., and Lottie Moon to Annie, May 3, 1912, owned by Charlotte Churchill.

92. W. W. Adams, "Miss Lottie Moon, Some Recollections and Glimpses."

93. T. W. Ayers, "Miss Lottie Moon—As I Knew Her," WMU. Also, Lottie Moon to her niece, Mattie, May 2, 1912, provided by Louise Haddock. Further details, Jewell Legett Daniel interview.

94. This story was often repeated by missionaries in the next generation—for example, by C. L. Culpepper, letter to author, June 12, 1978, and Anna Pruitt to Una Roberts Lawrence, April 22, 192?, URL

95. Lottie Moon to Mattie, May 2, 1912; Pruitt to Lawrence, ibid.

96. Mrs. Edgar Morgan interview, June 23, 1977.

97. Anna Hartwell, quoted by Eliza Broadus, "The Life of Miss Lottie Moon," manuscript in URL. This anecdote was omitted from the published version, "The Heavenly Book Visitor," WMU.

98. Interview with Charles H. League, 1978, and with Rachel Dickson Newton, 1978.

99. Lottie Moon to R. J. Willingham, July 24, 1912, LMLF.

100. Lottie Moon Bankbooks at Virginia Baptist Hospital Society and WMU; notations by W. W. Adams, her executor, July 21, 1925, URL.

101. *RH,* February 8, 1912, and March 12, 1912.

102. Ibid., March 9, 1912.

103. W. W. Adams to Una Roberts Lawrence, URL.

104. In addition to the various Adams recollections, letters from Jessie Pettigrew to J. McF. Gaston, October 28, 1912, and J. McF. Gaston to R. J. Willingham, November 10, 1912, J. McF. Gaston Letter File, FMB, summarize Miss Moon's last two months. Her absence from mission station meetings is noted in the Tengchow Minute Book, unclassified China Archives, Foreign Mission Board. See also letter from Cynthia Miller to R. J. Willingham, November 15, 1912, Cynthia Miller Letter File, FMB. Interviews with Mrs. Edgar Morgan and Jewell Legett Daniel and *RH,* June 26, 1913, add details.

105. Handwritten notes, source not indicated, URL. Also, *FMJ,* September 1884.

106. Recollections of Miss Florence Jones, interviewed by her great-niece, Anna Belle Crouch, professor at Chowan College, North Carolina. Miss Jones nursed Miss Moon for twelve days at a German hospital in Tsingtao until Dr. Hearn returned with Cynthia Miller. All assisted in transferring Miss Moon to the ship. Hearn stayed on board until the ship cleared Shanghai.

10
She Is
Immortal Till Her Work is Done

Fifty frail pounds filled with superhuman strivings were all that remained of Lottie Moon when she was carried on board the *Manchuria*. Cynthia Miller arranged to sleep in Miss Moon's cabin, for the patient could not be neglected for a minute. Dr. Hearn brought aboard a supply of Miss Moon's favorite grape juice and a special food for invalids. He conferred gravely with the ship's captain and doctor, who promised the best of care if she lived and a decent burial if she died. Hearn doubted that she could survive the trip, but he believed it was the only hope. He bade her a sad farewell.[1]

Cables and letters flew to Richmond. Edgar L. Morgan, the mission treasurer who had always received a gracious thank-you note when he sent Miss Moon her funds, outlined her melancholia to the Foreign Mission Board treasurer. "This has raised the question in the minds of some of us as to how much ought to be said about debt in letters to missionaries. Not even members of the Board can know how much it makes for depression."[2]

But the damage had been inflicted, and there was nothing to do but prepare to care for the shell of a missionary in America. Willingham made arrangements for Miss Lottie to go to Crewe, where her sister-in-law, Margaret, and Margaret's nephew agreed to care for her. Hearn had stressed the necessity for someone to meet the ship in San Francisco to take responsibility for the train trip. Willingham enlisted Miss Moon's friend, R. T. Bryan of Central China, to cut into his furlough and hasten to San Francisco. There he received not the vivacious heroine who had helped him in Chinkiang, but a little urn of ashes.

Cynthia Miller (FMB)

Miss Miller told him and all Southern Baptists the emotional story.

"It grieves us to give up one we loved and esteemed so highly—not only for her work's sake, but also for her own dear self's sake," Miss Miller said. Miss Moon had given up all will to live as the *Manchuria* sailed out of Chinese waters. She grew weaker, then quieter, and finally fell into a deep sleep. After several days, the rest cleared her mind. Late at night on December 18 she awoke, and Miss Miller hastened to give her some of the grape juice.

"Where did this grape juice come from?" the patient asked.

"Dr. Hearn brought it just for you," Miss Miller explained.

"Oh, Dr. Hearn is a good man," she said. She earnestly thanked the nurse for her care and apologized for being a troublesome patient. "Will you tell me why it is that Christian people are so good?"

"I think it is because Christ's Holy Spirit lives in their hearts, Miss Moon."

"Why don't you pray for him to come and fill up my heart?" begged the weak voice.

"I have been praying this very day, Miss Moon, that he would come and give you the peace and comfort that he alone can give."

"You have?" A little smile played across the worn face. "Well, he has come. Jesus is right here, now. You can pray now that he will fill my heart and stay with me. For when Jesus comes in, he drives out all evil, you know."

The *Manchuria* cabin became a temple as the nurse fell to her knees beside the shrunken form and conversed intimately with her Lord. Occasionally the trembling voice of Lottie Moon would find its familiar melody and join in the holy conversation.

Later, in the suspended beauty of the night, Miss Moon whispered, " 'Jesus loves me. This I know, for the Bible tells me so. Little ones to him belong. They are weak, but he is strong!' Do you know that song, Miss Miller?"

"Yes, ma'am. Many is the time you have taught that to the Chinese, haven't you?"

"Yes, but if we want him to stay with us, we must trust him, mustn't we? Will you sing 'Simply Trusting Every Day' for me?"

Miss Miller sang the hymn like a lullaby, and Miss Moon said, "Oh, but that is a sweet old song."

Through the long night she would rouse to say, "We are weak, but he is strong." By morning she no longer spoke, but pointed upward when Miss Miller approached her.

The ship slowly made its way through the Orient and stopped in Kobe, Japan, one of Miss Moon's most beloved spots, to take on coal. There, on Christmas Eve, the sleeper opened her eyes. She silently smiled and looked about. Then, with great effort, she raised her fists together in the fashion of a fond Chinese greeting. Her spirit went out to meet the One coming for her.

As the ship sailed out of the harbor, Miss Miller notified the doctor and the captain. In his report the captain wrote: "Tuesday, December 24, 1912, Harbor of Kobe, Japan. Miss Lottie Moon, age 72, died of melancholia and senility. The remains were cremated at Yokohama on December 26. Personal effects consisting of one steamer trunk taken care of by Miss Cynthia Miller, her traveling companion and friend."[3]

Miss Charlotte Digges Moon was returned to the Foreign Mission

The New Lottie Moon Story

Board in a small brown package delivered by the expressman to the hands of a young woman working as a clerk.[4]

A modest group of foreign missions people and a small handful of relatives gathered on January 28, 1913, at the Second Baptist Church of Richmond for a memorial service. The pastor, the president of the Board, and the secretaries of the Board participated in the ceremonies. Willingham "spoke feelingly" of her noble character, her thirty-nine years of service, her faithfulness, and her rare judgment on which the Board relied heavily.[5] On the next day, the little silver casket of ashes was buried in Crewe beside Isaac Moon.[6] Across the country, from Maryland to Georgia, small groups of women held their own memorial services for her.

The *Foreign Mission Journal* tersely summarized her life—one of the oldest women missionaries, one of the first single women missionaries, educator, evangelist among women, alone in her station for months at a time, brave, devoted to Chinese women and girls, "the best man among our missionaries."[7]

Her passing had left a sorrowful gap in Tengchow. In China the executor of her estate, W. W. Adams, with a broken heart, sold off her personal property and cleared her bank account of $254 (in inflated local currency). The heiress of Viewmont did not have enough estate to pay her way back to Virginia.[8]

Both Christians and non-Christians wept at the news of her death. Those in Tengchow felt that justice had been abused because she had not been allowed to die in the city. They hastened to erect a monument "to bequeath the love of Miss Lottie Moon, an American missionary." The marker simply said, "The Tengchow church remembers forever."[9]

The mission's report to the Southern Baptist Convention described Lottie Moon as "a life poured out as a cup of cold water," and saluted her gift of home, salary, and self in Christian social service.

The missionary circle missed her. The young set grieved over her absence in planning and decision making. One wrote to Willingham, "You do not know how lonely our station is without the presence of our dear Miss Moon. Her going away has drawn us all closer to the Master, for we have had to carry everything to him. We don't have Miss Moon to tell us how the Chinese would look at this thing and that, and we don't want to do any thing that will hinder the Master's cause."[10]

Another said, "Our station is lost without Miss Moon. We need more than ever your constant prayers." He looked to the future with confidence that the forces set in motion by Miss Moon would not be lost energy, but would be felt in the work for many years.[11]

And it was. For twenty or more years, new converts would testify, "When I was a child, I followed Old Lady Moon and learned hymns from her." Successful businessmen would say, "She gave me my start." And women in remote villages would ask, "When will the Heavenly Book Visitor come again?" The Chinese people who mourned Lottie Moon did not speak of her noble education, her brilliant mind, or her lofty ideals. They simply said, "How she loved us."[12]

The mission voted that a biography of Miss Moon be written to beckon others to service in missions. Many of the group felt that her life's purpose was not yet fulfilled.

In the United States the reaction to the late Miss Moon was curiously profound. In life alone she had served remarkably, but so had others. But in dying as she did, completely submerging every shred of self in the needs of others, she made a contribution that nobody else had.

Her old schoolfriend, Bettie Fowlkes, tried to capture for publication the shocked admiration and devotion many felt. In poetry she vainly searched for meaning in a life so gloriously spent and so hideously ended. "But this we know, what master so employeth life as with life's Truth, its pupils to inspire, doth do a work immortal; for things not seen shall live and live eternal. Sleep well, beloved worker, then; rich is thy gain. Rest safe, dear ashes here; thy friends are near."[13]

Miss Miller's account of the death broke like a cloud of guilt across the Southern Baptist Convention. "It is infinitely touching that those who work hardest and make the most sacrifices for the Master should suffer because those in the homeland fail to give what is needed," she wrote.[14]

Across the Convention groups large and small in Woman's Missionary Union stopped to mark the fall of this great woman. "She sank into a state of melancholy, refusing to eat, lest she might further impoverish her people or the Board," the story went. "This thought should sink deeply into the heart of every careless, indifferent Christian woman of the homeland."[15]

"She Being Dead, Yet Speaketh," wrote Mrs. Hatcher in the *Religious Herald.* She wrote because "the facts concerning her death struck me as so pathetic, so tragic, and soul-stirring, that I feel they should be known to all Southern Baptists.[16]

"This learned and brilliant Christian woman should not have been allowed to so overtax herself that she would waste away to fifty pounds! What are we going to do about it?" she asked. "Is there not some shame mingled with our sorrow? Shall we not, as a fitting tribute to her memory, lift at once the debt from the Foreign Mission Board? Is it not the memorial she herself would choose?"

Mrs. Hatcher echoed the word that seemed to everybody appropriate. "Immortal." Her eminent qualifications, her devotion, and her courage and spreading virtue through China could not be forgotten. "Her views on China were statesman-like. She could have graced a throne with signal ability," Mrs. Hatcher wrote.

"Is it strange that this noble woman will receive the homage of many people on two continents? The world in its final estimate, makes no mistakes. It sings no paeans to the selfish."

The Southern Baptist Convention annual for 1913 called her a "queenly saint." Thus rolled the emotions about the cut-down "flower of Virginia womanhood."[17] All obituary comments said something to the effect that "her name will forever be linked with the foreign mission work of Southern Baptists in honorable and useful distinction."[18] Just how this prophecy would be carried out was not yet clear, but the commitment to the idea was strong.

Women in Virginia quickly rose to collect funds for a monument at her gravesite. The funds came in small, heartfelt offerings from women who had known of Miss Moon. Later the Crewe Baptist Church installed a beautiful stained-glass window to portray her work in the Master's harvest field. But works of stone and glass would not make an immortal.[19]

Back in China, the missionaries of North China held their first meet-

Memorial window honoring Lottie Moon,
Crewe Baptist Church, Crewe, Virginia

ing without Miss Moon. "Our hearts were put to shame as we measured our lives by the plummet line of the Holy Spirit," they reported. They voted courageously to ask Southern Baptists to send them thirty evangelistic missionaries within the next three years. They echoed with new urgency a challenge that Lottie Moon had trumpeted across the United States many years earlier—"thirty seed-sowers for North China!"[20]

Pastor Li was said to have baptized more people than any other man in China, but he told the missionaries, "We must stop receiving new members until we can train those we already have." In the year of Lottie Moon's death, 2,358 persons had been baptized, almost doubling the Baptist population of the area. The mission was operating on a new level of mutual leadership with the Chinese. Miss Moon's old philosophy of official self-support, softened by personal charity, was fully adopted as a principle of work. "Was this growth to be the lasting tribute to her?"[21]

At Christmastime 1913 came the annual WMU offering for foreign missions. Agnes Osborne, leading woman journalist in the denomination, wrote, "This is Miss Moon's first Christmas in Heaven. It would be a beautiful thing for the women of the Southland to make the largest Christmas offering this year as a living memorial to Miss Moon." She reminded readers that it was Miss Moon's suggestion and situation that launched this offering. "Many thousand dollars must be brought into the Lord's treasury before we can again lift our heads as a denomination and look the world in the face and say, 'There is no debt on our Foreign Mission Board,' " she said.[22]

Miss Moon's pessimism about the debt was not misplaced. In the year of her death, the debt grew alarmingly as Southern Baptists foundered for lack of a financial plan. Yet the Convention bravely insisted that appointment and support of missionaries proceed with expectation of sufficient income.

Gradually Miss Moon's precepts and example, and the concepts of women's work she had fostered, bloomed and multiplied in the land of Southern Baptists. The debt was paid; systematic giving for missions and the Christmas season offering relegated deficit financing to the archives of mission strategy.

In 1918 Annie Armstrong, the woman who refused marriage to a China missionary in order that she could fulfill her calling as the leader of mission support among Southern Baptist women in the homeland, broke the silence of her retirement years. "Miss Moon is the one who suggested the Christmas offering for foreign missions. She showed us the way in so many things. Wouldn't it be appropriate to name the offering in her memory?"[23]

Woman's Missionary Union captured the idea at once. The Lottie Moon Christmas Offering for Foreign Missions became a fixed name and a fixed event in the Southern Baptist calendar. After ninety years of continuous observance, the Lottie Moon Christmas Offering had elicited a phenomenal total of more than $400,000,000; and never a penny of it had been spent in promotion or homeland operations.

The Lottie Moon Christmas Offering became more than a practical channel of missions finance. It was also a holiday tradition. Amid an increasingly self-centered season, giving to the offering was a tangible and welcome way to participate in the true message of Christmas. With the appeal for money always went a week of prayer, and with prayer went study. The name of Lottie Moon spoke of more than dollars and cents. It conveyed the ideals of life commitment, sacrifice, personal holiness, and daily submission to the will of God.

In 1927 the Baptist Sunday School Board published the biography *Lottie Moon.* Written by Una Roberts Lawrence at the request of Woman's Missionary Union, the book was readily studied. The Lottie Moon story became living history.

Because much emotion went with the money, the Lottie Moon offering escaped the hard handling that at times accompanied denominational progress. When the Convention established, in cooperation with Woman's Missionary Union and the state Baptist conventions, the financial system known as the Cooperative Program, all offerings were to be merged. But because of popular love, the Lottie Moon Christmas Offering for Foreign Missions and its twin, the Annie Armstrong Easter Offering for Home Missions, were carefully excepted. The Cooperative Program and the Lottie Moon Offering became parallel tracks of foreign mission support, each providing approximately half of the

Foreign Mission Board's resources. At times the crusty hands of denominational leaders have dealt lightly with Lottie Moon's sacred name. Always younger leaders, softly touched by the ever-fresh story of Miss Lottie, have snatched their heritage to safety.[24]

Some of her friends later suggested that Miss Moon would have been mortified to see her name painted across the churches and publications of Southern Baptists. On the other hand, it would be characteristic for her to sacrifice even her personal privacy if missionaries could be called, sent, and sustained.

Miss Moon would be the first to insist that she did nothing to lay up exceptional merit among hundreds of other remarkable missionaries. Others also have achieved "firsts," suffered privation, touched spiritual heights, blazed frontiers of thought, risen to the heroic, been martyred. Yet the Lottie Moon story is retold, not only for what she did, but more for the way in which she did it; for where and how she stood in history; for who she was in life and what she meant in death. As long as there are peoples and cultures who have not witnessed the living of a Christ-like life, as long as there are women and men who have not explored the Christian calling, the Lottie Moon story should be retold. As she said herself, "I have a firm conviction that I am immortal till my work is done."[25] She was speaking of her life; but the truth lay in her reputation, which lights the way of missions into all the world.

Notes———— See pp. 302-303 for Key to Sources.

1. T.O Hearn to R. J. Willingham, December 22, 1912, T. O. Hearn Letter File, Cynthia Miller to Una Roberts Lawrence, May 21, 1923, URL. Cynthia Miller to R. J. Willingham, Cynthia Miller Letter File, FMB.

2. Edgar L. Morgan to R. R. Gwathmey, December 3, 1912, URL.

3. *The Commission,* December 1969. The United States consul attributed death to "carbuncle back of ear, general debility, and old age," records of Department of State Consular Post, Shanghai, dated March 31, 1913, National Archives.

4. Blanche Sydnor White was the young clerk, and she related the experience to Rees Watkins, who told the author. Cynthia Miller was so upset by her experience in this cruel death, and so moved by her privilege to attend Miss

Moon, that she was forever affected. Through many years and many questionings, she repeated the story just as she wrote it in letters to Willingham. When she sailed from China for the last time, she took with her a coffin so that she might be properly provided for in case she did not survive the voyage, according to reports from WMU leaders who knew her in retirement.

5. *RH*, March 6, 1913.

6. Eyewitnesses in Crewe, Virginia, in reports to Charlotte Churchill.

7. *FMJ*, February 1913.

8. Margaret A. Moon, Lottie's sister-in-law, was the legal heir. Reports on settlement of the estate and inventory, dated July 25, 1913, one found in records of United States Consulate, Chefoo, Docket Book, Civil, Criminal, Probate Matters, December 10, 1898—May 23, 1939, and Records of Department of State Decimal File 393.113/11. Inventory showed no real property; personal propery appraised at $368.90 in local currency; and a deposit in the Hong Kong and Shanghai Bank at Shanghai of $254.27 local currency. Miss Moon's personal property was mostly sold among the missionaries. United States value of the currency would have been less than Chinese value.

9. Lawrence, *Lottie Moon.*

10. Mrs. J. V. Turner to R. J. Willingham, April 24, 1913, J. V. Turner Letter File, FMB.

11. W. W. Adams to R. J. Willingham, January 21, 1913, W. W. Adams Letter File, FMB.

12. From notations of W. W. Adams, Mrs. T. O. Hearn, and Mrs. J. McF. Gaston.

13. *RH*, February 13, 1913.

14. *WR*, February 13, 1913.

15. Mrs. T. J. Collings at Memorial Service for Lottie Moon, Crewe, Virginia, July 21, 1915.

16. *RH*, March 6, 1913.

17. *RH*, June 26, 1913.

18. Ibid., January 23, 1913.

19. Ibid., March 20, 1913, and many weeks following.

20. Ibid., August 14, 1913.

21. Ibid.

22. *WR*, December 18, 1913.

23. WMU Minutes, 1918.

24. Mrs. R. L. Mathis, destined to serve as president of WMU, Auxiliary to Southern Baptist Convention, for thirteen years, was one of those who helped preserve the name of the Lottie Moon Christmas Offering. While attending a WMU Executive Board meeting as a young people's leader in the 1940s, she was instructed to represent the president of Texas WMU during a business ses-

sion. She was shocked to find the older, famous leaders seriously considering dropping Lottie Moon's name from the offering. With shaking voice and trembling knees, Mrs. Mathis rose to insist that "the women of Texas won't like that." She swayed the decision in favor of tradition. Later, as president of WMU, she fostered the idea that WMU should sponsor and promote the offering as a churchwide activity in which both women and men participate. This concept helped increase the intake of the offering.

25. Lottie Moon in newspaper clipping, January 22, 1895, Virginia Baptist Historical Society.

GUIDE TO SPELLING

The spelling style used latest by Miss Moon and her contemporaries has been used throughout this book. This style will be of aid to researchers using materials contemporary with the subject. The following table will indicate some of the historic variations. The Pinyin spelling will aid students in relating history to present-day China.

Spelling used in this book (Wade-Giles system with exceptions):	Variations in historic documents:	Pinyin:
Chefoo		Yentai
Hwanghsien	Huanghsien	Huangxian
	Hwanghien	
	Hwangshien	
	Whanghien	
Laichowfu		Laizhou
P'ingtu	Pingtu	Pingdu
	Pengtu	
	Pingdoo	
Sha-ling	Saling	Shaling
	Sah-ling	
Shanghai		Shanghai City
Shantung		Shandong
Taian	Tai-an	Taian
	Taianfu	
Tengchow	Tungchow	
	Tengchowfu	Dengzhou
Tsingtao		Qingdao

ACKNOWLEDGMENTS

Woman's Missionary Union, Auxiliary to Southern Baptist Convention, and the author thankfully acknowledge the extensive and intensive aid of many persons who have shared in the preparation of this book.

General guidance and assistance in research

Lee N. Allen, professor of history and dean of Howard College of Arts and Sciences, Samford University (loyal husband and co-worker of the author)

Irwin T. Hyatt, Jr., chairman of Department of History and associate professor, Emory University

F. Wilbur Helmbold, librarian, Samford University

Significant research or investigation on behalf of the author

Kathy Affolter
Margie Black
Kathryn Bullard
Maxine Bumgarner
Mike Crain
Leo Crismon
Paul M. Debusman
Barbara Elder
Mrs. Frank Ellis
Elaine K. Evans
Wilma Franks
Louise Haddock
Waldo P. Harris
Helen L. Harriss
Eugene Hill
Johnni Johnson Scofield
The late Fon Scofield
Mrs. Peyton Thurman
Rees Watkins
Bill Weatherford
B. B. Williamson

Family of Lottie Moon who provided papers and oral history

Mr. and Mrs. Ernest Andrews
Mrs. J. S. Andrews
Mary Virginia Andrews Andrews
Mrs. R. C. Churchill
Mrs. Henry Davis
Grayce Fitzgerald
Mrs. Charles E. Goode
Katherine Hancock

Lilla Hancock
Mrs. William Barry Harmon
Mrs. John Lynch
Cary Nelson Moon
Mrs. Russell B. Moon

Mrs. George W. Snead
Mrs. L. R. Shadwell
Mrs. Russell Thomas
Elizabeth N. Tompkins
Mrs. Rita Watkins

Southern Baptist missionaries in China and their descendants

Children of missionaries acquainted with Miss Moon:

F. Catharine Bryan
Rachel Newton Dickson
Charles H. League
Lucy Ayers Pitman
Ida Pruitt

Personally worked with Miss Moon:

Mrs. W. W. Adams
Jewell Legett Daniel
Jane Lide
Mrs. Edgar Morgan

Later missionaries and families who passed on oral traditions and papers:

C. L. Culpepper
Martha Franks
Carl Hunker
Mrs. Frank Lide
Lynn New
Paul D. and Lucy Wright Parker

Susan Herring Taynton
Ruth Thornhill
Minnie Pettigrew Voyles
Lila F. Watson

Librarians and archivists who personally aided in research

Jenkins Library and Archives, Foreign Mission Board, Nancy Nell Stanley

Samford University Special Collections, Elizabeth Wells, Marilyn Sessions, and staff

Woman's Missionary Union, Auxiliary to Southern Baptist Convention, Doris DeVault and Betty D. Hurtt

Southern Baptist Historical Commission, Lynn E. May and Charles Deweese

Presbyterian Historical Society, Gerald Gillette

Historical Foundation of the Presbyterian and Reformed Churches, Ruth D. See

Disciples of Christ Historical Society, David I. McWhirter

Furman University, J. Glen Clayton

Virginia Baptist Historical Society, Mrs. H. Edward McGahey and Ellen Douglas Oliver

The Southern Baptist Theological Seminary, Ronald F. Deering, Paul M. Debusman

Hollins College, Shirley Henn

University of Virginia, Anne Freudenberg

Medical College of Pennsylvania, Sandra Chaff

Harvard University, William W. Whalen

University of North Carolina, Michael G. Martin, Jr.

The New Lottie Moon Story

University of South Carolina, Allen Stokes
National Archives, Civil Division, Diplomatic Branch, Kathryn M. Murphy
Cornell University
Duke University

Persons who provided assistance with content

Mrs. Henry C. Bailey
Mrs. Ernest Baird
Vanita Baldwin
Mrs. Waller Batson
W. S. Beane
Susie Blair
Luther Bootle
Ben P. Bryant
Nellie Carson
Jane Toy Coolidge
Mrs. G. H. Collings
Luther Copeland
Anna Belle Crouch
Mr. and Mrs. Edward Dorrier
Mrs. W. Yancey Ellis
Mrs. W. W. Ernsting
Eulalia Estep
Mrs. Charles Fuller
Mrs. Robert Gandy
L. Carrington Goodrich
Daniel Grant
Mrs. Robert Alexis Green
Frances Grove
Nina Brice Gwin
Mrs. Raymond Hale
Mrs. Hendon M. Harris
Alden L. Hicks
Embra Hearon
Eula Mae Henderson
Mrs. Douglas Hills
Mrs. Purser Hewitt
Princeton Hsu
Alma Hunt
Mrs. John Meekin Hunt
Mrs. John E. Hunter
Donald A. Irwin
Kathryn Jasper

Margaret D. Jefferson
Elise Jones
Helen Jordan
Mrs. Harold Lambert
Ken Lawson
Mrs. Robert L. Lewis
W. L. Lumpkin
Clara McCartt
Thomas Miller
Virginia Moore
Leila Mundy
Mary Jane Nethery
Mrs. George Omohundro
Marjean Patterson
Wesley M. Pattillo
Claudette Peterson
Mrs. Ed Price
Dorothy Pryor
Cosa Elizabeth Reynolds
Ruth Compton Reynolds
John E. Roberts
Mrs. Floyd Searcy
John Earl Seelig
Murial N. Showalter
Sarah S. Smith
Mrs. E. W. Springs
Mrs. X. O. Steele
Frances Stroope
Mrs. Ray Summers
Carrie S. Vaughan
Wang Myan-jai
Robert Walls
Rita Watkins
Mrs. John D. W. Watts
Carolyn Weatherford
Dean Weaver

Those who assisted with clerical work, typing, and editorial review

Ruth Ann Archer	Glenda Parker
Joyce Bates	Carolyn Roberts
Sharron Cosby	Bobbie Sorrill
Charlotte Dick	Esther Worsham
Judy Elliott	Glenda Yarborough
Mary Hines	Barbara Yeager

The editorial team wishes to thank The Southern Baptist Seminary for permission to use the painting of Lottie Moon on the jacket cover. The editorial staff also wishes to thank Professor Sheldon T. Ma, Vanderbilt University, for consultation on translations from Chinese.

KEY TO SOURCES

BB	*Baptist Basket,* The Southern Baptist Theological Seminary, Louisville, Kentucky; limited copies available on microfilm from Southern Baptist Historical Commission, Nashville, Tennessee.
CI	*Christian Index,* available on microfilm from Southern Baptist Historical Commission, Nashville, Tennessee.
CR	*Chinese Recorder,* Library of Congress.
CWPLF	C. W. Pruitt Letter File, Jenkins Library and Archives, Foreign Mission Board.
FMB	Foreign Mission Board of the Southern Baptist Convention, Richmond, Virginia.
FMJ	*Foreign Mission Journal,* Foreign Mission Board; available on microfilm from Southern Baptist Historical Commission, Nashville, Tennessee.
HH	*Heathen Helper,* The Southern Baptist Theological Seminary, Louisville, Kentucky; partially available on microfilm from Southern Baptist Historical Commission, Nashville, Tennessee.
HFB	Hartwell Family Papers, Yale University Divinity School Library.
JBHLF	J. B. Hartwell Letter File, Jenkins Library and Archives, Foreign Mission Board.
KW	*Kind Words,* The Southern Baptist Theological Seminary and The Southwestern Baptist Theological Seminary, available on microfilm from Southern Baptist Historical Commission.

LMLF	Lottie Moon Letter File, Jenkins Library and Archives, Foreign Mission Board.
LMR	Lottie Moon research data at the Foreign Mission Board.
MFCD	Martha Foster Crawford Diary, Duke University Library.
RH	*Religious Herald,* available on microfilm from Southern Baptist Historical Commission, Nashville, Tennessee.
TPCLF	T. P. Crawford Letter File, Jenkins Library and Archives, Foreign Mission Board.
URL	Una Roberts Lawrence Papers, including rough notes, much primary data, and first draft of *Lottie Moon,* The Southern Baptist Theological Seminary, Louisville, Kentucky.
WMU	Library and Archives of Woman's Missionary Union, Auxiliary to Southern Baptist Convention, Birmingham, Alabama.
WR	*Western Recorder,* available on microfilm from Southern Baptist Historical Commission, Nashville, Tennessee.
WWC	*Woman's Work in China,* Cornell University and Yale University Divinity School.
WWFE	*Woman's Work in the Far East,* Library of Congress.
WWW	*Woman's Work for Woman,* Library of Congress.

SOURCES CONSULTED

BOOKS AND ARTICLES

Allen, Lee N., *The First 150 Years: First Baptist Church, Montgomery, Alabama, 1829-1979*. Montgomery: First Baptist Church, 1979.

Annual, Southern Baptist Convention, 1872-1913.

Annual Reports, Woman's Baptist Foreign Mission Society of Maryland.

Ayers, T. W., *Healing and Missions*. Richmond: Foreign Mission Board, 1930.

Baker, Harriet (Lumina Silvervale, pseudonym), *Orphan of the Old Dominion*. Philadelphia: J. B. Lippincott and Co., 1873.

Barr, Pat, *To China with Love*. Garden City, New York: Doubleday & Co., Inc., 1973.

Beach, Harlan P., *Dawn on the Hills of T'ang or Missions in China*. New York: Student Volunteer Movement for Foreign Missions, 1905.

Beaver, R. Pierce, *All Loves Excelling*. Grand Rapids, Michigan: William B. Eerdmans Publishing Co., 1968.

Black, Margie, "Our Own Lottie Moon," *Viewpoints, Georgia Baptist History*, vol. 4. Atlanta: Georgia Baptist Historical Society, 1974.

Blair, Susie N., *Scottsville Baptist Church: A History*. Scottsville, Virginia: n.p. 1961.

Broadus, J. A., *Memoir of James Pettigru Boyce*. Nashville: Sunday School Board, 1927.

Bryan, Ferrebee Catharine, *At the Gates: Life Story of Matthew Tyson and Eliza Moring Yates*. Nashville: Broadman Press, 1949.

Burnet, David Statts, *The Jerusalem Mission*. Cincinnati: American Christian Publication Society, 1853.

Cauthen, Eloise Glass, *Higher Ground, Biography of Wiley B. Glass, Missionary to China*. Nashville: Broadman Press, 1978.

China Baptist Centenary. Canton, China, 1936.

Sources Consulted

China Centenary Missionary Conference Records. New York: American Tract Society, 1907.

Crawford, T. P., *Evolution in My Missions Views: A Growth of Gospel Mission Principles in My Own Mind.* Fulton, Kentucky: J. A. Scarboro, 1903.

Crumpton, Washington Bryan, *A Book of Memories, 1842-1920.* Montgomery: Baptist Mission Board, 1921.

Dalton, Elizabeth Landress, *Twenty Years and More.* Chattanooga: Central Baptist Church, 1978.

Encyclopedia of Southern Baptists. Nashville: Broadman Press, vols. 1 and 2, 1958; vol. 3, 1971.

Evans, Elizabeth Marshall, *Annie Armstrong.* Birmingham: Woman's Missionary Union, 1963.

Fisher, Daniel W., *Calvin Wilson Mateer, a Biography.* Philadelphia: The Westminster Press, 1911.

Fitzgerald, C. P., *The Horizon History of China.* New York: American Heritage Publishing Co., Inc., 1969.

Foster, L. S., *Fifty Years in China: An Eventful Memoir of Tarleton Perry Crawford, D.D.* Nashville: Bayless-Pullen Co., 1909.

Goodrich, L. Carrington, and Nigel Cameron, *The Face of China, As Seen by Photographers and Travelers, 1860-1912.* New York: Aperture, Inc., 1978.

Graves, R. H., *Forty Years in China.* Baltimore: R. H. Woodward Co., 1895.

Haddock, Louise, "Lottie Moon's Family in Oklahoma." *Oklahoma Baptist Chronicle,* Autumn 1977.

Hipps, Margaret Stroh, *Neighbors Half a World Away.* Nashville: Broadman Press, 1945.

Hsu, Princeton S., *A History of Chinese Baptist Churches,* vols. 1 and 5. Hong Kong: Baptist Press, 1972.

Hunt, Alma, and Catherine B. Allen, *History of Woman's Missionary Union,* Revised Edition. Nashville: Convention Press, 1976.

Hunt, Billy Grey, "Crawford Howell Toy: Interpreter of the Old Testament." Unpublished doctoral thesis, Southern Baptist Theological Seminary, 1965.

Hyatt, Irwin, T., Jr., *Our Ordered Lives Confess.* Cambridge: Harvard University Press, 1976.

In the Spirit of Christmas. Birmingham: Woman's Missionary Union, 1973.

Johnson, John Lipscomb, *Autobiographical Notes.* Privately published, 1958.

Jeffries, Susan Herring, *Papa Wore No Halo.* Winston-Salem: John F. Blair, 1963.

Latourette, Kenneth Scott, *China.* Englewood Cliffs, New Jersey: Prentice-Hall, Inc., 1964.

Latourette, Kenneth Scott, *History of Christian Missions in China.* London: Society for Promoting Christian Knowledge, 1929.

Latourette, Kenneth Scott, *A History of the Expansion of Christianity, A.D. 1800 to A.D. 1914,* vol. 6, *The Great Century in Northern Africa and in Asia.* New York: Harper & Brothers, 1944.

Lawrence, Una Roberts, *Lottie Moon.* Nashville: Sunday School Board of the Southern Baptist Convention, 1927.

Leonard, Charles A., Sr., *Repaid a Hundredfold.* Grand Rapids, Michigan: William B. Eerdmans Publishing Co., 1969.

Li, Dun J., *The Ageless Chinese, a History.* New York: Charles Scribner's Sons, 1965.

Liu, Kwang-Ching, *The Americans and Chinese.* Cambridge: Harvard University Press, 1963.

Maddry, Charles E., *Christ's Expendables.* Nashville: Broadman Press, 1949.

Marshall, Clara, *The Woman's Medical College of Pennsylvania.* Philadelphia: P. Blakiston, Son, and Co., 1897.

Mather, Juliette, *Light Three Candles.* Richmond: Virginia Woman's Missionary Union, 1972.

Mateer, Robert McCheyne, *Character Building in China, the Life Story of Julia Brown Mateer.* New York: Fleming H. Revell Co., 1912.

Memorials of Protestant Missionaries to the Chinese. Shanghai: American Presbyterian Press, 1867.

Minutes, American Christian Missionary Society, 1849-1860.

Minutes, Albemarle [Virginia] Baptist Association, 1840-1880.

Minutes, Middle Cherokee [Georgia] Baptist Association, 1873.

Minutes, Woman's Missionary Union, Auxiliary to Southern Baptist Convention, 1888-1914.

Moon, Anna Mary, *Sketches of the Moon and Barclay Families.* Chattanooga: Privately printed, 1939.

Moon, John William, *The Moons and Kindred Families.* Atlanta: Steen Printing Co., 1930.

Moon, William H., *History of the Moon Family.* Conyers, Georgia: The Times Publishing Co., 1920.

Moore Virginia. *Scottsville on the James.* Charlottesville: The Jarman Press, 1969.

Nevius, Helen S. Coan, *The Life of John Livingston Nevius.* New York: Fleming H. Revell Co., 1895.

Nevius, John L., *Demon Possession and Allied Themes.* New York: Fleming H. Revell Co., 1894.

Nichols, Frederick D., "The Two Viewmonts," *The Magazine of Albemarle County History,* vol. 8, 1953.

Patterson, Marjean, *Covered Foundations: A History of Mississippi Woman's Missionary Union.* Jackson: Mississippi Woman's Missionary Union, 1978.

Pruitt, Anna Seward, *The Day of Small Things.* Richmond: Foreign Mission Board, 1929.

Pruitt, Anna Seward, *Up from Zero in North China.* Nashville: Broadman Press, 1939.

Pruitt, Ida, *A China Childhood.* San Francisco: Chinese Materials Center, Inc., 1978.

Rabe, Valentine H., *The American Home Base of China Missions, 1880-1920.* Cambridge: Harvard University Press, 1978.

Rawlings, Mary, *The Albemarle of Other Days.* Charlottesville: The Michie Co. Publishers, 1925.

Records of the General Conference of the Protestant Missionaries of China. Shanghai: Presbyterian Mission Press, 1878.

Robertson, Archibald Thomas, *Life and Letters of John Albert Broadus.* Philadelphia: American Baptist Publication Society, 1901.

Ryland, Garnett, *The Baptists of Virginia, 1699-1926.* Richmond: Virginia Baptist Board of Missions and Education, 1955.

Smith, Ophia D., *Oxford Spy Wed at Pistol Point.* Oxford, Ohio: Callen Printing Co., 1962.

Taylor, George Braxton, *Virginia Baptist Ministers,* Third Series. Lynchburg, Virginia: J. P. Bell Co., Inc., 1912.

Tiers, M. C., *Christian Portrait Gallery.* Cincinnati, Ohio: n.p., 1864.

Tsui Yuan-Ting, *The History of P'ingtu County Baptist Churches, 1887-1935.* P'ingtu, China: P'ingtu Baptist Business Office.

Tupper, Henry Allen, *A Decade of Foreign Missions, 1880-1890.* Richmond: Foreign Mission Board of the Southern Baptist Convention, 1891.

Tupper, Henry Allen, *Foreign Missions of the Southern Baptist Convention.* Philadelphia: American Baptist Publication Society, 1880.

Walsh, Mary Roth, *"Doctors Wanted: No Women Need Apply."* New Haven: Yale University Press, 1977.

White, Blanche Sydnor, *Saved to Serve, a Brief History of the Development of WMUs in Other Lands.* Richmond: Rice Press, 1937.

Williams, Samuel Wells, *The Middle Kingdom,* vols. 1 and 2. London: W. H. Allen, 1883.

Woods, Edgar, *History of Albemarle County, Virginia.* Bridgewater, Virginia: C. J. Carrier Co., 1900.

Worswick, Clark, and Jonathan Spence, *Imperial China, Photographs, 1850-1912.* New York: Penwick Publishing, Inc., 1978.

PAMPHLETS

Ayers, T. W., "Miss Lottie Moon—As I Knew Her." Birmingham: Woman's Missionary Union.

Adams, Mrs. W. W., Mrs. C. W. Pruitt, W. W. Adams, Mrs. J. McF. Gaston, "Miss Moon As We Knew Her." Birmingham: Woman's Missionary Union.

The New Lottie Moon Story

Broadus, Eliza S., "The Heavenly Book Visitor." Birmingham: Woman's Missionary Union.

PERIODICALS

The Alabama Baptist, 1850-1979.

Baptist Basket, 1888-1893 Louisville.

The Cartersville [Georgia] American, 1884.

The Cartersville [Georgia] News, 1913.

The Cartersville [Georgia] Semi-Weekly Express, 1871.

The Christian Evangelist, 1906.

Christian Index, 1869-1875, Georgia.

The Christian Standard, 1866-1966, Cincinnati, Ohio.

The Chinese Recorder and Missionary Journal, 1868-1913, Foochow and Shanghai.

Foreign Mission Journal (including *The Mission Journal* and *Home and Foreign Journal*), 1870-1914, Richmond, Foreign Mission Board of the Southern Baptist Convention.

Heathen Helper, 1882-1888, Louisville.

Kind Words, variously published under auspices of Sunday School Board and Domestic Mission Board, Southern Baptist Convention. Random issues.

The Millennial Harbinger, 1857-1860, Bethany, Virginia.

The News and Courant, 1902, Cartersville, Georgia.

The Religious Herald, 1847-1914, Richmond, Virginia.

Royal Service (including *Our Mission Fields*), 1906-1979, Woman's Missionary Union.

The Standard and Express, 1871-1873, Cartersville, Georgia.

The Sun, 1873, Baltimore, Maryland.

The Weekly Standard and Express, 1871-1873, Cartersville, Georgia.

The Western Recorder, 1865-1914, Louisville, Kentucky.

Woman's Work in China, 1877-1889, Shanghai.

Woman's Work in the Far East, 1890-1911, Shanghai.

Woman's Work for Woman, 1872-1891, Philadelphia, Woman's Foreign Missionary Society of the Presbyterian Church.

MANUSCRIPTS AND PAPERS

W. W. Adams Papers, Samford University Special Collections, Birmingham, Alabama.

Albemarle County Courthouse, Charlottesville, Virginia, Will Books and Deed Books.

James Turner Barclay Biographical File and Julia Ann Barclay Correspondence, Disciples of Christ Historical Society, Nashville, Tennessee.

John A. Broadus Papers, The Southern Baptist Theological Seminary, Louisville, Kentucky.

Caldwell Institute Catalogs, Centre College, Danville, Kentucky.

Records, First Baptist Church, Charlottesville, Virginia, 1850-1865, University of Virginia Manuscript Division, Charlottesville, Virginia.

China Letters, Board of Foreign Missions of the Presbyterian Church of the U.S.A., Microfilm Reels 198-207, 211, 256, 258, Presbyterian Historical Society, Philadelphia, Pennsylvania.

Cocke Papers, Manuscript Division, University of Virginia.

Confederate States of America, Records of Army Commissioned Officers, National Archives, Washington, D.C.

Jane Toy Coolidge, "Some Notes on the Toy Family," unpublished manuscript, 1963.

Martha Foster Crawford, Diary and Papers, Duke University Library.

Records, Crewe [Virginia] Baptist Church.

Records, First Baptist Church, Danville, Kentucky.

Fife Papers, Manuscript Division, University of Virginia.

Sara Graves Strickler Fife Diary, Property of Anne Fruedenberg, Charlottesville, Virginia.

Foreign Mission Board of the Southern Baptist Convention, Jenkins Library and Archives:

Letter Files for the following missionaries:
W. W. Adams, T. W. Ayers, T. P. Crawford, Jewell Legett Daniel, E. E. Davault, Mattie Dutton, James McFadden Gaston, Jessie Pettigrew Glass, Rosewell Graves, N. W. Halcomb, Anna Hartwell, J. B. Hartwell, D. W. Herring, J. L. Holmes, J. M. Joiner, W. D. King, Fannie Knight, Jane Lide, J. W. McCollum, Cynthia Miller, Lottie Moon (including Edmonia Moon), W. C. Newton, C. W. Pruitt, Ida Taylor, Laura Barton Taylor, Emma Thompson, Mary Thornton, Crawford H. Toy, J. V. Turner, Lula Whilden, Matthew T. Yates.

China Archives Unmarked
Letter Copy Books and assorted files of J. B. Hartwell and family.
Manuscript of North China Baptist Mission History by Jane Lide.

Minutes, Foreign Mission Board, 1845-1914.

Photo Files.

Lottie Moon Research Files of Johnni Johnson and Fon Scofield, prepared for the movie, "The Lottie Moon Story."

Copy Books for Corresponding Secretaries and Treasurers, 1872-1913.

Minutes, North China Mission.

Miscellaneous Personal Effects of Lottie Moon.

John Harris, Record of Will and Probate, Ledger Owned by Cary Nelson Moon, Charlottesville, Virginia.

Records, Hardware (Pine Grove) Baptist Church, Virginia Baptist Historical Society, Richmond.

Hartwell Family Papers, Yale University Divinity School Library.

Harrison Papers, Letters from Lottie Moon, Virginia Baptist Historical Society.

Hollins College Catalogs and Student Records, Hollins College, Virginia.

Ella Jeter, Photo Albums and Miscellaneous Photographs, contributed to Foreign Mission Board by Ruth C. Thornhill.

Joel T. Kidd, "Scottsville Baptist Church," unpublished manuscript, Virginia Baptist Historical Society.

Una Roberts Lawrence Papers, The Southern Baptist Theological Seminary, Louisville, Kentucky.

Lottie Moon Letters, miscellaneous writings and family papers shared by the following:

First Baptist Church, Montgomery, Alabama

First Baptist Church, Newberry, South Carolina.

Second-Ponce de Leon Baptist Church, Atlanta, Georgia.

First Baptist Church, Cartersville, Georgia.

Mary Virginia Andrews Andrews, Daleville, Virginia (now in Woman's Missionary Union Archives).

Mrs. Henry (Orie Andrews) Davis, East Flat Rock, North Carolina (now deceased, copies at Woman's Missionary Union Archives and Foreign Mission Board).

Mrs. L. R. (Genevieve) Shadwell, Richmond, Virginia.

Cary Nelson Moon, Charlottesville, Virginia.

Mrs. Russell Thomas, Roanoke, Virginia.

Mrs. R. C. (Charlotte Thomas) Churchill, Crewe, Virginia.

Grayce Fitzgerald, Crewe, Virginia.

Mr. and Mrs. Ernest Andrews, Roanoke, Virginia.

First Baptist Church, Roanoke, Virginia.

Mrs. J. S. (Mildred) Andrews, Pearisburg, Virginia.

Lottie Moon File and Moon Publications, Woman's Missionary Union Archives, Birmingham, Alabama.

Lottie Moon File, Southern Baptist Historical Commission, Nashville, Tennessee.

Letters of Mary Moon to Capt. J. H. Stafford, Property of Lila F. Watson, Darlington, South Carolina.

Orianna Russell Moon File, Faculty Minutes, Other Records, Medical College of Pennsylvania, Philadelphia.

Photo Albums of William Carey Newton, given to Woman's Missionary Union
Archives by Rachel Newton Dickson, Richmond, Virginia.

Anna Cunningham Safford Diary, Correspondence, and Biographical
Sketches, Historical Foundation of the Presbyterian and Reformed
Churches, Montreat, North Carolina.

George Braxton Taylor Diaries, Virginia Baptist Historical Society, Richmond,
Virginia.

United States Census, Albemarle County, Virginia. Population Census for
1830, 1850, 1860, 1870, 1880. Agricultural Schedule for 1850. Slave Census
for 1850.

United States Consular Records, Chefoo China, Shanghai, China, National
Archives, Diplomatic Branch, Record Group 84.

The Willard School Catalogs (Troy Female Seminary), Troy, New York.

Minutes, Woman's Missionary Society, First Baptist Church, Cartersville,
Georgia, 1873-1913.

Woman's Missionary Society Record Book, Scottsville Baptist Church, property
of Susie Blair.

PERSONAL INTERVIEWS

(Transcripts and tapes or notes in Woman's Missionary Union Archives. Interviews conducted by the author unless otherwise indicated.)

Mrs. W. W. Adams, Birmingham, Alabama (now deceased).

Mr. and Mrs. Ernest L. Andrews, Roanoke, Virginia.

F. Catharine Bryan, Atlanta, Georgia.

Nellie Carson, Anderson, South Carolina.

Mrs. R. C. (Charlotte Thomas) Churchill, Crewe, Virginia.

Jewell Legett Daniel, Dallas, Texas.

Mrs. Henry (Orie Andrews) Davis, East Flat Rock, North Carolina (now
deceased).

Rachel Newton Dickson, Richmond, Virginia.

Mrs. Charles F. Goode, Chattanooga, Tennessee.

Katherine and Lilla Hancock, Richmond, Virginia.

Embra Hearon, Bishopville, South Carolina.

Mrs. William Barry (Linda Lynch) Harmon, Richmond, Virginia.

Charles H. League, Nashville, Tennessee.

Jane Lide, Darlington, South Carolina (now deceased).

Mrs. Russell B. Moon, Scottsville, Virginia.

Mrs. Edgar Morgan, Columbia, South Carolina. Interviewed by Mrs. Carter
(Agnes) Morgan and later by author.

Lucy Ayers Pitman, Birmingham, Alabama.

Ida Pruitt, Philadelphia, Pennsylvania.

Mrs. L. R. Shadwell and Mrs. John Lynch, Richmond, Virginia.

The New Lottie Moon Story

Mrs. Russell Thomas, Roanoke, Virginia.
Elizabeth N. Tompkins, Richmond, Virginia.
Minnie Pettigrew Voyles, Memphis, Texas. Interviewed by Mrs. Frank Ellis.
Lila F. Watson, Darlington, South Carolina.

INDEX

Adams, Wayne Womack and Mrs. Floy White 255-257, 262-264, 271, 276, 288

Alabama 46, 48, 50, 67, 71, 89-91, 177, 239, 264

Albemarle Baptist Association 70, 200

Albemarle County, Virginia 12, 22, 29, 45, 47, 58, 71, 112, 161, 238, 244

American Christian Missionary Society 21

American Philological Society 136

American Tract Society 104

Andrews, Isaac M. 238, 261, 269

Andrews, John Summerfield 46-50, 56, 110-111

Andrews, Orianna Russell Moon (Mrs. John S.) 16, 22, 27-29, 32, 39-40, 45-50, 55-56, 71, 193, 237-238

Andrews, William Luther 48, 238, 258, 269

Annie Armstrong Easter Offering for Home Missions 293

Anniston, Alabama 231, 239

Annuities for Missions 230, 261, 269

Armstrong, Alice 65

Armstrong, Annie 65, 174-175, 177-178, 201, 239, 242, 293

Atlanta, Georgia 102, 199, 240, 254

Ayers, Harry 230

Ayers, Lucy 247

Ayers, T. W. and Mrs. 228, 239, 241, 244, 250, 253, 272

Baker, Harriet 65

Ballinger's Creek Baptist Church 16

Baltimore, Maryland 60, 65, 68, 71, 193, 200

Baptist General Convention of Texas 187

Baptist Sunday School Board 293

Baptists, English 121, 126

Baptists, Northern 66, 119

Barbour, Lewis G. 54, 58

Barclay, Anna Maria (see Moon, Anna Maria)

Barclay, James Turner 15-21, 39-40

Barclay, Julia Sowers (Mrs. James T.) 16

Barclay, Mary Elizabeth (see Moon, Mary Elizabeth Barclay)

Barclay, Mary Hoops 15

Barclay, Robert 15

Barclay, Sarah Coleman Turner (see Harris, Sarah)

Barclay, Thomas 15

Barclay, Thomas II, 15, 19

Barton, Laura (Mrs. Z. C. Taylor) 177, 181, 196, 206

Bell, T. P. 137-138, 153 (fn. 42), 161, 188

Bible Women 95-96, 214-215, 245, 251

Biblical Recorder 127

Bishopville, South Carolina 48

Blackwell, Elizabeth 29

Bostick, George P. and Mrs. No. 1 (see Thornton, Mary J.) 177, 181, 186-187, 196

Boxer Rebellion 222-227, 250, 273

Broadus, John A. 29, 32, 34, 35-39, 45, 48, 60, 62, 102, 112, 136

Bronaugh, William N. 33

Brown, A. B. 31

Bryan, Robert T. 175, 224, 285

Buh Ko 217

Burnside, Ambrose 47

Burton, G. W. 54

316

The New Lottie Moon Story